By the same author:

Victoria History of Somerset (ed.) (Oxford University Press, 1967–)

Local Sources for the Young Historian (Muller, 1973; reprinted as *Local History for Beginners*, Phillimore, 1980, 1983)

Christianity in Somerset (ed.) (Somerset County Council, 1976)

Victorian and Edwardian Somerset (with David Bromwich) (Batsford, 1977)

A History of Somerset (Somerset County Council, 1978, 1987)

A History of Somerset (Phillimore, 1983)

The Monmouth Rebellion (Dovecote Press, 1984)

Monmouth: the Road to Sedgemoor (Lion Publishing, 1985)

Somerset in Domesday (Somerset County Library, 1986)

Some Somerset Country Houses (Dovecote Press, 1991)

SOMERSET AND AVON

ROBERT DUNNING

ALAN SUTTON

First published by John Bartholomew & Son Limited in 1980

This revised edition first published in the United Kingdom in 1992 by
Alan Sutton Publishing Ltd. · Phoenix Mill · Far Thrupp · Stroud · Gloucestershire

First published in the United States of America in 1992 by
Alan Sutton Publishing Inc. · Wolfeboro Falls · NH 03896–0848

British Library Cataloguing in Publication Data

Dunning, R.W. (Robert William), *1938–*
   Somerset & Avon.
   I. Title
   942.38

   ISBN 0 7509 0069 5

Library of Congress Cataloging in Publication Data applied for

Typeset in Baskerville 11/13 and 9/10.
Typesetting and origination by
Alan Sutton Publishing Limited.
Printed in Great Britain by
The Bath Press Ltd., Avon.

Contents

Acknowledgements

Anyone who writes on the history of the old counties of Somerset and Gloucester is conscious of the work of antiquarians, archaeologists, and historians of the past two centuries and more. Their work, enshrined in monographs, pamphlets, articles, and guides, and so essential for a proper understanding of the countryside and the town, could be little more than sampled for this volume. I am grateful to David Bromwich, Local History Librarian of Somerset County Council and honorary librarian of the Somerset Archaeological Society, for his great help throughout the writing of this book, and for reading the whole when it was finished.

Visitors to the two counties in the past have in different ways brought our local heritage into the heritage of England. St Augustine's visit, probably to Aust, is recorded by Bede in *A History of the English Church and People*, translated by Leo Sherley-Price (Penguin Books 1955); the description of 12th-century Bath is from *Gesta Stephani*, edited and translated by K. R. Potter (Nelson's Medieval Texts, 1955); *William Worcestre's Itineraries* are translated and edited by J. H. Harvey (Oxford 1969); *John Leland's Itinerary* is edited by Lucy Toulmin Smith (reprinted Centaur Press 1964); *Gerard's Survey of Somerset, 1633*, edited by E. H. Bates (Somerset Record Society 1900, reprinted 1973). Kilvert's description of a visit to Cheddar is from *Kilvert's Diary*, edited by W. Plomer (Cape 1977); the bells of Bitton and Kelston are recalled in the poem 'Bristol' from *John Betjeman's Collected Poems*, compiled by the Earl of Birkenhead (Murray 1958); the entrance to East Coker is from T. S. Eliot's *Four Quartets*.

If modern visitors to Somerset and Avon are led through this book to appreciate better the countryside around them, then its purpose will have been served. But the book itself could not have been written without cost to my family – sometimes grudgingly afforded by two small children, who will, I hope, grow to understand. My wife has supported in a marvellous way: she found time to type the script as well as to cope with the consequences of its compilation. It is hers as much as mine.

Robert Dunning
Taunton
August 1979

Preface

The counties of Somerset and Avon lie on the southern shore of the Severn Estuary, and cover some of the most rich and varied scenery in the British Isles. The coastline has, perhaps, more interest for the geologist than attraction for the holiday-maker, though the resorts of Clevedon, Weston-super-Mare, and Minehead were among the pioneers of seaside leisure. But the traveller who ventures from the relative security of the motorways, which cross the counties for Wales and the South-West, is amply rewarded for his temerity. From the southern fringes of the Cotswolds on the Gloucestershire and Wiltshire borders; across the Avon Valley with the twin cities of Bath and Bristol; to the contrasting limestone country of the Mendips, and then through the fascinating low moorlands of central Somerset or the golden Ham stone and flint country of the south; and then narrowing to the western hills, to the Quantocks, the Brendons, and finally to Exmoor – still in Somerset until well after Dunkery – here is an area that has been known and marvelled at by generations of the discerning, and by those who in increasing numbers seek retirement within its friendly and welcoming bounds. There may still be some excuse for not knowing exactly where is the county of Avon, created in 1974 out of parts of Somerset and Gloucestershire, the city and county of Bristol, and the county borough of Bath; but ancient Somerset, created 1,000 years ago, has too often been thought of simply as the introduction to the South-West, the Jordan to be crossed before the Promised Land of Devon and Cornwall. Part of its charm is, undoubtedly, its relative immunity from the outward trappings of tourism; a certain reluctance to be commercial. Yet here, within bounds partly of the 20th century, but largely dating back to Saxon times, are sites that have been attracting visitors for generations – dramatic creations of nature like Cheddar Gorge; the great Roman and 18th-century spa of Bath; Glastonbury, the cradle of Christianity in the West; the port of Bristol whence Cabot and others sailed to seek the New World; or the little medieval microcosm that is Wells.

These are some of the highlights, the magnets that attract whatever the field; and Dunster and Montacute, Dyrham or Dodington too have an appeal that is universal. And yet, take away any from its context and it is not the same. It is the context, the counties of Somerset and Avon, the country of Arthur's Camelot, the heart of Alfred's Wessex, 'King' Monmouth's land, that is the subject of this book; a country where history and legend are still quite hopelessly entangled, whatever the experts may decide; where villages are attractive for themselves as well as for their people; where small towns may have lost their cattle markets, but are not entirely swamped and made anonymous by the super variety; where manufacturing industry, often with impressive international significance, has mostly an acceptable face; and where, even within sight from the centre of Bristol, the landscape of the country declares itself in all its variety and interest.

Introduction

The Foundation of the Landscape

The motorway traveller on the M5 from the north, coming into Avon from Gloucestershire, has already for miles been in the wide valley of the Severn. To the right, northwestwards, the countryside falls gently away to the widening river, and then to the higher ground of the Forest of Dean beyond. To the south-east, on the left of the motorway, the long Cotswold scarp, running like a spine up through the centre of England to the southern tip of Lincolnshire and down the east and south of Somerset to the Dorset coast, forms through southern Gloucestershire and Avon something like a wall nearly 50 miles long between Chipping Campden and Dyrham. The Mendips across Somerset form a second scarp south of Bristol overlooking the Somerset Levels. The dramatic, two-tiered route of the M5 west of Bristol on the edge of the Gordano Ridge, and the descent into Somerset over the Bleadon Ridge appear the more dramatic as they stand, like Brent Knoll, above the flat marshlands of the Yeo Valley and the much more extensive Somerset moorlands. Thereafter the motorway skirts the Polden Ridge and the southern edge of the Quantocks, which stand a rim around the Levels as their ancient name suggests. Then on into the vale of Taunton Deane and up the side of the Blackdowns into Devon, glimpsing the Brendons across the valley and Exmoor beyond.

The M5, as its designers and builders discovered, runs through a great range of geological formations and soil types. The Severn Valley, bounded on the east by the Cotswold scarp and on the south by the Bristol Avon, rises gradually from the river towards the scarp in an area of some complexity. In form it is flat, with a wide band beside the river below the 50 ft contour, a parallel ridge chosen as the sites of the villages of Alveston and Almondsbury and followed by the M5 and the older A38; then the valley of the River Frome and its tributaries the Laddon and Stoke brooks, followed by the gradual rise to the foot of the Cotswold scarp. In fact this geological area continues to the south and east of Bristol, as far as the Mendips, forming an equilateral triangle between Cromhall in the north, Frome in the east, and Nailsea in the west, and comprises old coal-bearing rocks and Pennant Sandstone, sandwiched between the older Carboniferous Limestone. North and East of Bristol the Lower Coal Measures are covered with clays, and the Middle Lias also yields some iron ore at Iron Acton, Downend, Rangeworthy, Bitton, and even in the Royal York Crescent in Clifton. Haematite (red peroxide) was found at Frampton Cotterell, and some 68,000 tons were extracted between 1862 and 1874. The area between Yate and Wickwar also yielded most of the celestine in the world, the source of strontium hydroxide still used in German beet-sugar refineries, but now largely exported to the United States to make tracer bullets, signal flares, fireworks, and rockets. Most important of all, however, was coal, for two centuries and more the major industry north and east of Bristol. Mining played a significant part from the Middle Ages in clearing much of South Gloucestershire of its native woodland, and from the 18th century was the basis for other local industries such as metal smelting and hence for the general economic strength of Bristol.

In contrast to these old rocks which produced such mineral wealth and the plentiful Pennant Sandstone and Dolomitic Conglomerate which provided much of the building materials of the area, the Cotswolds are young. The scarp is formed by a tipping of the strata, exposing the older, Inferior Oolite, while the Great Oolite is nearer the surface on the more gently sloping country towards Oxfordshire, the source of the best Cotswold stone. The name Cotswold must have referred in the beginning to a very small area, for it signifies the forest of some pioneer settler called Cod.

The Cotswold oolite continues in a narrow band along the eastern edge of Somerset, providing the county with its most characteristic building material. The cream-coloured Bath stone, whose qualities Ralph Allen, the 18th-century Bath developer, appreciated, was quarried first on Combe Down and Bathampton Down, and was brought to the river and later to the Kennet and Avon Canal and to the city by tram road. The quarries, subsequently overtaken by the more extensive workings at Box in Wiltshire, provided expanding Bath with a fine stone so fitting in colour and texture for the clear lines of the Classical style.

The spine of oolite, heavily indented in places and forming abrupt grassy gradients around Bruton and South Cadbury, runs into Dorset near Sherborne and then turns west along the Somerset boundary to form a landscape of the greatest charm. The stone here, known as Ham stone from the quarries of the best quality on Ham Hill, is limestone heavily encrusted with shells and impregnated with iron, producing a fine golden stone which is the glory of churches, houses, and cottages not only in Somerset but also in Dorset and Devon. The surrounding soils, known as Yeovil Sands, are light both in colour and texture, produce characteristic hollow-ways in the narrow lanes, and are so fertile that open-field agriculture survived here longer than in most parts of Somerset.

The limestone curve from Bath to Ham Hill holds in its lap the rich clay plain of the Parrett and the Yeo, draining into the Levels of the central basin. The landscape of the plain is green and wide and many-towered, its houses and churches in the lias of the country, blue turning to white, and shown off by Ham-stone doors and windows bought by the foot on Ham Hill, and by intricate pinnacles, tracery, arcades, and panels which make the buildings of the plain some of the most outstanding products of the mason's art.

The view over the clay plain and the Levels beyond from Ham Hill shows to the north-east the distant height of Mendip. Limestone again, and much of it fine for building, but interspersed in complicated fashion with marls and coal measures, Old Red Sandstone, and Keuper marls which have made the area south of Bristol, as that north of it, a centre of industrial activity. Lead was certainly mined since Roman times at Charterhouse (see The Mendips), and was heavily exploited during the Middle Ages and into the 17th century; Shipham and Rowberrow produced calamine; and coal was mined at least from the 14th century in several places, modern mining being concentrated around Radstock and stretching as far north as Pensford.

The visitor now sees little of this activity, and much more evidence of the production of stone. The grey and red-brown of the limestone and conglomerate, sometimes a little grim in chapel and cottage under grey slate or pantile; and the cliff-like scars of quarry faces or lorries heavily laden with roadstone and aggregate are warning enough of the insatiable demands of modern living and travelling. The more sophisticated product of an earlier age was the cream freestone of Dundry, above Bristol, the source of stone for St Augustine's Abbey and St Mary Redcliffe; and Doulting, whence the stones of Glastonbury and Wells were hewn.

Below Mendip is a different scene. Abruptly, at the foot of the scarp, spreads a flat plain north and west to the sea, south to the Polden Ridge and its outliers between Somerton and Langport, and then on again up the river valleys towards Yeovil and Taunton. It is a landscape of droves and willows; peaty pastures with, apparently, only a gate to keep in cattle, for the rhines (*pron.* reens) and drains are more effective barriers than any hedge. Geologically, the Levels are the result of flooding in a deep clay basin, followed by gradual recession, leaving a landscape of shallow pools and a recovering vegetation. Decaying plant life in such conditions created on the wet clay floor a thick brown fibrous layer that is peat. Occasional outcrops of clay and lias formed low 'islands' in the marsh, where earliest settlement has been found, and the rather mysterious higher knolls – the best known being Glastonbury Tor – nearly all show traces of religious activity in the early Middle Ages. Pumping engines and sea defences keep the waters usually at bay, providing rich grassland and a fine source of peat. The clay that forms the rim of the Levels produced bricks and tiles in quantity, and an 18th-century street development in Bridgwater marks the beginning of widespread use of brick first for quality building and later for more general use until the present century.

Bridgwater lies on the Parrett, sheltered from the west by the Quantock ridge, a mass of red sandstone and slate which changes the Somerset scene yet again. The same, rather forbidding, materials make up the Brendons and Exmoor. The Quantocks are just near enough to Ham Hill for a prosperous parish like Kingston St Mary to buy Ham stone for the dressings and details of its fine church, a picture in red and gold. Further west, sandstone and a grey ashlar are the usual materials for churches and prestige buildings; cob, whitewash, and thatch are an indication of poorer soil and smaller returns as well as a simple lack of fine building stone. Rare here, for instance, is the tall and decorated tower of other parts; rare the mansion. This is the land of scattered hamlets and isolated farms in narrow, remote valleys, a contrast to the ample vale of Taunton Deane so short a distance away. That is a vale of marls and orchards, the core of the rich manor of Taunton, for long the prized possession of the Bishops of Winchester. Red stone here, too, and little ancient manor houses like Cothay and Greenham Barton (*see* Wellington). And then, abruptly, south again, are the Blackdowns, the boundary with Devon and Dorset stretching down to Chard. Well-wooded country, with ancient trees from a medieval forest and modern plantations, for here are greensands, clays, and valley gravels, by no means as fertile as the vales below. The Yeovil Sands reach up almost to Ilminster, so Ham stone and its shades are near enough for quality work; but for the modest building, for cottage, barn, and byre the local flint adds its own colour and character to what is, in so small a compass, almost infinite variety.

The Occupation of the Land

The investigation of ancient life in an area now heavily populated depends not only on survival but on opportunity. The probability that many of our villages can be traced back as settlements at least to the Iron Age means that excavations have to be limited ones and that destruction in 2,000 years of continuous settlement is likely to have been great. The open areas of the Cotswolds, the Mendips, the Quantocks, and Exmoor reveal many aspects of the past: cave remains illustrate the natural history of the Mendips and Man's early attempts to hunt his quarry; burial mounds reveal not only funerary customs but their exact positions may indicate boundaries and roadways. And while hill-forts, barrows, and enclosures have been found in great numbers, the more informative settlement sites are all too elusive. The construction of the M5 through Avon and Somerset enabled a different view to be taken. From 1969 archaeologists working in a wide band in advance of road construction in what was southern Gloucestershire revealed how much more intensively settled was this part of the countryside than had been imagined, the motorway course producing on average through its whole length to the Devon border more than two sites in every mile.

The archaeological story of the Severn Valley within Avon suggests that the natural forest was cleared in the third millennium B.C., but that it returned during the second and first millennia, without any trace of Bronze or Iron Age settlement. Roman occupation from the later 1st century A.D., however, is significant, perhaps a consequence of the Roman port of Abona (Sea Mills) and the road thence to Gloucester. The largest site was exactly under the course of the motorway at Alveston, occupied from the 1st to the 4th centuries, and has been interpreted as a farm, largely for sheep, part of which was later given over to metal-working.

Somerset's archaeology has much richer prizes. Palaeolithic implements from the river gravels of the Blackdowns and Watchet, implements and animal remains from Cheddar, Wookey, and other Mendip caves; and the more recent discovery of *Homo erectus* at Westbury sub Mendip (or rather evidence of his existence there) have established a spread from the Avon at Pill to the Devon border. The Mesolithic period of small flint implements is represented on Mendip and Exmoor, on the coast at Watchet again, and at Clevedon, and on the Levels at Shapwick and Middlezoy where flints have been found. Curiously, the Neolithic pattern is different: habitations in Mendip caves, probably settlement on Ham Hill and at Cadbury Castle, and the intensive use of the Levels through the appearance of wooden trackways, the oldest in Europe if not in the world, linking areas of dry ground across the marshes. The Quantocks and Exmoor seem to have been unexplored in this phase of settlement, though there are a few long barrows on Mendip.

Bronze Age round barrows are found in all the upland areas from Bath to Exmoor, but although no settlement sites are known, the large number of trackways on the Levels suggest a concentration there. During the Iron Age the area that is Somerset and Avon seems to have been shared by two tribes with some sophistication of government and economic life: the Dobunni, who had influence down at least to the Mendips from the south Midlands, and the Durotriges, based at Dorchester (Dorset) with a secondary capital at Ilchester, who ruled the south. Hillforts of the period are impressive, notably Solsbury Hill near Bath, Dolebury on Mendip, Cadbury Castle, and Ham Hill. And two villages have at last been found, the so-called Lake Villages of Glastonbury and Meare, in reality lakeside settlements in the swampy ground of the Levels.

In four centuries the Romans left more traces of their civilization than is often realized. There were only two towns in the area, Bath (Aquae Sulis) and Ilchester (Lendinis), but townships at Camerton and Catsgore (north of Ilchester) and a port at Sea Mills. There are few military sites, though a notable one on the much-occupied Ham Hill; but the Fosse and its branches, so important for military and economic reasons, made a complex road network whose details are not fully known. The Fosse itself later became the boundary line of many a medieval parish, probably not so much for itself as for its own rôle as the limit of many Roman estates. In the central clay plain around Ilchester were rich arable farms, still to be traced, radiating from substantial villas. Roman lead- and silver-mining on the Mendips and associated pewter production at Camerton and Lansdown above Bath were the centre of the Roman industrial scene, and some iron may have been mined on the Brendons. The whole area was clearly of great economic value. Temples on Pagan's Hill in the Chew Valley, on Creech Hill near Bruton, in Henley Wood near Yatton, and on Brean Down are important evidence for Roman religious observance in the countryside as the great temple complex in Bath is for the more sophisticated, even international, society that was the Roman Empire. The great question now being asked is when did Roman religious observance become Christian? The mosaic pavement from the Low Ham villa (now in the County Museum at Taunton) could not be more pagan, but the evidence in other places, notably at the cemetery in Cannington Park, is equivocal. That site dates from the 2nd century A.D. and was in use until the 8th, but where do the Christian burials begin?

The sub-Roman problem is considerable and fascinating: was there continuity of settlement, even of civilization, after the formal withdrawal of Roman government? The legends of King Arthur will perhaps ever cloud the issue, but the West Country, if anywhere, is likely to provide many of the answers. The identification of Avalon with Glastonbury seems to have been the work of a brilliant late-13th-century publicist for Glastonbury Abbey; and Camelot is not known to be equated with Cadbury Castle until Leland's time. But excavations on Glastonbury Tor and at Cadbury indicate clearly the presence of a warrior chieftain whose rôle as leader of a people threatened by invading hordes and as representative of a Christian civilization facing a pagan onslaught has been translated into the most popular and enduring legend in history.

*   *   *

The names of our towns and villages, our lanes and our fields, are in themselves the history of our landscape. Nowadays their study is a specialist subject, involving ancient languages, dialects, and phonetics, but the results of all this learning are of the greatest interest to anyone who would understand the history and development of the country-side. Somerset and Avon may have more than their fair share of poetry and euphony in names like Temple Cloud or Huish Episcopi, Chipping Sodbury or Mudford Sock, but they, like every village or hamlet name, give more than a clue to origins and early owners and to the shape of the land.

INTRODUCTION

Some of the names on the maps of the two counties date back to Celtic times, a feature particularly common in Somerset where native traditions survived better the Saxon conquest. Rivers and hills have commonly kept their British names which even the experts cannot explain: names like Parrett and Frome and Boyd, which the Saxons took over; the common Avon, which even the Romans accepted, calling their port on the Bristol Avon *Abona* (Sea Mills). *Sabrina* was the name by which Tacitus knew the Severn in the second century A.D., and it has remained, not much changed but still unexplained, for 18 centuries. The Britons thought of the Quantocks as a circle or rim sheltering the lands they knew; the name Mendip comes in part from the Welsh word *mynydd* for hill; the River Boyd from the Welsh for dirty, the Tone from the Welsh word for fire. Rivers and hills, the basic elements of the landscape, thus prove as unchanging in their names as in their shapes and courses. They are the elements of the land of our ancient peoples.

The Saxon village and hamlet names spread throughout the two counties mark the advance of the conquerors. After the Saxon Hwiccas defeated the native Celts at Dyrham in 577 A.D. and again at Penselwood in A.D. 658 the west was open. Settlement was sparse up to the Bristol Avon in the late 6th century, but as they reached further west they settled more thickly and more systematically; they were now both Christian and more organized, establishing as they went not only rural settlements but also mission stations and military strongpoints. Just outside Taunton, where they fortified a settlement by the 720s, they found a hill which the natives called *Cructan*, their name for a beacon hill. The Saxons also called it by their name for hill, *beorh*, and, putting the two together, made it *Crycbeorh*, now Creechbarrow. And when the Saxons went a little further west, on the borders between Halse and Fitzhead, they used as a boundary marker an ash tree, which (as they recorded in a charter) had long been thought sacred by the superstitious natives. In such ways could Celt and Saxon live together.

The hundreds of names between the north Avon border and Devon tell the story in their earliest elements of the centuries of settlement; the story of claims to land and the establishment of hamlets and farms; the story of cultivation and development; of roads and fords and bridges and boundaries; the existence of natural resources, of flora and fauna. So was each place-name born, often a description of a farm or hamlet, enclosure or clearing, bearing the elements *tun*, *stock*, *wick*, and *ley*. The rarer *ney* or *zoy* reveal the islands of the Somerset Levels, the *combes* show where shelter was to be found in the irregular scarps, and the *worths* the ancient woodland.

These place-names tell us more about the Saxon settlers than any written history. One tells us that a local chieftain or head of family called Hafoc chose a sheltered site half way up the Cotswold scarp, high enough to be defended if necessary and giving a splendid view over the plain below. And Hafoc and his village are still remembered in the name of Hawkesbury, a memory well over 1,000 years old. The farm of Dodda or Dudda and his people is recalled in Dodington, a few miles south, and also at the Dodington in the Quantocks in Somerset. And from Mangoda's country (Mangotsfield) and Soppa's *beorh* (Sodbury) in the north to Wifela's combe (Wiveliscombe) in the far west and the *tun* of Heardred's people (Hardington) in the south, early settlers made their mark and left their names for ever on the land.

They knew, of course, that they were not quite pioneers. Out in the depths of the countryside they cleared or settled in primary woodland and their *leys* and *worths* remain. But in the more open country others had been before. Some of the *beorhs* were fortresses of prehistoric times, like the old *beorgh* at Oldbury (on Severn); many another site with a pure Saxon name might have been a Roman farm or prehistoric village, just as others were abandoned and forgotten. But the great Fosse Way was a permanent feature of the land which could not easily be lost. Where the Saxons settled on it, their names recall the fact: Stratton (on the Fosse) and Street are still quite obvious; Radstock means '*stock* on the road' and South Harp in South Petherton refers to the *harepaeth* or military way, which was, of course, exactly the purpose of the Fosse as it crossed Roman Britain from Lincoln to the port of Axmouth in South Devon. Ilchester, the Roman settlement on the River Yeo or Ivel, may not have been fully occupied by the country-loving Saxons but they recognized its importance, and if they forgot its Roman name, Lendinis, they remembered and were impressed by its walls in part of the name they gave it, *Givelcestre*. So, too, at Bath, where the hot springs were the distinguishing feature, and then the walls; the Saxons called the town *Bathum* or *Acemannesceaster*, a far cry from the classical *Aquae Sulis* after the healing waters of the goddess Sulis Minerva.

The newcomers found much to be done and many places in which to settle. Simple names they gave, like the place under the hill (Christon) or on the ridge (Dundry), the place in the river's bend (Cromhall) or the farm on the neck of land (Halse). Frampton (Cotterell) and Frenchay are the *tun* and the wood on the River Frome, the river already with a name; North and South Petherton, though far apart, are both on the river Parrett, whose name the Saxons learnt from the native Celts. And when the lie of the land was not easily recognizable, then its trees and plants might be the key – the *tun* by the oaks (Acton); the farm near the ashes (Ashton); the places with thorns (e.g. Thornbury), or reeds (Redwick), or alder trees (Aller) or broom (Brympton) or rushes (Ruishton). Staying longer they might notice other features like the deer at Dyrham, the otters at Otterford or the stags at Horton.

Permanent settlement led to regular cultivation and established topography: well-worn routes to fields and mill and market. Saxon charters and perambulations – the best descriptions of estate boundaries until maps – followed the property from landmark to landmark, often noting bridges and fords and ancient ways, like the 'made way' of the Olveston charter (955–9 A.D.), or the 'Redway' and the 'salt-carriers' way' of the Cold Ashton charter (931 A.D.). These routes were vital even in a primitive economy; the mills no less so for grinding the corn grown on the measured arable lands at Fitzhead or Fivehead (five hides) or Nynehead (nine hides), or on the *infurlanges*, the near plough-lands whose boundary was mentioned in the Aust charter of 929 A.D. And once measured out, the land was marked by boundary stone or ditch or post, giving us Alwih's stone (Alveston) or Cippa's post (Chipstable). And, just as the local owner staked out his land, so the tribe or people knew where theirs began and ended. Tormarton (hill-boundary-*tun*) and Marshfield (open land on the boundary) are both near the old Gloucestershire–Wiltshire county border; and so is Rimpton (*tun* of the *rima*) near the border of Somerset with Dorset.

After a generation or two of settlement and cultivation came expansion, as village communities sent out offshoots a mile or two away. The many Nortons and Suttons, Eastons and Westons, and their variants like Northwick and Southill, Eastham or Westerleigh chart the new foundations to all parts of the compass. The land is filled almost as far as the eye can see, but still there is forest and woodland, moor and marsh to be tamed and exploited; and later still come the scars of other exploitation. Iron was found at Acton by the end of the 13th century, and Coalpit Heath is clearly enough the product of 19th-century industrialization; less permanent were the lead diggings on the edge of Clifton Down, recorded in the perambulation attached to the Stoke Bishop charter of about 883 A.D., the slag mentioned in the Pucklechurch charter of 950 A.D., and the stone quarries in the Cold Ashton charter of 931 A.D.

To reach the 11th century is by no means the end of the story; indeed, only a complication, for the introduction of the new landed class of Norman-French families introduces the euphony that makes the study of place-names so enjoyable. To add the family name to a new estate was as much common sense as vanity, for Somerset settlers had proved so unimaginative that the Suttons and the Thorns, the Stokes and the Sheptons (sheep *tuns*) had somehow to be distinguished the one from the other. So family names were added to make Sutton Montis (Montacute), Sutton Mallet, and Sutton Bingham; Thornfalcon and Thorn Coffin; Stoke Pero, Rodney Stoke, Stoke Trister, and Stoke Gifford; and Shepton Beauchamp, Shepton Mallet, and Shepton Montague (Montacute again). And when for lay families is read the Church, then Huish Episcopi, Kingsbury Episcopi, and Bishops Lydeard signify the estates of the Bishops of Bath and Wells, and Stoke Bishop and Bishopston the episcopal estate of Worcester; Abbots Leigh (St Augustine's, Bristol), Stanton Prior (Bath), Abson (Glastonbury Abbey), Gaunts Earthcott in Almondsbury and Stockland Bristol, two holdings of Gaunt's Hospital, Bristol (now the Lord Mayor's Chapel), Temple Combe and Temple Fee, Bristol, owned by the Order of Knights Templar, Hinton Charterhouse and Witham Friary by the Carthusians; all are remembered from their names as estates of medieval religious houses. But some anomalies still remained even after these distinctions; there were still simple Stokes to be had in Somerset, so they became known, to mark them from the others, after the dedications of their churches, as in Stoke St Mary, Stoke St Michael, and Stoke St Gregory; and so, in the same way, were born Lydeard St Lawrence, Thorn St Margaret, Kingston St Mary, Lawrence Weston, and Norton St Philip.

Names on a map are not the exclusive preserve of the distant past, although a craze for the antique 100 years ago gave us Magnas and Parvas for simple English Great and Little, and made almost any medieval house with 'ecclesiastical' windows or carvings an Abbey or a Priory without the slightest historical justification. There was a time when Newtown, New Street, or New Inn were names borne with pride, but human nature is such that names like these last for centuries. Just as the modern map is dotted with names given by Saxon settlers who came to exploit the soil, so it includes names and features planted by 18th-century settlers who came to 'improve' the landscape with their mansions and parks, or who came to disfigure it with mines and factories. Modern awareness of the conservation lobby and of the needs of our over-mobile society to have some roots in the past now give rise, particularly in new streets and roads, office blocks and local government areas, to the resurrection of old names to clothe a naked modernity with some sort of respectability.

The Settlement of the Shires

The stages by which the Saxons of the upper Thames reached over the Cotswolds to the Severn Valley and then pushed west across the Avon to Mendip and beyond can only be traced in the barest outline. The victory of Cuthwine and Ceawlin over the British kings at Dyrham in 577 is the starting point, the battle of Penselwood in 658 marks the next phase, and the defeat of Geraint by Ine in 710 is the completion of at least the military conquest of the area. Ine himself was evidently more than a nominal Christian, and there is a close connexion, for instance, between his settlement at Taunton and a religious foundation there, established formally, it is said, by his successor's wife Frithogyth, but probably first planted in the wake of the advance. So it seems likely that in the period between 577 and the beginning of the 8th century, the political masters in the newly conquered lands were establishing the church on a firm footing.

The presence of St Augustine in futile conference with the Welsh bishops at Aust c. 603 certainly does not imply total Christian Saxon success even in the conquered territories, and after c. 628 until his death in 654 the offensive pagan Penda of Mercia had control of the former West Saxon land up to and probably beyond the Avon, almost certainly to the line of the West Wansdyke between Maes Knoll and Horsecombe, south of Bath. Effectively, therefore, the Christian settlement of the Saxons begins in the second half of the 7th century, marked by the establishment of a bishopric based on Worcester for the Hwiccas in 680, and by the foundation of religious houses at Bath (676) and Gloucester (681), the last two by Osric, Under-king (*Subregulus*) of the Hwiccas with the consent of Ethelred, King of Mercia. With slightly less precision, or rather on the basis of charters which in their surviving form are clearly forgeries, and traditions which at least have not been disproved, Ine of Wessex founded Muchelney (? by 693), Athelney may well predate Alfred's foundation, and Frome was established by St Aldhelm, perhaps by 687. All these were upstarts compared with the claims that Glastonbury was later to make for itself, though archaeologists can produce material no earlier in date than the 7th century.

There was, of course, an earlier, British tradition, not only at Glastonbury but on many sites within reach of the sea and the Celtic world: the links with Wales, Ireland, and Brittany are no less real for being much less precise. Glastonbury claims St Patrick; St Indracht, St David; Porlock, St Dyfrig; Congresbury, St Congar; Watchet, St Decuman; Timberscombe, St Petroc; Carhampton, St Carantoc; Brean, St Bridget of Kildare; Street, St Gildas and St Kea. The links have often survived to the present as church dedications; to the Reformation some survived as cults, and claims were made that the Somerset bishopric was based at Congresbury. Such suggestions were unhistorical in several senses, notably because Celtic bishops were itinerant pastors without need of fixed abode. Yet the claims establish religious sites which the Saxons adopted as bases for work in the countryside.

Were they minsters or monasteries? A precise line between religious communities of regular and secular rule can hardly be drawn in a period before the Benedictine revival, but by the beginning of the 9th century mission stations had been established at Westbury on Trym and Yate. The former was clearly linked with the Worcester bishopric perhaps from its beginnings and certainly from *c.* 691 when Bishop Oftfor was given the estate of Henbury by Ethelred, King of Mercia. In Somerset there were similar mission stations at Wells and Taunton, and early claims for Banwell and Bruton; and by King Alfred's time, though the monastic life had proved at least fragile, the pattern of minsters was established, a pattern that has become an integral part of the history of the countryside.

By its function the minster was the centre of missionary activity and its clergy, successfully preaching in the country, established first a regular preaching station, then a Christian community, and finally a place of worship. The links thus forged between 'mother' churches and their 'daughters' were the key to the formation of these huge early parishes, and often exerted a profound effect on social and economic ties. Hawkesbury, now a remote church under the Cotswold scarp not far from the Avon–Gloucestershire border, was evidently one such church. Its size bespeaks something more than a simple parish church; and links with other churches that surround it, once its daughters – Little Badminton, Hillesley, Tresham, and Wast – are a common minister characteristic. Probably all were part of a single Saxon estate which was given to Pershore Abbey. Later, when parishes were formally grouped together in deaneries, the minster at Hawkesbury stood at the head of its group.

Tell-tale place-names ending in 'minster', a church surrounded by chapels and other factors, show how widespread was the system in the West: Bitton, with its Saxon sculpture, the 'mother' church of Oldland and Hanham; Keynsham later (like many minsters) a house of Augustinian canons; Bedminster, embracing the whole of medieval Bristol south of the Avon; Chew Magna, reaching to Chew Stoke and Dundry, and itself an episcopal manor; Crewkerne, a royal manor whose 'daughters' of Misterton (once Ministerton) and Wayford still recognized their dependence in the 18th and 19th centuries; South Petherton, whose 'daughter' at Barrington copied the shape of its tower from the mother church; Taunton, whose 'daughters' were to be found spreading between the Quantocks and the Blackdowns on the Bishop of Winchester's huge estate of Taunton Deane. Thus the Saxon church developed in the countryside, forming its pattern of parish and deanery of significance far outside the confines of religion; some perhaps inherited from Roman estates or influenced by Roman roads, some dictated by natural features, some imposed by conquest. Somerset's bishopric founded at Wells in 909 naturally strengthened and concentrated the civilizing power of the Church, and by the time of Domesday its estates in both Somerset and Gloucestershire were extensive, though still much smaller than those of the Crown, whose lands in Somerset included not only the ancient demesne of Edward the Confessor but the large holdings of his Queen, Edith, and the forfeited properties of Harold and the royal house of Wessex. So the Conqueror held the huge royal estate of Somerton, possibly the ancient tribal capital of the county; Cheddar, Axbridge, and Wedmore, long associated with the Saxon kings; Bruton, Frome, and Milborne Port in the south-east; Bedminster on the banks of the Avon; Williton, Cannington, and Carhampton, held for the defence of the coast in the west. Over the Avon the King held the barton of Bristol, where the great royal castle was probably already begun, Marshfield on the top of the Cotswolds, and Thornbury overlooking the Severn.

Harold's lands, too, were extensive; strong in the west at Dulverton, Brompton (Regis), Old Cleeve, Nettlecombe, and Winsford; the minster estate at Crewkerne that had once been Alfred's and which William was soon to give to his favourite monastery at Caen; Congresbury in the marshes, Coker and Hardington in the fertile south. The Bishop of Winchester's property at Taunton heads the list of the Church's holdings in Domesday, followed by the Bishop of Salisbury (Seaborough, now in Dorset, and Chilcompton), the Bishop of Bayeux (Temple Combe) and the Bishop of Coutances. Bishop Giso of Wells already held the core of what his successors retained until the confiscations that followed the Reformation: radiating from Wells itself, the estate spread to Combe St Nicholas on the Devon border, to Wellington and Wiveliscombe in the west, and north to Chew Magna and Yatton. In contrast the estates of Bath Abbey were concentrated, evidence of its early foundation under Mercian influence: Bath, Bathford, Batheaston, Bathampton; up towards the Cotswolds to Charlcombe and Cold Ashton, and then across the Severn Valley to Olveston; to Priston, Stanton Prior, and Ashwick on Mendip, and south to Lyncombe, Monkton Combe, and Freshford – all save Olveston within 15 miles of the city. Glastonbury's property was both huge and scattered, though the central core, the 'Twelve Hides of Glastonbury', lay on the moors around the abbey. But they stretched from Stogursey in the west to Mells and Whatley in the east and to Wrington and Marksbury in the north; and then into Gloucestershire at Pucklechurch, and further, to Berkshire, Wiltshire, and Dorset. Worcester cathedral priory had wide lands too, its possessions coming as far as Westbury on Trym and Stoke Bishop by way of Redwick and Aust.

The Landscape in View

The estates that the great landowners had acquired by the late 11th century can, with the help of Domesday Book, be not only plotted but in outline described; and the story of Somerset and southern Gloucestershire during the next five centuries – indeed its story until the present – can be read by the discerning in the landscape. The name Kingswood is an obvious pointer to the great tract of woodland and heath to the east of Bristol which in Edward's I time had become known as the Forest of Chase of Kingswood, and which towards Keynsham merged into the Chace of Fillwood. The history of the countryside there is one of gradual encroachment for mining and settlement, proved, if proof were needed, in the name of Iron Acton, meaning 'the settlement in the oak wood known for its production of iron'. Further north, Alveston was the site of a royal park on the edge of the Forest of Horwood, an ill-defined area which seems to have stretched eastwards (in fact if not in law) in a wooded band around Hawkesbury and over the Cotswold scarp. Underwood rather than woodland proper was apparent around Bath, but further into Somerset woods were plentiful over the lias clay plain except, curiously, around Ilchester; among the hills and valleys of the north-east; along the Mendip slopes; and in the Quantock and Exmoor combes. Occasional large tracts were found in the south near the Blackdowns and in the far west around Porlock. Relatively bare were the Exmoor and Quantock uplands and the Levels.

So the great royal forests of medieval Somerset, Selwood along the Wiltshire border, Neroche on the Blackdown slopes, Exmoor, Mendip, and Quantock, and the royal parks of North Petherton (where Geoffrey Chaucer was once an official and where the Alfred Jewel was found) and Somerton were chosen areas of land where the pleasures of the hunt took precedence in law over the unfortunates who lived near by. Place-names, surviving ancient tree species, field shapes, and the character of settlement still mark out these areas. Stag and fox are still hunted over many of the areas that medieval kings made peculiarly their own.

Medieval landowners, eagerly emulating the Crown, created small parks for themselves on their own estates, each surrounded by ditch and bank and pale, so designed to encourage deer to enter but to prevent them from leaving. These, too, are traceable, for the fields within and the lanes without still often proudly bear the name. Park Lane on the south side of Montacute village is not planted with hotels but with trees, marking the boundary of a park which the Counts of Mortain had established before 1100. The National Trust now owns a footpath that follows the park pale and gives a fine view of a landscape feature created 800 years ago. As an added bonus, part of the park reaches to the ramparts of the Iron Age hillfort on Ham Hill, and an area was later converted into a rabbit warren. At the end of the warren is a small copse, known in the 19th century as the Dog Trap, a practical arrangement for excited hounds that had been chasing rabbits in the warren or deer in the park.

The low-lying areas of Somerset where trees were so conspicuously absent in the 11th century were those where more change was to come in the next two centuries than in any other part of the landscape. Under the encouraging hand of the landowners, principally Glastonbury Abbey but also involving the canons of Wells and the abbeys of Athelney and Muchelney, the tenants in the 'island' villages began to drain small parcels of marshland. The result was, for instance, to add 1,000 acres to the area of Middlezoy, Othery, and Weston Zoyland on the old 'island' of Sowy by 1240; an achievement every bit as important and economically beneficial to Glastonbury as the new port facilities at Bristol at the same period. This was not to say that the Levels were then fully drained; work on the rhines and on sea walls, and river embanking continued throughout the Middle Ages, and only in the middle years of the present century has flooding been largely eliminated by means of pumping engines, though extreme winter conditions can still put acres of grassland under water, showing how safe was Alfred's island refuge against the Danes in the 9th century (see Athelney). But medieval drainage certainly recovered vast acres of the low marshes; villages like Portbury, Wraxall, or Weston Zoyland became as large as some of the old small towns of Somerset, and farming was so improved that by the late 14th century Glastonbury Abbey could keep large flocks of sheep on the recovered soil.

Sheep were not only an important element in Glastonbury's farming. Somerset and Cotswold wool had been of equal value in the mid 14th century, though East Anglia and Kent then produced more for the continental market. Not much more than a century later Somerset was the second largest producer after Suffolk, but the wool was now being woven, dyed, and prepared at home and exported through Bristol, Bridgwater, and the southern ports in the form of finished cloth. Such a change had come about largely because of general trading changes, but it was made possible through the invention of the fulling mill, which occurred from the beginning of the 13th century. Thus when in the mid 14th century it became possible to export finished cloth rather than raw wool, the lines of collection and distribution were already established by the network of country markets that had grown up largely in the previous century. There were fewer markets in the Severn vale of southern Gloucestershire than in Somerset, because settlement was sparse there and Bristol so near – Chipping Sodbury, Bitton, Hawkesbury, and Marshfield were followed by Tockington, Pucklechurch, Wickwar, Almondsbury, and Frampton all founded between 1227 and 1285 to add to the ancient market of Thornbury. Clothiers like John Chapman, only a shadow of the famous woolman William Grevell of Chipping Campden, came from Gloucestershire for the Mendip fairs each year and in his will left money for the churches of Norton St Philip, Hinton Charterhouse, Priddy, and Binegar, places where he had done good business in the past. A century later merchants like John Smythe of Bristol were importing Spanish dyestuffs for the producers and sending their finished cloth to France and Spain.

John Chapman's will is tantalizing for Somerset historians. There is plenty of evidence to connect the Cotswold woolmen and clothiers with the churches of Northleach and Fairford and Chipping Campden, to whose rebuilding and decoration they gave generously. Thomas Compton (d. 1510), clothier of Beckington, gave a chapel there. The gift of a pair of tucker's shears to Old Cleeve (1533) and of cloth to the tower building fund of St Mary's, Taunton (1488–1514), the shuttle carved at Kingston St Mary (1522) or the fuller at Spaxton are clear indications that the cloth trade was at the heart of things on the Quantocks. But the basis was, in fact, as the popular contributions to the new works at Croscombe imply, very much wider than one industry, however prosperous. The Perpendicular style in Somerset and Gloucestershire was a glorious flowering made possible by industrial and agricultural prosperity, the exploitation of superb building stone, and possibly by changing emphasis in liturgical practices.

Natives are apt to blind enthusiasm, architectural historians are often interested in the technicalities of proportion and detail. The visitor to Avon and Somerset may recall the 'cathedrals' of East Anglian parishes and, influenced by sheer scale, give Somerset second best. And yet, for its contribution to the landscape the Somerset church tower is supreme. The delicately pierced crown of what was only a chapel, not even a parish church, at Dundry (1482) beckons over the hill from Bristol to the glories beyond; it may, too, have been something of a mason's sample, for it stood on the edge of a quarry that provided stone for a wide area. In the centre of Bristol a similar tower, that of St Stephen, is a direct link with the cradle of Perpendicular – Gloucester; towers in Bristol with pierced parapet and one higher pinnacle, spread their influence for miles into the hinterland. But over the hill from Dundry can be traced a triumphant progress of tower building, a progress that experts have on more than one occasion tried to trace by types and styles. What is certain is that from the 1380s to the 1540s many towers and most churches in Somerset and Avon were rebuilt, extended, refurnished, or refashioned by what must inevitably have been a small number of craftsmen of the highest skills.

Itinerant masons, chosen by inspecting churchwardens, agreed for the work to be done and used their own or some master mason's approved pattern. The contract between John Marys of Stogursey and the parishioners of Dunster in 1442 was that he would complete the tower 100 ft high within three years, the parish bringing all the materials and providing ropes, winches, and other essentials. The mason agreed to a detailed specification including windows made to the pattern of Richard Pope, free-mason. That great tower is relatively plain, with strong diagonal buttresses in fine proportion to its red sandstone bulk. The parishioners had not far to go for materials, and the sandstone of the Brendons or Exmoor, the light grey freestone which looks so well in contrast, often topped with grey-blue Treborough slates, are used to good decorative effect. This decoration was important; there was a practical element in the quality of individual stone types, but the masons could not have been unaware of the effect of the bands of conglomerate and Pennant stone at Iron Acton, the gold and red of Kingston St Mary or the gold and blue of Huish Episcopi. A lowering sun on towers like these reveals a depth of colour and a delicacy of shadow which is Somerset Perpendicular at its best.

Towers are not, of course, the only Somerset speciality. There are bench ends in splendid variety, often dated or signed, and displaying the imagination of local craftsmen in secular as well as religious themes (though Glastonbury St John's bought a full set of pews in 1500 from David Carver of Temple Fee, Bristol, which were brought from there by sea and river). There are screens and rood-lofts probably marking a significant change in liturgical practice and chantry chapels through which the rich could display their piety with the maximum of exuberance.

Beside the parish churches and cathedrals of medieval England stand religious houses and castles as popular reminders of a vanished past. Pre-eminent here stands Glastonbury, where antiquity and legend have carved out for this place dreams that were never dreamed when religious observance gave life to the place. So Glastonbury and Muchelney and Bath were old when St Dunstan (himself from Somerset) reformed them in the 10th century. After the Conquest came the Norman foundations of Stogursey, Montacute, and St James's in Bristol, the second the only Cluniac house in the area. During the 12th century houses of Augustinian canons were founded, often in succession to Saxon minsters: Taunton led the way *c.* 1120, followed by Bruton, St Augustine's, Bristol (later the cathedral), Keynsham, Barlinch (in the far west near Dulverton), Buckland (in Durston parish), all founded in the 12th century, and Worspring and Stavordale (see under Weston-super-Mare and Wincanton) in the 13th. The strict Carthusians came to Witham in 1178–9 as part of Henry II's penance for Becket's murder and the first house of the order to be founded in England; and the Cistercians chose a remote valley in the parish of Old Cleeve (see Cleeve Abbey). Becket's murder brought the Knights Templar an estate at Williton before their commandery at Temple Combe is known to have been founded, and before they acquired the valuable property in Bristol known as Temple Fee. In the 13th century the friars came to the towns, to Bristol, to Bridgwater, and Ilchester, but not to Wells or Bath; and the Knights Hospitaller, the Order of St John of Jerusalem, added the former Templar property in 1312 to the house for the sisters of the order at Durston acquired from Augustinian canons *c.* 1180. The remains of St Augustine's, Bristol, Glastonbury, Muchelney, Cleeve, Worspring, and Hinton Charterhouse survive to demonstrate well the external features of the monastic life; in other places the work of destruction has been thorough and precise sites of buildings are not even known. At Taunton the great burial ground has been discovered, but neither the church nor the conventual buildings. Athelney, too, is unexplored; so is the church and cloister at Montacute. Amateur and professional have uncovered several sites, none more successfully than a former owner of Hinton Charterhouse, whose work on the great cloister and its tiny individual cells and gardens provided clear proof of the strict simplicity of life achieved by the Carthusians and sustained until the Dissolution.

That great event is a watershed in landscape history, for it marks not only the end of the regular religious life but, with the other changes of the Reformation, it is the end of pre-eminent religious expression. The medieval landowner, anxious for his soul's salvation, gave generously to the Church; endowed, sustained, built, and protected it. And the Church, landowner in its turn, built, endowed, and sustained. At Dunster William de Mohun built his castle on the hill and his priory at the gate; Robert, Earl of Gloucester, strengthened the great fortress in the centre of Bristol and, so it is said, gave every 10th stone brought for his great keep from Caen for the building of St James's priory across the Frome. The model survives at Dunster, at Bristol hardly at all.

The other castles of the area are a reflection of local political history. The one other Domesday castle apart from Dunster, the great, largely natural motte that gave its name to Montacute (*Mons acutus*), ceased to be a fortress with the disgrace of the Count of Mortain and passed to the passive hands of the Cluniac monks in the new priory at its foot. In the anarchy of Stephen's reign, when Bristol and the West played so prominent a part, castles at Nether Stowey, East Harptree, Castle Cary, and Glastonbury took on a temporary importance, but survive now as more or less impressive earthworks. Taunton's castle had a different role from the beginning; its low riverside site makes that obvious, and its first buildings were not military in purpose. Its great keep, built in the mid 12th century, was there to impress rather than to defend, though a strictly military rôle was later several times thrust upon it. The castle was, in fact, an administrative centre for the great estates of the Bishops of Winchester, and now aptly serves as home for the Somerset County Museum and the Somerset Archaeological and Natural History Society, while the base of its great keep forms a garden for a fine hotel.

Three later castles are similarly well preserved. Fairy-tale Nunney in its valley site, Farleigh Hungerford on a bluff above the Frome, and the unfinished splendour of Thornbury are in essence fortified mansions and not military strongholds at all; the tradition of towers and battlements and gatehouses ignored the military advances of the day, and were put to shame when owners tried to defend them in the Civil War. They were, of course, the exception; settled times had given rise to homes in the domestic style, rare at first (at least in survival) like the late-Norman Saltford or Horton, some still retaining a pretence of defence with a gatehouse or tower like late-medieval Clevedon Court or Clapton, but more often claiming no more than an elegant domesticity. Lytes Cary and Cothay in Somerset, Congresbury vicarage or the prebendal houses at Yatton and Horton in Avon, are examples among many of the style and scale of the homes of the late medieval middle class; field work is almost every week producing a new example of the smaller medieval house, almost always disguised behind a later façade, but evidence enough both of the remarkable survival of buildings and of the high quality of living conditions in the West Country.

After the Reformation changes a new element came into the picture. The sale of the monastic sites and the end of masses for the dead together brought potential new houses and spare cash to buy and build. The Church ceased to be the object of a man's generosity and devotion; treasures on earth were now worth accumulating. A house might be formed from the remains of a monastery as at Hinton Charterhouse, or the abbot's lodging might be adapted as at Montacute, Muchelney, or Cleeve. At Barrow Gurney (Avon) a new mansion was built where the old nunnery once stood. The profits of government and of land dealings might be invested to the same end: the manor house at Mells, formerly belonging to Glastonbury, or the new mansions at Montacute, Poundisford, Long Ashton, and Barrington were built by men who in one way or another had risen from humble origins and accumulated wealth in the age of opportunity when ex-monastic land had stimulated the market and trade was both respectable and good. Dyrham in the late 17th century and King's Weston in the 18th were similarly products of wealth acquired in political and government service, and Dodington the result of successful investment abroad.

There were, of course, remarkable cases of continuity, notably at Dunster where the Luttrells lived from the early 15th century, changing their home, not always by design, from castle to mansion; or Hinton St George, acquired through marriage by the Pouletts not many years later. Dunster, thanks to a 19th-century architect, has retained its character as a medieval fortress, but the medieval house at Hinton is difficult to trace among the additions and alterations of successive owners, and is now divided. Its park, now almost entirely farmed, never achieved the perfection Nathaniel Kent and the 4th Earl Poulett planned – lakes and belts of trees to add to the earlier deer park, oak and lime walks and terraces – but the essential outlines still survive. Similar parks, revolutionary and sometimes ruthless in their creation, are a permanent and important feature in the history of the landscape.

John Leland in his travels in the 1540s through Gloucestershire and Somerset had a keen eye for the towns through which he passed, if a rather repetitive turn of phrase.

Chipping Sodbury was 'a praty little market towne', Wickwar 'a pratye clothinge toun-let'; at Thornbury trade had seen better days, and Keynsham was 'sumtyme a good, now a poore, market town, and ruinus'. Pensford and Chew Magna, Wells, Glastonbury, and Bruton were prospering, though Ilchester was 'in wonderful decay' and Crewkerne 'nothing very notable' and 200 houses at Bridgwater had decayed 'in tyme of remem-braunce'. Dunster and Minehead had respectively a 'celebrate' and a 'praty' market.

Towns are clearly not the stable features of the landscape we often take them for; their fortunes vary. There were in medieval Somerset a relatively large number of towns, a legacy of Saxon settlement, and their numbers were increased by new plantations. Axbridge, Langport, Watchet, and Bath were parts of the defensive system initiated by King Alfred, and by the time of Domesday Ilchester, Milborne Port, Bruton, Taun-ton, Frome, and Milverton were calling themselves boroughs, and Crewkerne, Ilminster, and Yeovil had urban characteristics. Bristol and Thornbury were the nearest towns across the Avon. In size Bath came first, but was still by present standards small, with a probable population of approx. 1,000. Bath was followed in Somerset by Ilchester, soon to be the county town, about half the size; then Taunton, Milborne Port, Langport, and Axbridge. The phenomenal growth of Bristol in the 12th century clearly had its effect on urban development within a wide radius, but particularly in south Gloucestershire. Wells, though, apparently devastated in the late 11th century by the removal of the bishop, became by the 14th century and for long remained the largest Somerset town, as much by natural growth as by the return of ecclesiastical administration. Bridgwater, not recognizably urban in Domesday, developed into the county's largest port within two centuries, thanks to its position on the tidal Parrett.

The most notable development, however, was the 'new town', converted from a village by the grant of trading privileges and often by a physical extension. So the Counts of Mortain laid out plots below their castle at Montacute before c. 1100 to create what is now Middle Street; the Mohuns of Dunster before 1197 gave the people in the village below a charter which marks the creation of its wide and picturesque High Street. The Lord of Somerton in the late 13th century totally reorganized the streets there to ensure that trade passed through his new market, the Market Place which is still the focus of the town's business. And so the story continued, with varying success, at Nether Stowey and Stogursey, Chard, Rackley in Compton Bishop, Downend in Puriton, Lower Weare, Stoford, Marshfield, Wickwar, Pensford, and Chipping Sodbury.

By the early 14th century there were 17 places in Somerset described as towns, and other places like Frome, Shepton Mallet, Bruton, Bedminster, Crewkerne, and Glaston-bury which were worth, for tax purposes, almost as much. There were only five in the southern part of Gloucestershire. The Somerset list begins with Wells, followed by Bridg-water, Bath, and Taunton. Bristol obviously dominates the Gloucestershire list, followed in the county as a whole by Gloucester, Cirencester, and then by Marshfield. Thornbury, Chipping Sodbury, and Wickwar come well down the list.

One great change for some towns had come about just as Leland was in the West Country: Glastonbury, Keynsham, and (despite what he said) Bruton would never be the same again with the fall of the monasteries, though an attempt to make Glastonbury the county town of Somerset might have changed the course of subsequent events. Thornbury, affected a few years earlier by the fall of the Staffords, was never to fulfil the flamboyant promise of its castle. And small towns depending too much on a dwindling cloth trade were already dying; those that survived depression in the 16th century found themselves on the wrong trade routes in the next. Taunton, Wellington, and Shepton Mallet could flourish on cloth despite the threats of northern industrialization in the 18th century, and Frome in the early 1800s grew faster than any and reminded Cobbett of Manchester. But Wickwar was off the main routes, and so were Nether Stowey, Somerton, and Langport. They could just survive, but did not grow. Bridgwater's trade was never so good after the great cloth days of the late 15th century, but what port could expect to thrive in the shadow of Bristol? Its 18th-century expansion was modest but real, and it remains the most industrialized of all Somerset's towns. Ilchester's story is perhaps the saddest of all, its death prolonged over six centuries by political machinations, finally yielding its anomalous claim to be the county town when it was little more than a village.

Precise growth can only be measured in modern times. In 1801 Frome was by some distance the largest Somerset town after Bath, but was outstripped by Taunton within the next 40 years. Shepton Mallet and Wells came next, but though Wells grew a little, both gave place to Yeovil, Midsomer Norton–Radstock, and to the fast-growing Weston-super-Mare, which outstripped all but Bath by the 1920s. More modern figures show a different pattern. The sprawling subsurb has given way to the dormitory and the new town; Kingswood is almost Bristol, Keynsham and Saltford are the homes for workers in Bristol and Bath. Clevedon and Portishead are not now those quiet seaside retreats; Nailsea, Yatton, and Congresbury, Thornbury and Yate, have grown beyond recognition. The County of Avon itself is an acknowledgement of Bristol's magnetic field.

The town in the old sense of a gradually developed centre of population has been set aside; numbers are what matter. But numbers do not create community, and streets need a focus in more than a simple design sense. The attractions of Chipping Sodbury and Marshfield, Somerton or Crewkerne are not simply visual, though that is a factor of importance. Each is the creation of a community over a long period of time, not the sudden inspiration of a draughtsman or the dream of a planner.

The prehistoric trade routes, like the saltways of the Severn Valley or the ridgeways on the spines of higher ground, gave way to the Roman Fosse and its branches giving access to sea ports and lead mines and providing speedy communication between developed towns. The railways in their turn, their axis on Bristol, were built for speed. Brunel's plan to make Bristol the last landfall before the New World, and the later idea of making Brean Down a great port of embarkation, had to be abandoned for more modest achievements: links with the Channel resorts of Portishead, Clevedon, Weston, and Minehead and co-ordinated paddle-steamer trips to Barry, Ilfracombe, and Lundy. The tracks, mostly laid down by the 1860s with loops and other improvements continuing until 1910, brought stations within easy reach of most villages and an impetus to farmers and manufacturers alike. The London market was open for perishables like butter, milk, and strawberries, and for bulk goods like coal and ore, paper, gloves, and shoes. And then, perhaps, began the disease that has in some ways been Somerset's salvation. The railways made the old county of Somerset almost a non-stop express route. Holiday-makers from Leeds and Bradford, on their way down the Midland line through Gloucester and Bristol for South Devon, sped along the gentle curves of the track through the Somerset Levels and Taunton. From Manchester they took a more dramatic route from Bath across the Mendips to holidays in Bournemouth. They could change at Bristol for the iodine of Weston, but the urge was to be gone.

The motorways encourage the same attitude of mind. Almondsbury is the unfortunate axis for the routes from Wales, the North, and London which beckon the driver with the same siren song. The new routes opened up new landscapes as well as swallowing up old land, but there is no time to enjoy them. The old routes are at least less crowded; and those who venture on them have their own reward.

Road patterns are, of course, an important factor in the landscape and the rise and fall of trade routes are part and parcel of the history of our land. Since its rise as a port, roads have converged on Bristol for obvious reasons, though until the turnpike era their quality was variable both according to the season and the efficiency of each parish in maintaining its section. The main routes north and east from Bristol, marked by the medieval markets at Almondsbury and Thornbury on the Gloucester road, at Chipping Sodbury – a 'new town' c. 1227 – on the Oxford road, and Marshfield or Bath on the direct London road, could be modified even in antiquity so that Wickwar (1285) took business from Gloucester traffic attracted to Chipping Sodbury; and then, in the late 14th century, both were bypassed, giving new life to Winterbourne (1393). The southern routes then and later were confined by difficulty in crossing the Levels. The main reliable route, marked again by a 'new town' at Pensford, probably a late-12th-century foundation, passed through Wells, Glastonbury, and Somerton to Crewkerne and the south coast, with a less reliable route to Axbridge, Bridgwater, Dunster, and Minehead. Three roughly parallel routes gave direct access from London, the mail coming through Yeovil, Crewkerne, and Chard, the cattle more likely over Salisbury Plain and, skirting Selwood, passing through Somerton to Taunton. The third route was through Frome, Shepton Mallet, Glastonbury, along the Poldens to Bridgwater and then by the Great Road over the Quantocks to Exmoor.

The turnpike era adopted new routes and established new standards. The demands of Bath brought the first Turnpike Trust to Somerset in 1707–8, and for the next century improvements came thick and fast, to which J. L. McAdam's employment on the Bristol–Bath road in 1816 was a fitting climax. The pattern was thereafter set until the phenomenal rise in the number of vehicles demanded more radical measures than road-widening and limited dual carriageways. There are still, happily, many miles of roads not built for the motor car; the characteristic hollow-ways of the Yeovil area, their sides often like bare cliffs of sandstone, or the grass-covered stone banks and high hedges of the Brendons and Exmoor; even the deceptively straight by-roads on the Levels, given to sharp corners and flanked by ditches too deep and wet for comfort. There are those who complain of lack of signposts; others with a good sense of direction will surely be challenged to the full if they travel far without a map. But what is wrong with being lost in such delectable country?

*　　*　　*

The present has come out of the past. That is a statement of rather obvious truth; but there are some parts of the country where the signs of the past are less easy to see and its reality more difficult to imagine. The West Country has not by any means been totally untouched by industry, only by industry that has not kept to itself. A popular radio programme offered as a first prize a week in Severn Beach, and as a second prize two weeks; there is a factory at Bridgwater that produces an effect more reminiscent of experiments in chemistry at school than of the manufacture of modern clean packaging. That smells and smelters are so obvious is a measure of the freshness and beauty of their surroundings. On the high upland acres of the Cotswolds in summer, or a winter's day on Mendip; in the mist of early morning on the Somerset moors, or on autumn afternoons on Quantock and Exmoor, the past can often be very near and the present far away. But that experience might be possible in many parts of the world. What is so attractive about this part of the West Country is that its beauty is not remote but close at hand; and so normal that its natives (like natives everywhere) often need others to show it to them. And because it is normal, the dangers of making it picturesque and popular have, with a few exceptions, been avoided.

Close at hand is certainly the key; even the largest urban sprawl is somehow within manageable proportion. Bedminster Down is still green, Dundry church stands sentinel over its fields, and Clifton and Durdham Downs provide at least western Bristol with its greatest asset – a vision of the country beyond brick and concrete. Bath's surrounding hills keep it in compass, though the thunder can roll around the city and make one sigh for cooler air. And at no distance from either are places of peace and quiet which the mad world has mercifully passed by. North of Bath, in the folds of the dying Cotswolds, there are villages and hamlets like St Catherine and Tadwick, Langridge and Woolley, whose links with the city are still more redolent of their ownership by the Abbey before the Reformation than of their proximity to Beau Nash's spa. True, Woolley church was rebuilt by Wood the Younger, but Langridge still has Norman work which makes it as old as John de Villula's cathedral, and St Catherine has a chancel and glass given by Prior Cantlow of Bath in 1490 and parts of a house where he and other priors had a country retreat. Similarly, beyond the urban spread of Bristol there are villages like Publow and Woollard, Abbot's Leigh or Failand, more obviously affected by the city but still providing near at hand the natural beauties of the Chew Valley or Leigh Woods (NT), as well as the flavour of village life which is the most valuable asset of the English countryside. Taunton is not urban in the same sense, but from High Street both the Quantocks and the Blackdowns can be seen, and unspoiled hamlets like Nailsbourne and Orchard Portman can be found long before the hills are reached.

And the past is not just close at hand physically. Somerset folk are not quite as Cecil Sharp found them when he was gathering songs at the turn of the century – simple country people of great age, guardians of a primitive culture; and yet many of the traditional activities of country life are thriving. They may be revivals, and occasionally with just a hint of commercialism, but at least not obviously altered for the tourist calendar. Wassailing in the orchards of Carhampton in January or holding a Punkie Night lantern on a late October night are not put on as a show for outsiders, they are live community events. Sampling last year's cider is a more serious purpose than firing guns in the orchard to ward off evil spirits and ensure a good crop, though any publicity the event might attract is good for a product that is for some synonymous with Somerset. Mangold lanterns at Lopen and Hinton St George, it is claimed, have no more sinister and primitive meaning than to recall how the visit of village husbands to Chiselborough fair was unduly prolonged, and how the wives, equipped with these makeshift lights, frightened their befuddled spouses when they went en masse to look for them. The Minehead Hobby Horse, stolen from Padstow or the other way about, may or may not have driven off the Danes, but it is more kind to visitors, appearing on the first three days of May and sometimes coming as two or even three. That he now emerges from a van makes him no whit the less mysterious when the dance begins, the drum takes up the rhythm, and the collecting tins are shaken in unison. The 'animator' ceases to exist, just as the Marshfield mummers on Boxing Day become impersonal under their costumes of newspaper strips.

Everywhere in a countryside with memory there are ghosts and rumours of ghosts. Legends are legion, but none so moving and so widely influential as those of Glastonbury, of St Joseph of Arimathea and the boy Jesus, of the Holy Grail and the Holy Thorn, of Arthur and Guinevere. And no event is so live as the battle of Sedgemoor: emotions still run high, and events however unhistorical and easily disproved are recounted with relish and absolute belief. The beams from which Jeffreys' victims were hanged near 300 years ago are pointed out with the pride of those who would have joined in Monmouth's support had they been there.

Tradition, of course, is a dangerous mistress. As early as the end of the 18th century cheese made in Cheddar was being sold in London as Double Gloucester, only the beginning of the injustice that now allows the housewife to buy Cheddar cheese from Ireland, Holland, and Canada. Bath, on the other hand, seems to have a monopoly of chaps and chairs, buns and olivers. A recent visitor wanting to buy local clotted cream could find none in the shops not made in Devon. But cream is made, like cheese and cider, in the farmhouses of the countryside, and often sold at the door, as it was long before the milkman and the off-licence were invented. Crafts, too, are flourishing and cottage industries thrive – pottery, spinning wheels, corn dollies, furniture, weaving, leather work – products not of this area in particular, but the work of artists and craftsmen inspired by the local scene. But all is done with reticence, without commercial display.

There is, so people claim, a different air. The pace even in Bristol is not metropolitan. Further west the humidity rises, softens the speech, even enervates. But who complains? Does not the spring come earlier to Porlock, and is not the grass more lush and green on Aller moor? Political, religious, and economic pressures have forced the native to seek refuge or a better future in many parts of the world, but the fond link with home is written on the map wherever he has gone. Somerset will ever be that land of summer, as the Welsh describe it; Avon is only a name, ancient indeed, but as a county how can it yet be welded to the traditions of the land it now embraces after so short a time? But what does name and county matter? Somerset itself occurred first as a people and only later as a unit of administration. It is people who make community, not government; and it is people who make or mar the landscape in which they live. In the countryside that is now called Somerset and Avon are the legacy of the people of the past and the challenge to the future; here is the fascinating pattern of English building at its most varied, the rich fabric of the English countryside within compass, the glory of English provincial history illustrated to perfection.

Short-Stay Guide

A few days will not be enough to appreciate to the full the attractions of Somerset and Avon, but a few days are better than nothing at all. They will be enough to persuade the traveller to a second visit. The following list is highly subjective and in order of neither preference nor merit.

Cities and towns
Bath
Bristol
Chipping Sodbury
Clevedon
Crewkerne
Frome
Marshfield
Somerton
Taunton
Thornbury
Wellington

Villages
East Coker
Great Badminton
Iron Acton
Montacute
Norton St Philip
Selworthy
Tintinhull

Castles
Farleigh Hungerford
Nether Stowey
Nunney

Landscape and Nature
Brendons
Cheddar
Exmoor
Ham Hill
Mendips
Quantocks

Churches and Abbeys
Bristol Cathedral
Clifton Cathedral
Croscombe Church
Glastonbury Abbey
Hawkesbury Church
Hinton Charterhouse Priory
Huish Episcopi Church
Muchelney Abbey
Stogursey Church
Stoke sub Hamdon Church
Wells Cathedral

Mansions
Dodington
Dunster
Dyrham
Montacute

Gazetteer

Abbreviations

BTA   for British Tourist Authority
DoE   for Department of the Environment
NMR   for National Monuments Record
NT   for National Trust

Entries in the Gazetteer

The first figure of the map reference supplied to each entry refers to a page number in the map section at the back of the book. The subsequent letter and figure give the grid reference.

Alfoxton Som. *see* **Nether Stowey**

Aller Som. *see* **Athelney**

Almondsbury Avon 5 B3

Almondsbury is at the centre of a large parish which once included the modern suburbs of Filton and Patchway. Its former manors can still be traced in the late-16th-century Knole Park, with its 15th-century tower; the Elizabethan Over Court (2 miles sw) on the site of a 14th-century house; and the 16th-century manor house at Gaunts Earthcott (2 miles E), a place called after the Gaunt family who by 1259 had given it to their hospital at Billeswick, Bristol, usually known as Gaunt's Hospital. The hospital's chapel survives as the Lord Mayor's chapel on College Green, opposite Bristol Cathedral.

Gloucestershire's historian, Samuel Rudder, referred to the 'vulgar opinion' that claimed that the body of Offa, King of Mercia, was first buried at Over and was later taken out of a tumulus there – a local and fanciful explanation of the burial mounds that perhaps marked the settlement of the Saxon named Aethelmod or Ealhmund who gave the place its name.

The church of St Mary has suffered severely from 19th-century restorers, though they at least revealed what the 18th century had tried to conceal. They pulled down the nave, destroying the arcades of an impressive Norman church. The lower part of the N porch and the font now stand alone from the period. The church is said to have been consecrated by four bishops in 1148. There was considerable rebuilding in the mid-13th century when the chancel, crossing, and transepts were reconstructed. The beautiful E window was blocked in the 18th century by a Classical screen or altarpiece which Rudder, typical of his time, thought handsome. Restoration in 1834 revealed the triple lancet with Purbeck marble shafts, leaf capitals, and corbels with human heads. The graceful rib-vaulted roof supports an upper chamber. How much had to be restored is difficult to determine. The tower belongs to the 13th-century rebuilding, though not its splendid leaden spire.

Former owners of the great houses of Almondsbury lie in the church, but the oldest memorials, contemporary with the chancel, probably include a former vicar. Edward Veele (d. 1577), lord of the manor of Over, and his wife Catherine (d. 1575) have an impressive pillared tomb about 6 ft high, he wearing armour heavy enough to inhibit any kind of martial exercise. She wears a Paris hood, ruff, stomacher, padded sleeves, and full skirt. The calf and wheatsheaf under their heads were symbols on the family arms.

The large monument to the Chester family, who lived at Knole after Thomas Chester, Mayor of Bristol, built it *c.* 1570, was put up in 1763 on the death of another Thomas by his 'deeply afflicted' and 'venerating' widow. Thomas was M.P. once for Gloucester and five times for

the county; and if his wife's words are to be believed he was an exemplary party man of 'inflexible attachment to what he thought the true interests of his country. From these he could never be prevailed on to swerve, nor during so long a service, by one Vote, or conniving Absence, to desert, or disappoint the Expectations of his Constituents'. He was, in fact, a Tory who sat in Parliament 1727–8 and 1734–63, largely with Beaufort support, and is only reported to have spoken in the House of Commons once in his whole career, during a debate on the cider tax. On that occasion, it was said: 'Old Chester was seen to speak, but not heard, a gentle murmur on all sides filling the House as he spoke'.

Medieval Almondsbury lay on the main route between Bristol and Gloucester, and a market was established in 1285. The village grew rapidly in the 1870s, from 600 to 2,188, and its Cottage Hospital and Institute (1891) mark the beginnings of its urbanization. But if that means a concentration of people, a more modern development, the motorway, has had a fragmenting effect. The M4 and M5 have divided Almondsbury parish, and their junction, the first four-level interchange in the country (1966), swallowed up much of its farmland.

Alveston Avon *see* **Thornbury**

Ammerdown Avon *see* **Radstock**

Athelney Som. 2 B2

The isle of Athelney, beside the A361 between LYNG and BURROWBRIDGE, is perhaps the most fascinating and yet elusive of all the sites in the Somerset Levels. A persistent tradition tells of King Alfred, so concerned with problems of state that he allowed his hostess's baking to spoil. Certainly Athelney, which means 'island of princes', was for him a turning point in his reign. He came here in the winter of 877–8, a fugitive from the seemingly unbeatable Danes who threatened to destroy the Saxon Kingdom of Wessex. Here 'amid the woods and fen tastnesses' of the Somerset marshlands he recovered his strength. At Easter 878, according to the *Anglo-Saxon Chronicle*, Alfred built a stronghold on land only a little higher than the marshes. Then, with some local people, he rode to Egbert's Stone, E of the great forest of Selwood beyond Frome (q.v.), and was there joined by all the people of Somerset and Wiltshire and from parts of Hampshire. And two days later they defeated the Danish army at Edington (Wilts.).

Some weeks afterwards the Danish king, Guthrum, with 30 leading men, came to Alfred at ALLER, across the marshes from Athelney, and in the church there, on its own island (4 miles E) he was baptized in a public declaration that henceforward the Danes were Christian, part of the civilized world.

Athelney continued to be important to Alfred. He joined it by means of a bridge or causeway to another fort 'of most beautiful workmanship'; and this causeway,

The Severn Bridge

sometimes now with bundles of withies leaning against its banks, still links Athelney with the fortified village of LYNG, though the only traces of its ancient earthen banks are the rise and fall of the road and the position of the church and churchyard.

Alfred founded, or perhaps revived, a monastery on the island to spearhead his campaign to re-establish learning in England. He filled it with foreigners under John the Old Saxon; but the monks were unhappy with the arrangement, and two of them planned to kill John and leave his body in a house of ill-fame. The abbot managed to fight off his assailants.

The Abbey was neither large nor rich, but it survived until 1539, when an abbot and six monks surrendered. All traces of buildings have disappeared, but medieval floor tiles were recently discovered *in situ* by the monument. William of Malmesbury, writing in the early 12th century, tells of a church with apsidal chapels all built on piles – normal building practice when the foundations rest on peat.

A mile NE at BURROWBRIDGE is an isolated hill called Burrow Mump (NT), bought as a memorial to Somerset's dead in the First World War. The natural hill was the site of a fortification in the 12th century, if not an Alfredian fort earlier. This was replaced by a medieval church dedicated, of course, to St Michael, which was rebuilt in the 15th century and again in the 18th. On the latter occasion, however, the work was never quite finished. The parishioners endured the exertion and exposure for a little longer, but built a replacement in the village in 1836.

Aust   Avon   5   B3
Aust is tucked away beside the M4 motorway and beneath the Severn Bridge approaches. Its name seems to come from a Roman river crossing to Caerleon-on-Usk and Caerwent, the *Trajectus Augustus* used by the Augustan Legion of the Roman army. Ever since that time Aust has been important as a crossing. In A.D. 603 St

Augustine of Canterbury may well have come here or hereabouts to 'a place still (when the Venerable Bede wrote) known to the English as Augustine's Oak, which lies on the border between the Hwiccas and the West Saxons'. There Augustine met bishops and other church leaders from Wales.

> He began by urging them to establish brotherly relations with him in Catholic unity, and to join with him in God's work of preaching the Gospel to the heathen. Now the Britons did not keep Easter at the correct time ... Furthermore, certain other of their customs were at variance with the universal practice of the Church. But despite protracted discussions, neither the prayers, advice, nor censures of Augustine and his companions could obtain the compliance of the Britons, who stubbornly preferred their own customs to those in universal use among Christian Churches.

And despite a test of Augustine's spiritual stature which almost rivalled Elijah on Mount Carmel, no decision was reached, and the Welsh Church continued on its separate way.

In 1966 the last ancient ferry-crossing ceased to operate when the Severn Bridge was opened. Designed by Sir Gilbert Roberts, the main span is 3,240 ft and its side spans 1,000 ft long. It is a suspension bridge of the box-girder type and has been described (in *Gloucestershire, The Vale and the Forest of Dean* by David Verey) as 'a consummate expression of the civil engineer's art in that although it appears so impossibly fragile in its lightness and grace, it is capable of carrying vehicles up to 200 tons in weight'.

The church has timber roofs in both nave and chancel which are largely original and which date from the 15th century, when the whole was evidently rebuilt. It was linked at least from 1297 with the college of Westbury on Trym, an estate at Aust forming a prebend at the college for the support of one of the canons there. In 1362 Pope Urban V granted the prebend of Aust to a young Oxford don from Yorkshire called John Wyclif. He was never the parish priest, only one of the many distinguished clergy of the time who took their income from a parish and left the pastoral work to others.

At the time of his appointment Wyclif was a traditionalist, a philosopher, the 'flower of Oxford'. In the 1370s he began to publish his anti-clerical opinions which made him popular with John of Gaunt and an opponent of the ecclesiastical hierarchy, and his writings included a denial of the doctrine of transubstantiation. Condemned by his colleagues at Oxford and then by a synod in London, he was left to die unconvicted at his country home at Lutterworth in Leicestershire in 1384. There is no evidence that he ever visited Aust, but his ultimate influence as inspirer of the Lollards, particularly strong in and around Bristol, and as precursor of the Protestant Reformation make the prebendary of Aust a man of the greatest importance in our national history.

Axbridge Som. 4 H5

Axbridge somehow shows its age, not because there are particular signs of decadence, but because timbered houses and the church cluster around the sloping market place. Close grouping has always been the problem, for Axbridge has never been able to expand naturally, squeezed as it is between the Mendip scarp and the moors. Its name suggests an early fortified settlement commanding the River Axe and defending the Saxon royal palace at Cheddar (q.v.) (unless it was a bridge, in which case the river has been moved a long way). In the 11th century Axbridge had a mint and a market, and its 32 burgesses had a continuous history until 1886, when the Mayor and Corporation were finally dissolved. The borough records, still preserved in the town, are a remarkable collection and tell the history of the place in great detail.

King John gave the town some autonomy from county government; Henry III gave it a fair on St Barnabas's Day, Edward I another on St Bartholomew's Day – or rather gave the fairs to the lords of the town, William Longsword in the first case and the Bishop of Bath and Wells in the second. Axbridge sent representatives to Parliament between 1295 and 1344. The place no longer depended on Cheddar after the Conquest, and its trade was presumably in Mendip wool and cloth. A covered market cross, like the one at Cheddar, survived until the mid 18th century and there is still a stone and bronze pillar dated 1627 outside the Town Hall, once used either as a place to pay cash or to stand scales. The medieval Guildhall was pulled down in 1833 and the present Town Hall is on another site. King John's Hunting Lodge (NT) has nothing to do with King John; it is a fine jettied, timber-framed merchant's house of c. 1500, and contains a museum. Many of the Georgian fronts in the town centre undoubtedly hide similar houses.

It is difficult to believe that the railway came to Axbridge, for by the 1860s there was little business but market gardening, though its early potatoes (Axbridge Jacks) and peas were well known. The course of the line is now a welcome bypass, but the station still stands, as if awaiting ghostly passengers and stopping trains.

Overlooking the market place and dominating the town is the church of St John, splendid Somerset Perpendicular, beginning with chancel and transepts of the end of the 14th century. Special features are its w porch with little adjoining rooms, part of an imposing western façade, and the nave roof, 'a most romantic piece of Jacobean Gothicism', as Pevsner describes it. Instead of the wood panelling of the aisle roofs, there is plaster, divided by thin ribs into lozenges and octagons with pendants, and dated 1636. Another surprise is a piece of embroidery, an altar frontal, the work of Mrs Abigail Prowse, daughter and first biographer of her father Bishop George Hooper of Bath and Wells. The frontal is said to have taken seven years to complete. Its design shows

St John's, Axbridge

an altar table with plate, books, and surroundings; its ends bear the dates 1703, when the Bishop was translated from St Asaph to Wells (actually 1704 New Style), and 1720. The Prowse family was, if monuments are any guide, prominent in Axbridge for a century until the 1760s.

Babington Som. *see* **Mells**

Backwell Avon 5 A4
Rodneys lived at Backwell from the 12th to the 17th century, and it was both won and lost by affection. Walter de Rodney was given half the manor for his support for the Empress Matilda against King Stephen. The other half went to the Sor family, hence Sore's Court and the tithing of Backwell Sore. The Rodneys, admirable local gentry, stayed in a house E of the church until Sir George Rodney fell in love with a young widow; and when she preferred a rather elderly Earl of Hertford to a mere knight, he shut himself in the village inn at Amesbury, it is said, wrote the lady a poem of 140 verses in his own blood, and then fell on his sword. When his goods were listed there was one sword among them, worth 6s. 8d. So ended the Backwell Rodneys.

Backwell is in several parts, now merging as it expands for its Bristol-commuting inhabitants. Farleigh is on the main road, where the fair was held from 1269; Moorside or Backwell Common was squatter territory; Church Town speaks for itself, the heart of the Rodney manor, marked by the tall and rather curious tower of the church standing out nobly against Backwell Hill.

The church was already substantial in the 13th century, with a chancel, nave, and two aisles; *c.* 1300 a porch was built and the first N chancel chapel. Later in the century the nave and chancel arch were rebuilt and the s chapel added. The windows were renewed in the 15th century and the tower perhaps in the 16. The N chapel was apparently rebuilt by Elizabeth Rodney (d. 1536), but it seems to have been 're-edified' by Rice Davis (d. 1638) whose memorial is in the chapel with that of Sir Walter Rodney (d. 1467). Sir Walter was married to Margaret, a daughter of Lord Hungerford; and in 1449 she inherited from her father a black-and-green silk bed, a possession valuable enough to have been brought back to the manor house at Backwell.

Among the clergymen to be rectors of Backwell were Thomas Cornish (1484–5) who was consecrated Bishop of Tenos in order to act as suffragan in the diocese; and Lord John Thynne, rector from 1823, who as Sub-dean of Westminster when Queen Victoria was crowned, is said to have been the only one to have kept his head in the unrehearsed ceremony.

Badminton Avon *see* **Great Badminton**

Banwell Avon 4 H5
'Banwelle standith not very holsomly ... the fennes be

almost at hande', declared Leland; and much of the large parish certainly lies below the level of high tide. In the Middle Ages Banwell was, indeed, divided between Upland and Marshland; and the upland, where the village lies, has produced evidence of man's activity from the time of the worked flints in Banwell camp on the top of the hill E of the village. But more remarkable are the Bone Caves on Banwell Hill, w of the village, discovered in 1821, opened in 1824, and excavated over the next 40 years, which produced the remains of prehistoric mammals washed into these limestone caves from above – bison, horse, reindeer, bear, and wolf, marten, otter, wild cat, and fox – the animals that roamed the Mendips before Man.

About A.D 885 a 'monastery' at Banwell was given by King Alfred to Asser his Welsh adviser, together with as much incense as a strong man could carry. From that time with few breaks Banwell belonged to the Church. The rectory was given to the monks of Bruton and, after the Dissolution, to the Dean and Chapter of Bristol; the

The font, Banwell church

Puxton church

manor to the Bishops of Bath and Wells. Bishop Bekynton (Bishop 1443–65) rebuilt or altered the manor house (now the Abbey) and planted a splendid orchard. Bishop Godwin (1584–90) spent much time in the old house and built a new one on his own estate near by at Towerhead. He entertained generously at Banwell, for there were at least 28 beds, 60 feather beds, and 40 pairs of sheets in the house when he died. In fact there was more bedding than furniture and plate. Later bishops let the house and it was much altered in the 18th and 19th centuries.

The discovery of the Bone Caves encouraged Bishop Law (1824–45) to build a romantic *cottage orné* in 1827 and to create a park around it sprinkled with pyramids, arches, cells, and garden houses. Suitable poems were carved to catch the eye of the stroller as he made his way to the tower on the hill. The house was enlarged in 1833 and is known as the Caves. Banwell Castle, on the hill above the village, is less romantic: a ponderous and very obvious Victorian pile. Above the castle a cruciform earthwork has been the subject of speculation for more than a century. The latest suggestion of a rabbit warren is the most plausible.

Banwell church is notable for its tall tower and its screen. The former, of the Bristol type with a single turret, has on its w side a representation of the Annuncia-

tion, with the lilypot in the adjoining window. On the opposite face, but inside the nave, is St Andrew, the patron saint, holding his cross and the fishing net of his occupation. The building is largely of the 15th century, even the Norman font having been decorated to match the new style. The screen, however, can be exactly dated to 1520–1: the wardens paid 4d. for paper on which to draw the design, 8s. 4d. to draw up the agreement with the carver, and nearly £40 for the carver himself. The rood was painted then, but the loft was gilded later. The top of the w gallery was once part of Bishop Godwin's pew.

The monastery or 'minster' at Banwell was in Saxon times the mother of at least three neighbouring churches. PUXTON, 3 miles N, with its short leaning tower and charming Jacobean furnishings, was consecrated, presumably after extensive rebuilding, in 1539. The N porch was added in 1557. The ends of the rood beam above the base of the stone screen can still be seen in the walls. CHRISTON, 1 mile sw, is Norman, partly genuine and partly of the 19th century; genuine the remarkable arches that support the central tower. CHURCHILL, 3 miles E, is distinguished less for its architecture than for its monuments and family connexions. On the floor of the s aisle is a brass to Ralph Jennys (d. 1572), who is said to have been ancestor of Sarah, the 1st Duchess of

Barrington Court

Marlborough. John Latch seems to be looking at his shrouded wife Jane (d. 1644) with some alarm, though the inscription claims that he is simply 'doting' on death, 'preparing how to die'. There, too, is the helm of Sir John Churchill (d. 1685), Recorder of Bristol and Master of the Rolls, who bought the manor and Churchill Court from the penurious Jennings family in 1652. Sir John was descended from the Churchills of Rockbeare (Devon); and so, too, was that other John Churchill, later 1st Duke of Marlborough, ancestor of Sir Winston. And the military John married Sarah Jennings whose father had sold out to Sir John.

Barlinch Som. *see* **Dulverton**

Barrington Som. 2 B3
In the heart of the Ham stone country and carefully preserved, this village has more than its share of typical thatched and golden houses, several of them dating from the later Middle Ages. The building traditions of the area died hard, and the village school, only a little more than a century old and still in use, is built in the shape of a medieval barn. The church, in the centre of the village above the remains of the green, has an octagonal tower like its 'mother', South Petherton.

A villager much opposed to its restoration wrote that the church had been totally gutted in the 1860s; and cer-

tainly the work was nothing if not thorough. The crocketed ogee decoration outside the porch, however, seems genuine, a fine example of local craftsmanship. The church dates from the late 13th century, probably rebuilt in celebration of its independence from South Petherton in the 1240s, when the Bishop allowed the villagers to bury their dead in their own churchyard, and not take them all the way to Petherton.

Many of the older houses belonged to tenant farmers whose obvious wealth came not so much from the open fields, which still survive on the ridge above the village, but from common grazing in Neroche Forest (q.v.). The manor house, known for the last century or so as Barrington Court (NT), stands in its own grounds at the E end of the village. The house, which used to be considered an early example of Renaissance work, has now been found to date from *c.* 1570. It replaced an earlier, moated building which had been the home of the ancient Breton family of Daubeney since *c.* 1225. But the Daubeneys, or rather the eldest branch, came to a sad end. Giles, in his youth, joined the rebellion of the Duke of Buckingham in 1483 and lost all his lands, but Henry VII restored them and made Giles a baron in 1486 and a KG in 1487. His son, a flamboyant character, set his sights on an earldom. Although without an heir, he spent vast sums on people of influence and finally achieved the Earldom of Bridgwater, but was left with no estate to speak of. Barrington was held only for his life, and he died in 1548. About 1552 the property, then probably ruinous, was bought by William Clifton (d. 1564), a London merchant looking for an investment for the money he had made on the Customs in London. The house was perhaps started by him and finished by his son.

The magnificent Ham stone mansion, whose stones bear the signs of the Ham Hill masons, is an E-shaped building with a central block of traditional medieval plan with two long wings, one including a kitchen, and a central porch. The third floor is formed into a long gallery. The mullioned and transomed windows and diagonal buttresses are remarkably plain but the roof line is a delight with its finials with ogee caps, twisted chimneys, and octagonal buttress tops.

Beside the house the mellow brick stable block was built in 1674 by William Strode. From the mid 18th century the house was occupied by a succession of tenant farmers, and by 1905 it was largely a ruin, threatened with demolition and possible rebuilding in America. It was then acquired by the NT, and was restored by Col. Abraham Lyle, the lessee. The gardens were laid out by Gertrude Jekyll, and the farmhouses and buildings in the rear were designed by Forbes and Tate, architects for the house; they include a barn that was one of the first buildings to use reinforced concrete.

One mile s, over the hill, the village of STOCKLINCH has two churches, each belonging to one of the two manors, Stocklinch Magdalen and Stocklinch Ottersay. The former (Pevsner has them reversed), in the village and still in use, has a charming interior, which includes an 18th-century gallery, pulpit with tester and reading desk, and the Royal Arms forming a tympanum in the chancel arch. St Mary's, Stocklinch Ottersay, now redundant, stands alone in the former park; it dates from the 13th century, and has a beautiful traceried window in the s transept.

One mile SE from Barrington, SHEPTON BEAUCHAMP lies in the rich sandy soil that still bears marked traces of its medieval open fields. The church of St Michael has a fine tower in Ham stone and lias with a beautiful fan vault including the 'bat's wing' badge of the Daubeneys. There was once a N tower, added c. 1300 to a church that can now only be traced in outline. The s aisle is an enlargement by G. E. Street. The Tractarian tradition of the parish began under V. S. S. Coles (rector 1872–84), whose 'spiritual power ... penetrated the whole Anglican Communion'. The former rectory, now called Beauchamp Manor, was built in 1874 to house Coles, his curates, and visitors, and served as the centre of numerous social and religious organizations in a parish which, unlike most of its neighbours, felt the agricultural depression of the late 19th century more acutely and sent its sons in some numbers to the New World, the Colonies, or the mines of South Wales.

Barwick Som. *see* **Yeovil**

Batcombe Som. *see* **Bruton**

Bath Avon 5 C5 (*pop.* 84,670)

'The Georgian City' is the most obvious though by no means the only phrase used to describe Bath in tourist literature. The city has, perhaps more than most, many faces. There is a world of difference between the elegance of Milsom Street and the atmosphere of the 'bus station on a Saturday afternoon, just as there always was between the social élite of Beau Nash's spa and the street sweepers and domestics who made it all possible. Bath's fine squares and crescents had façades for the eye to see and to appreciate; behind were pipes and drains and areas which any industrial town could boast. This is not to say that Bath was a sham; only that it had, and still reveals, many sides and angles, for it has been throughout its long history several different places.

First of all Roman Bath, 7 ft down below street level and only now being so brilliantly reconstructed by Professor Barry Cunliffe after a series of difficult excavations beneath the Pump Room. Only the centre of Roman Bath is yet known with any accuracy, but the story of the settlement clearly began with the hot springs in the second half of the 1st century, which became so famous that by the early 3rd century visitors were coming from all over the Roman world. By this time there were public buildings – a temple, a forum or theatre, the enormous bathing establishment, and other structures – within an area defended first by an earthen rampart and later, in the 3rd century, by a stone wall, but measuring only some 23 acres. There is some sign of a contemporary N settlement which might have been military in origin. All this poses a problem: in size it seems much too small to have been a local administrative centre but besides its importance as a spa it was strategically placed in its curve of the Avon in an area of important communications; and still in the 4th century it was a market centre in a region rich in prosperous farms.

But there is much less doubt about the public buildings that were the glory of Bath. They stood in the area w and sw of the present Abbey, a massive group with the temple of the goddess Sulis Minerva at its centre, and the bathing establishment on its s side. Five building phases have been identified around the baths, beginning in the late 1st century with the Great Bath, lined with lead, at the centre of an aisled hall, with a small swimming bath at one end and hot and cold baths at the other. Additions in the next 200 years and more included the circular bath and curative immersion baths.

The temple seems to have changed less. It stood in the centre of a large colonnaded courtyard, approached by six wide steps. It was built of freestone, and above its pillared portico was a carved pediment with winged Victories flanking a gorgon's head. Also on the pediment were to be seen an owl and a dolphin, known attributes of the Roman goddess Minerva. But there was something different about the gorgon: it was not purely Classical, but a modification, with characteristics of the Celtic goddess Sulis. Here was a supreme example of Roman compromise; native religion and the religion of the Empire here triumphantly merged.

In the centre of the courtyard before the temple stood a sacrificial altar, placed so that the bathers could have a direct view of it across the spring from the great hall of the baths. Two corners of this altar have been found, one with Bacchus and a female fertility goddess on site, the other, with the figure of Jupiter, forming a corner of the chancel of the church at Compton Dando (q.v.). Perhaps even more remarkable is the base of a statue that stood before this altar, which is inscribed with the name and title of its donor: Lucius Marcius Memor, Haruspex; that is, augurer, a man of considerable importance in Roman religious life, who told the future from the entrails of sacrificial victims or from the flight of birds. That Bath should attract such a man says much for the importance of its temple and its baths.

And Bath certainly attracted others who recorded their visits in just the way that 18th-century visitors had their more permanent sojourns recorded on the walls of the Abbey. The courtyard around the temple was highly decorated, with a façade showing the four seasons, and furnished with inscriptions and altars – inscriptions noting the visits of a stonemason from near Chartres, a native of Trier, and a worshipper from Metz. But popularity was not enough to save the baths, not from military withdrawal nor political collapse, but simply from flooding. There is some evidence that the temple was repaired in the 5th century but then there seems to be an uncanny gap, filled only by the defeat of the Britons at Dyrham (q.v.) in 577 which made Bath a frontier possession of the advancing Saxons. The Roman town survived in plan clearly enough to suggest some sort of continuity of occupation, but even in the 8th century the core of it all was derelict. Professor Cunliffe is convinced that the author of *The Ruin* was writing of Bath:

> Wondrous is this masonry, shattered by the Fates. The fortifications have given way, the buildings raised by giants are crumbling ... There stood courts of stone, and a stream gushed forth in rippling floods of hot water.

Early Saxon charters nearly always give cause for concern, for forgery was widely practised in defence of unwritten tradition. Bath's earliest charter, dated 676, records the gifts by Osric, Under-king of Mercia, to Bertana the Abbess, of a large estate for the establishment of a nunnery at Bath. The same man is said to have founded Gloucester Abbey. Nothing more seems to be heard of the nuns after 681, and by 758 monks were in residence, apparently under the influence of the West Saxon kings. Twenty years later the house was 'given back' to the great Offa of Mercia, and he was thought of by some later historians as the founder of the house, perhaps then a house of canons. Under Athelstan or Edmund a group of exiles from abroad seems to have settled there, and the life of the community was evidently regularized by St Dunstan before 970. The coronation of King Edgar, which took place at Bath on Whit-Sunday 973, and which has been the model for subsequent coronations in this country, presumably was performed in the monastic church; the townsmen still re-enacted the event in Leland's time. From then the regular monastic life seems to have continued without a break, and Bath was one of those rare houses which retained its Saxon abbot, Elsig, until the year of the Conqueror's death. Then there came a significant change: the Norman Bishop of Wells, John de Villula, *c.* 1088 transferred his cathedral to Bath. He became Abbot of the monastery and began a massive new church fit for the dignity of a cathedral, whose crossing piers are to be seen at the E end of the present Abbey. After a fire in 1137 Bishop Robert of Lewes, perhaps more interested in Wells, but still only Bishop of Bath, built a new chapter house, cloister, and conventual buildings to add to John de Villula's 'palace', of which a great square tower still stood in the 1540s.

The site of the Norman abbey seems to have been chosen with some deliberation to cut across Bath's main street and market centre, and its precinct gradually came to occupy the SE quarter of the little city. Leland suggested that Bath was given privileges by King Edgar after his coronation, and there was certainly a mint in Saxon times, suggesting some economic strength. The defended town, possibly now with stone walls, formed part of the West Saxon system of defence, the Burghal Hidage; and under a charter granted in 1189 its merchants received trading privileges comparable with those of the fortunate businessmen of Winchester. By 1230 Bath had a mayor, and in 1256 a new charter gave the citizens the right of self-government, a status which was recognized in modern times in the creation of Bath as a county borough. But this was not absolute independence, like that achieved by Bristol a century later; until Bishop Savaric's time (1192–1205) the Bishop was both Abbot and lord of the town, and when he bargained with the King for possession of Glastonbury Abbey as well, Bath passed to the Crown. Changes in Edward I's time gave Bath back to the bishops, though by that time they had returned to Wells, leaving the monks to play a secondary role in diocesan affairs, but giving the prior in practice much more immediate power in the city.

Since 1295, it is true, Bath had sent representatives to Parliament, chosen, apparently unhindered and uninfluenced by successive Priors, but the town remained very small, with an estimated population of only 855 in 1381 (perhaps still recovering from the Black Death, which had reduced the number of monks from 59 to 30). Cloth-making, in the tradition of most West Country towns, was its mainstay, the principal merchants (perhaps like the principal Romans before them) living in the northern suburbs and rubbing shoulders with their colleague the Wife of Bath. Inside the walls, according to a tax return of 1379, lived the rest, one-third of them labourers, nearly a quarter servants, and only one gold-

Bath Abbey

Queen Square, Bath

smith in the place.

During the 14th century Bath had to yield pride of place among Somerset's towns to Wells, but it had one asset which certainly a century later it exploited. Bishop Robert of Lewes was not only monk and Bishop, but also politician. His espousal of King Stephen's cause was clearly not wise, but it encouraged him to write a history of the events (anonymously, of course, but now recognized, both for its great value and for its authorship), in which Bath played a part; so he described

> a city where little springs through hidden conduits send up waters heated without human skill or ingenuity from deep in the bowels of the earth to a basin vaulted over with noble arches, creating in the middle of the town baths of agreeable warmth, wholesome and pleasant to look upon ... the sick are wont to gather there from all England to wash away their infirmities in the health-giving waters, and the whole to see the wondrous jets of hot water and bath in them.
>
> *Gesta Stephani*, trans. K. R. Potter

Three centuries later that precious monarch King Henry VI visited Bath and was clearly disturbed and embarrassed by what he saw. The Bishop was notified and warnings were duly issued in every church in the district in 1449 that the local practice of stealing bathers' clothing and holding it to ransom was to cease forthwith. By Leland's time three baths were in operation. The Cross Bath and the Hot Bath, both near St John's hospital, seem to have been reserved for the 'poor deseasid with lepre, pokkes, scabbes, and great aches'; the King's Bath was for gentlemen.

By the time Leland went to Bath a second time, in the 1540s, a great change had come to the city, for the cathedral priory was no more. On a previous visit he had seen graphic evidence of the decay of the monastery – the ruin of the great Norman abbey church 'laid to waste', unroofed, with weeds growing about the founder's tomb. The impetus had gone out of religious life long ago; the days of enthusiasm when Robert of Lewes had brought the body of St Euphemia and the alb and mitre of St Peter of Tarentaise, had disappeared. There were 41 monks in the house at the election of

ABOVE: *Prior Park, Bath*

BELOW: *Pulteney Bridge, Bath*

Bishop Jocelin in 1205, and *c.* 1260 a new Lady Chapel was built. But the Black Death was crippling; there were only 16 monks in 1377 and only 20 in 1539. The estates, at £617 the second most valuable in Somerset, were worth less than one-fifth of Glastonbury's.

But as elsewhere in the country the creaking finances were strained almost to breaking by an amazing enthusiasm for building, in Bath on the initiative of Bishop Oliver King (1496–1503) and of the last two priors, William Bird and William Holway alias Gibbs. Bishop King began a 'goodly new church' in the western end of the shell of the Norman abbey, employing the king's masons Robert and William Vertue, ordering cases of glass from Normandy and supporting their claim that the vault of their chancel would be better than anything to be seen either in France or England. Bird and Holway continued the work, and Bird's chantry chapel (*c.* 1515) on the s side of the sanctuary is perhaps the best piece of carving in the whole building. For the Vertue claims were certainly not achieved, and Bishop King's fine dream, enshrined as Jacob's Ladder at the w end, lost both its inspiration and its financial support. When the building had only just begun the Bishop died, and the arms of Bishop Hadrian de Castello (1504–18) on the chancel vaults show how far work progressed in his time. How much was done by the time the Abbey was surrendered to the Crown in 1539 is not precisely known, though some harm undoubtedly came from the removal of the lead from roofs soon afterwards. When Queen Elizabeth visited Bath in 1574 the attempt to disguise the state of the building with evergreens was perhaps an astute move by the citizens, who only two years earlier had bought the property. The Queen was moved to generosity, ordering collections throughout the country which proved so successful that the choir was usable by 1576 and the crossing and transepts were restored. Work on the nave was then delayed until the time of Bishop Montague (1608–15), whose tomb on the N side of the nave is an indication of his personal attachment to Bath.

The early 17th century completed the nave with a plaster vault and carved wooden ribs, in a style that still survives in the vestry. The present fan vault dates from the late-19th-century restoration, which perhaps accounts for a certain stilted quality which the Vertues would not have achieved. The whole is thus a disappointment; neither a last great statement of the Middle Ages – as found at St George's Chapel, Windsor, or at King's College Chapel, Cambridge – nor yet, beyond its open choir and congregational furniture, a genuine flowering of English Protestantism. And the building stands almost self-consciously amid the Classical splendours and monumental disgraces of later centuries; how would Wren, or even one of the Woods have treated the site?

The dissolution of the abbey thrust responsibilities on the people of Bath. A century before they had successfully shown their independence of the prior in a moral

victory in a bell-ringing dispute, but economically the town was not strong, and the death of three leading clothiers in the 1530s had left Bath 'sumwhat decayed'. Antiquity was not enough, and the end of the monastery brought a vacuum which the city fathers were forced to fill by acquiring monastic property, taking over education in the famous Bath tradition of the medieval scholar Adelard, running the old hospital of St John and in 1572 acquiring the patronage of the abbey church itself and its dependent churches. The citizens were incorporated under a charter of 1590 and their concerns, as shown in the accounts of the city chamberlains, were those of any other town seeking influence. People like Leicester, Ralegh, and Essex enjoyed a full share of their bounty and adulation, and the visit of the Queen herself was reason enough for much decoration, painting, and repair. Travelling bands of players were often on hand to keep the people happy (and might Shakespeare himself have come with Lord Strange's players in 1592?); but what bureaucrat sent a hue and cry to Bristol in 1587 to check on a rumour that London was burning?

Bath's royalism during the Civil War and its strategic importance then and during the Monmouth Rebellion gave it a significant rôle to play as host to a nearby battle on LANSDOWN in 1643 when the royalists who were left with the field under the mortally wounded Sir Beville Grenville could hardly be considered the victors. The refusal of the city to admit Monmouth – followed by a musket ball in the head of his herald – was an important factor in that reckless young man's defeat. And at the same time the baths still continued to bring relief, or at least the hope of improvement, to such as the Duke of York's unhealthy wife and Mr Pepys's flighty one. But here was as yet no popular attraction: the War Office found in 1686 only 324 beds and stabling for but 451 horses, still a long way behind Wells. The best inn was the Hart, later the White Hart, of *Pickwick Papers* fame. Bath, apparently, was no spa in the making, ready and eager to become the centre of the social scene. Indeed, when the antiquary William Stukeley came in 1723 he saw essentially the medieval city, its gates still standing, its walls patched with fragments of Roman carvings and inscriptions, its medieval churches still clustering round the former abbey church.

But changes had already come. Richard Nash had been in the city for nearly 20 years, Ralph Allen for 13; Orange Grove and Trim Street gave notice that new thoughts were abroad, and General Wade's house in the Abbey Churchyard, the work of an unknown though clearly talented architect for a great Bath figure, could clearly not stand alone. But an antiquarian might well not have noticed. Yet within the next 20 years or so the city had been transformed by a group of architects led by John Wood the Elder. Queen Square (1728–36), the Parades (1740–3), and the Circus (1754) burst out of the medieval confines; the Royal Mineral Water Hospital (1738–42) declared the essential purpose; Ralph Allen's

Royal Crescent, Bath

House in Lilliput Alley, recently restored, revealed the style and the incentive. And more was to come. Nash and Allen might have foreseen the scale, but could they have glimpsed the grandeur of the younger Wood's Royal Crescent (1767–75), Thomas Atwood's Paragon (1768), or Robert Adam's Pulteney Bridge (1769–74), leading through Thomas Baldwin's Great Pulteney Street (*c.* 1788) to Bathwick and beyond? So the city in graceful sweeps and fine vistas emerged from its walls in less than a century. Circus and square and avenue and parade, designed to please the eye, provided behind their elegant façades the lodgings for the social élite; and the city centre gave them entertainment in the Assembly Rooms (1768–71) for balls and card parties, the Guildhall (1776) for routs, and the Pump Room (1786–95) for conversation and even for a sip of the water. Proprietary chapels like the Octagon (1765–7) and Kensington Chapel (1795) provided sophisticated surroundings for pecuniary preaching when the city churches could not or would not expand.

And if all this seems impersonal, then at least the plaques by many an elegant door record the names of the famous who were lodged there; and tablets adorning (if that is the word) the Abbey walls immortalize those for whom Bath found no other permanent cure. Do not the names of the American Senator William Bingham (d. 1804), or Thomas Pownall (d. 1805), Lieutenant-Governor of New Jersey and then Governor successively of Massachusetts Bay and South Carolina, or Admiral Phillip (d. 1814), founder and first Governor of Australia, agents of a colonial power, read like the inscriptions in the Temple of Minerva a few yards away? And might not the epitaph upon James Quin by David Garrick be as good as any prophecy of Lucius Marcius Memor the augurer?

But there was always another side to Bath, the backs of terraces, the further, narrower streets, the cheaper lodgings. The city has an industrial history which needs revealing, for its suburbs have long provided both services and employment which any city needed. Twerton and Walcot produced yarn in the early 18th century but Richard Warner, historian of Bath at the end of the century, could assert that there was 'little trade and no manufactures, the higher classes of people and their dependents constitute the chief part of the population; and the number of the lower classes [is] small'. This simply

The banqueting room, Guildhall, Bath

will not do: in 1831, for instance, Lyncombe and Widcombe had 565 men making fine woollen cloth, and Twerton 284 in a factory area where earlier in the century several hundred women and children had also been employed. Elsewhere, nearer the city centre, there were tradesmen of all descriptions, and one-third of the total number of pastrycooks in the whole of Somerset. Side by side with the building of Norfolk Crescent (1798–1810) and the Theatre Royal (1804–5), George Stothert could change his ironmongery business to an iron foundry. Of course, the Kennet and Avon Canal and later the railways came to Bath more elegantly than to most places, but they came for sound economic reasons which were no longer based primarily on the city's social attraction. Bath is the home of engineering as well as the mecca of elegance.

The modern city is thus an amalgam of attractions, a city of museums and a museum of a city. Medieval Bath is hardest to find – a piece of over-restored wall, a water-gate hiding under a pavement behind the Empire Hotel, and the Abbey. Roman Bath, or rather the baths, are splendidly displayed, and 18th-century Bath is all around. If there is, perhaps, a touch of the Sham Castle about the city, it is for those who fondly imagine that façades are meant to be more than skin deep. What does lie deep is the city's culture, finding expression not just in the annual Bath Festival, nor yet in its gardens and floral displays. Bath is culture and refinement, tempered by a climate which makes it sometimes unbearable for the outsider. There is market town and industrial conurbation, but over all there is urbanity that is somehow unique.

Beckington   Som.   5 C6

Although Beckington is not a Mendip village, it was a clothing centre, for it lies on routes from the sheep-rearing areas of both Mendip and the Wiltshire Downs to Bath and Bristol. Mellow stone gables and mullioned and transomed windows dating from the 16th century show the prosperity of the place at that time; but Beckington can show earlier riches in its church, which holds the key to the parish's history.

The great Norman tower of St George's appears to dominate the village if you approach from the N; an imposing piece of work, with bold decoration, and outstanding in the county. Most of the rest is a Perpendicular building, as is usual in a Somerset clothing village, though two shields in the N aisle arcade suggest that the de Erleigh family, whose ancestors probably helped to build the tower, extended the church in the late 14th century. But not later, for they had to sell most of their land to pay the ransom of Sir John de Erleigh, captured at the battle of Najara (1367) fighting with the Black Prince. Perhaps Sir John is the knight lying with his lady in the chancel.

In the 15th century Beckington had a greater son: Thomas Beckington or Bekynton, son of a weaver, was

North Door, Lullington church

born here c. 1390, and was sent to Winchester College and New College, Oxford. Bekynton became an important figure in government, humanist, and diplomatic circles in the first half of the 15th century, holding the office of Secretary to King Henry VI from 1437 until his appointment as Bishop of Bath and Wells in 1443. His tomb at Wells Cathedral (q.v.), made several years before his death in 1465, shows him both as bishop in his robes and as a partly shrouded cadaver. Since he approved the work, could it be a portrait?

Bishop Bekynton left to the church where he had been christened a gilt and copper processional cross, a censer, and a green, gold, and red cope. None of these survive, but the church bears marks of other benefactors, like the great carved nave roof (c. 1470), a parish affair, and the SE chapel, probably given by John Compton (d. 1510), a wool or cloth merchant whose trade mark can still be seen there. The mark of Thomas Webb, 'clotheman', is also there, but richest of all must have been Robert Webb, 'clothier to the Queen', who in 1596 for licence to export unfinished woollen cloth for 21 years with a partner, managed to pay the huge sum of £2,000 a year to the Crown and £240 a year to poor London clothworkers.

Among the larger houses in the village are Beckington Castle, not a castle at all, but an imposing three-storeyed house with a tall porch, on a culde sac off the new main road; and The Abbey, not an abbey nor, very likely, the remains of a hospital founded here in 1502, though the house contains work of that date and an elaborate barrel ceiling in decorated plasterwork of the early 17th century. Seymour's Court (1 mile NE) is partly of the 16th century and is a reminder that the famous Seymour family (here spelt Seyntmaur) had been early settlers in the parish; the brass of John Seyntmaur (d. 1485) and his wife lies on the chancel floor at Beckington.

Another notable commemorated in the church is the poet Samuel Daniel (d. 1619), who retired to RUDGE, 2 miles E on the Wiltshire border. A poet, too, lies in the island churchyard of ORCHARDLEIGH (2 miles SW): Sir Henry Newbolt (d. 1938), author of *Drake's Drum* and of the famous line 'Play up! Play up! and play the game!' Orchardleigh is little more than mansion and church. The mansion, formerly the home of the Duckworths (Newbolt married a Duckworth), is a mid-19th-century house in the Elizabethan style, though there are earlier remains in the park, including a rotunda and boathouse of the 18th century, the gateway from LULLINGTON (early 19th-century) and 'Tudor' lodges of 1825–30.

Orchardleigh church, accessible normally on foot from Lullington (and worth the walk) is mostly of the 13th century with some fine detail in the chancel and some good 15th-century glass. Lullington church is a splendid Norman building with a spectacular N doorway and a highly decorated font.

Berkley (*pron.* Burkley)   Som.   5 C6

'The best Georgian church in any Somerset village', says Pevsner, and there is more than just rustic charm about the tree-lined path to the tower entrance, the tower topped by balustrade and vases. The dome inside and an octagonal lantern, supported by four large columns, recalls Wren's London churches, but this may be by a provincial, probably Thomas Prowse, who lived in the house behind. The registers give the date and progress of building. A marriage in October 1748 was held at Rodden (see below) 'when Berkely church was shut up in order to be repaired'. Then there must have been a change of plan (and probably of site): a wedding in November 1748 was held at Rodden 'while Berkley church was pulling down in order to be rebuilt'. And on Sunday 11 November 1750 'Berkley church had divine service performed in it the first time after its being rebuilt'.

The mansion behind, the home of the Newburghs in the 17th century (see their monuments in the church), was given a new front by Nathaniel Ireson in 1730–2. Edith Newburgh, second daughter of Roger Newburgh, married the rector, John Bayley, on 25 August 1632. They had a stillborn daughter almost exactly five years later, and the mother died the following day. The rector stayed until the Civil War, but he was removed on 12 October 1645. For the next four years, as he noted in the parish register, the church was served by outsiders; and the rector himself was kept out of his living until 1660 'by reason of the civil dissensions which then befell this Nacion'.

The chapel at RODDEN (1½ miles SW) is approached through the yard of Rodden farm. The old village has gone, but the church is a rarity in Somerset, for it was completely rebuilt in 1640, still in the Gothic tradition; presumably through the efforts of sad Rector Bayley of Berkley.

Berrow   Som. *see* **Burnham on Sea**

Bishops Hull   Som.   2 A2

Despite Taunton's expansion, the village of Bishops Hull still manages to retain its separate identity; and so it should, for as a settlement it is probably older than Taunton. This, at any rate, is the interpretation of the name, earlier spelt Hill or Hylle or even Hel, the hill which forms a steep scarp above the River Tone. Here was an admirable place to settle, commanding the river valley. And the people who chose this spot spread their influence, for the medieval parish of Bishops Hull reached the centre of Taunton, and included the Castle itself.

The rest of the village name came after the Bishop of Winchester bought the great manor of Taunton in 904; his successors owned the property until 1822. The church, however, was given c. 1120 to Taunton Priory, and priors and villagers between them must have put up the medieval building. The Prior of Taunton was certainly involved in the 16th-century rebuilding, for there was a dispute about the contract to build the chancel in 1522. In fact rebuilding took some time: the octagonal top was added to the 13th-century tower base, and the N chapel was added to the chancel (1536). The whole was not consecrated until 1540. Many of the pews date from the same period (see the night-watchman and the Resurrection scene), and one of the bells dates from 1550. What strikes odd, however, is the present shape of the church, more like a nonconformist preaching house because the church was more than doubled in size by an extension S in 1827. The contemporary Gothick box pews and gallery create an unbalanced but by no means unpleasing effect.

Bishops Hull village street was the main route from Taunton to Exeter until the 19th century and several of its houses suggest that the place attracted gentry as well as substantial farmers. The Manor House, built in 1586 by George Farwell (d. 1609, see his monument in the church), came first; Bishops Hull House is a nice brick home of the 18th century, and Netherclay House of the 19th.

Bishop's Lydeard   Som.   2 A2

The last element, '-eard', is the Welsh *garth* or hill, and the name here must refer to the Quantocks, the ever-

View over Cothelstone

present backdrop to this large and expanding village. The bishops who owned the village were first those of Sherborne and, after the see of Wells was founded in 909, the Bishops of Bath and Wells. In 1363 the income from the Bishop's estate was under £25 from a farm of *c.* 400 acres and properties including a fulling mill and a dovecote; but nothing at all from the woodland, partly because much of the timber had been felled and because no grazing was possible there due to the abundance of vipers.

The tall red sandstone tower dominates the village, and certainly makes the rest of the church look small. But inside there is much worth seeing: bench ends of the 16th century including a windmill, a ship, and a Quantock stag. The mill is a post mill; birds carefully avoid the sails and the miller stands below with his horse. The E end of the church is resplendent, all light and colour beyond the screen which embraces nave and both aisles. The work is by Sir Ninian Comper.

The village street is almost urban in proportion near the church, and until it was bypassed took the brunt of traffic from Taunton to West Somerset. In the late 17th century there were 60 beds to be had at its inns, and one, now the Lethbridge Arms after the squires of Sandhill Park (1 mile NW, 1720 and 1815), has a sadly defaced brick fives wall.

Two miles NE, under the Quantock scarp, is COTHEL-STONE, 'a place very remarkable', wrote Thomas Gerard in 1633, 'for that a long time it hath bin and still is the cheife seate of the ... familie of the Stawells'. The house and its gatehouse have curious baluster and candelabra shapes not only in windows and as colonnettes in the doorway but in other places too. The N side of the house was rebuilt in the 19th century from a virtual ruin, but the gatehouse is original and a splendid conceit. Pevsner supposes from the decorations a date rather before 1560 but is not entirely convinced. The Stawells were capable of anything (see Low Ham). There was certainly an earlier house on the site, for a medieval arcade can be seen in the wall of cottages on the way to the church. Is this the 'fair and ancient' house Gerard saw, making the present one the work of the eccentric Sir John of the Civil War?

The church, hidden behind the house, has a chapel of *c.* 1200 which contains Stawell tombs and some 15th-century glass including St Dunstan holding the pincers with which he tweaked the Devil by the nose. And here is the tomb of the ardent royalist Sir John Stawell, who left at his death in 1662 such elaborate plans for his funeral procession from his other home at Low Ham. Two conductors, two trumpeters, the 23 estate bailiffs, domestic servants; divines, a Deputy Lieutenant and the

High Sheriff; the insignia of knighthood borne by heralds; the body in a chariot covered in velvet and drawn by six plumed horses. A man capable of organizing his own funeral down to the refreshments taken en route is capable of building an eccentric, unfashionable, and yet fascinating house.

Bitton　Avon　5 C4

Bitton stands on the higher road between Bristol and Bath below Lansdown, and takes its name from the River Boyd, a tributary of the Avon. The road gave the village a bad name from the end of the 18th century through the activities of the Cock Road gang. Bitton was home to some of these ruffians, despite the treatment of at least one judge who thought he 'had hanged the whole of that parish'.

H. T. Ellacombe, successively curate and vicar (1817–50), was not only an authority on church bells but a tireless student of his own remarkable church, a Saxon minster whose parish once included Hanham, Oldland, and Kingswood (q.v.). Before the Conquest it had a long, wide nave, dominated by a huge stone-carved rood above the chancel arch. Additions include the fine N chapel built *c.* 1300 by Thomas of Bitton, Bishop of Exeter, one of a notable family of churchmen which included two Bishops of Bath and Wells. William of Bitton I (Bishop 1248–64) appointed his nephew Thomas to be Archdeacon of Wells in 1263. Thomas's brother, William of Bitton II, was Bishop from 1267 until 1274, and two or three members of his family held office under him. Thomas later became Dean of Wells, and was Bishop of Exeter 1291–1307. Bishop William II was noted as a holy man, and pilgrims to his tomb in Wells (q.v.) found him good for the toothache. Bishop Thomas left, among much else, 1d. each to 10,212 poor people and to 235 prisoners.

Bitton is on the edge of the East Bristol industrial area. The Golden Valley mill on the Boyd was built by 1769 as a brass battery mill, part of the Warmley complex. It became a paper mill in 1825 and in the present century has produced fibreboard. In the 19th century there was a pin factory above the old parish workhouse.

Two miles down the road towards Bath is KELSTON. A Saxon cross shaft in the church indicates its early foundation, when the village was part of an estate called Hesterige (still remembered in Henstridge hill). Kelston (Calves *tun*) was a name later given to part of the property which belonged for centuries to the nunnery of Shaftesbury (Dorset). After the Dissolution Kelston was given to Audrey Malte, probably a daughter of Henry VIII, when she married John Harington of Stepney. James Barrozzi of Vignola is said to have built Harington a house in 1567, its site now Tower House garden. This was the home of Sir John Harington (1561–1612), godson of Queen Elizabeth I, poet, and claimed as the inventor of the water-closet. Harington's son, also John, puritan lawyer and MP, left an important diary not confined

to the politics of its period (1646–53), but mentioning such personal matters as his sore toe and his constipation.

The house was pulled down in 1764–5 and Kelston Park, designed by John Wood the Younger for Sir Caesar Hawkins, was built to replace it. The plain house with a porch of Tuscan columns stands on a terrace above a wooded slope to the Avon.

John Betjeman's poem *Bristol* includes the verse:
Ringers in an oil-lit belfry – Bitton? Kelston? who shall say? –
Smoothly practising a plain course, caverned out the dying day
As their melancholy music flooded up and ebbed away.

Blagdon Lake　Avon *see* **Chew Magna**

Blaise　Avon *see* **Henbury**

Brean　Som. *see* **Burnham on Sea**

Brent Knoll　Som.　4 H6

Like a guardian by the M5, with a service area named after it, Brent Knoll was, so the story goes, put there by the Devil. In order to ruin the Mendip ridge he began by digging out Cheddar Gorge. He flung the first spadeful into the Bristol Channel, thus forming Steep Holm and Flat Holm; but the second did not reach the coast, and so the knoll was born. Or alternatively, for the hill needs some explanation, it was the home of three fierce ogres. King Arthur knighted a young man named Yder and charged him to put an end to their attacks on passersby. When Arthur and his knights arrived on the scene some time later they found the giants and the young knight lying dead together. Full of sorrow, the King bore his champion to Yniswithrin, which is Glastonbury, and there buried him. Glastonbury Abbey owned the knoll and all the rich land in Brentmarsh until the Dissolution.

On the top of the hill is an Iron Age hillfort (NT), later occupied by the Romans; and the name Battleborough Farm has long been taken as evidence of an Alfredian victory here against the Danes. The monks of Glastonbury still knew it as a castle in the 13th century, though any buildings were long ago destroyed by quarrying. On the slopes of the hill are two villages, both with churches of great interest.

EAST BRENT has a fine and elegant tower and spire, seen from miles away in this flat country. And there is much to see at close quarters, notably the medieval glass in the N aisle, one of the 21 medieval wooden lecterns in the country, and late-15th-century bench ends including one with the initials of John Selwood, Abbot of Glastonbury (1456–92), owner of the manor house in the village. But before all these details the eye goes upwards to the plaster ceiling of the nave, dated 1637 and similar in style to that at Axbridge (q.v.). Contemporary furnishings include the pulpit (1634) and the gallery (1635), formerly against the chancel arch. Gothic revival merges with late Perpendicular in perfect harmony.

From 1845 to 1896 the vicar here was G. A. Denison, Archdeacon of Taunton. Frequently controversial, he was defendant in a heresy trial for his advanced views on the Eucharist, an ardent opponent of State education, and founder in 1857 of the Harvest Home which still draws hundreds to eat roast beef and plum puddings each year.

Brent Knoll village was formerly called South Brent, for it clings to the s side of the knoll, with the church the highest of all. The history of the building begins with the Norman s doorway and the pillar piscina in the N aisle. But the oustanding features are the benches and a monument. Three carved bench ends recount a story which probably had political overtones in the 15th century, though quite what they were is still not certain. There is Reynard the Fox dressed as an ecclesiastic, though is it really the Abbot of Glastonbury, for he was owner of the village? Perhaps it is the Bishop instead, preaching to the birds, then put in the stocks, and finally hung by geese. Whatever it means, the carving is extraordinarily vivid.

The monument is to John Somerset (d. 1663), who, with his two wives, one with a fetching, wide-brimmed hat, and his family, is rising from the tomb at the last day. Somerset was not only a man of family and religion; he was a man of courage. At Easter 1645 this former captain in the Royalist army led the villagers of South Brent against the plundering of royalist troops, and was imprisoned for his impudence.

Bridgwater Som. 2 B1

Bridgwater's industrial sprawl, its 19th-century terraces in local brick, and its modern housing estates suggest a place quite foreign to Somerset. And so, in some ways, it has always been. Leland approached from the s and saw first a long stone causeway, then St Saviour's Chapel, then one of the four stone gates, then through a 'praty streate a while' into the market place. Beyond was the castle 'symtyme a right fair and strong peace of worke, but now al goyng to mere ruine'; to the w the former Grey Friars' house, turned into a dwelling by the local customs collector; to the E, over the great bridge to the suburb of Eastover, was 'a thing notable', the hospital of St John.

Bridgwater was not at its best when Leland was there. More than 200 houses had 'faullen yn ruine and sore decay' within the previous 20 years or so, for foreign wars played havoc with the overseas trade on which the town depended. It lies well inland up the Parrett, and the river is tidal well beyond the town, but its bridge prevented the passage of shipping and ensured that Bridgwater merchants controlled the county's trade. The port was, in fact, the most important between Bristol and Barnstaple, and by the late 15th century local merchants were

East Brent church

St Mary's Bridgwater

not only trading regularly across the Bristol Channel but also had close links with Ireland, France, and Northern Spain. A town account of 1400 was written on paper made in Piedmont and brought by some unknown Italian merchant probably from Genoa. A luxury import like this took its place beside dyestuffs, iron, wine, salt, and fish; and in return Bridgwater's merchants took Somerset's cloth, corn, and beans to Bordeaux and Bayonne. Very little evidence of all this medieval trade still remains in the town, for there is nothing to be seen of the once substantial Fransciscan friary, founded *c.* 1245 and a sure sign of mercantile prosperity; nor of St John's Hospital, founded by William Briwere, lord of the town, *c.* 1219, for the care of poor and infirm people, and later to provide a grammar school. Of the castle built by William Briwere (d. 1226), which must have dominated the town, only the Water Gate and some walling survives on the w quay, though it once con-

tained a hall, chapel, and bell tower and part was evidently turned into a residence for the Constable on the high ground that is now known as King Square. This was left as a ruin after slighting in the Civil War. Even the three-arched medieval bridge is gone, replaced by a single-span iron bridge from Abraham Darby's works at Coalbrookdale in 1795 and that in turn by the present one in 1883.

But there is the 'large paroch chirch' that Leland saw, with its fine medieval spire; and the names and arrangement of the streets are medieval to the core. Friarn Street recalls the house of Greyfriars, Dampiet Street, the dam on the Town Brook made to drive a mill. The quaint Penel Orlieu was formerly two streets named after two local families, the Pynels and the Ordlofs. Between them they encircle the church in its triangular market place, and lead direct to the quay.

The church demonstrates the wealth of Bridgwater's merchants well enough, though there is surprisingly little apart from its plan to suggest that it had chantry chapels, a rood, and late-medieval decorations as elaborate as any in the country. That is a reflection of 17th-century Bridgwater, not of the medieval town, which financed this large building, and in 1366–7 raised £137 and employed Nicholas Waleys on the tower. There are a few fragments that date back to the 13th century and a little later, including parts of the decoration of the N doorway and the crypt below the N transept, but the church is largely of the 14th century, with big windows of the 15th century, the chancel roof of c. 1422, and late-medieval chancel screens, the fine carved pulpit, and the remains of stalls used as sedilia.

Post-Reformation Bridgwater, like many other towns of its kind, had Puritan and Nonconformist opinions. Robert Blake (d. 1657), the Parliamentarian commander in the Civil War, who presides over the town in bronze, was born in the town (his birthplace in Blake Street is the local museum), and John Pym (d. 1643) of Brymore in nearby Cannington (q.v.), who led opposition to the Crown in Parliament, personify the town's sympathies in the 17th century, sympathies evident in the town's support for Parliament in the Civil War and for the Duke of Monmouth in 1685; and evident, too, in the curious lack of medieval furnishings and monuments in the parish church, and their replacement by the splendid Jacobean Civic Pew. The brick Unitarian Chapel in Dampiet Street, founded as a Presbyterian one in 1688, was logical progression.

The port was never so thriving again as in the later Middle Ages, but its Channel trade continued, and Bridgwater's own products – glass, bricks, tiles, and Bath bricks – were developed in the 18th and 19th centuries. This mild prosperity is seen clearly in the buildings along West Quay, most notably in the house called the Lions (1725), put up by a local builder, Benjamin Holloway, but now less impressive since the pavilions are derelict. Holloway's work is also seen in Castle Steet, 'the most

West Bower Farm, Durleigh

perfect Georgian street in Somerset' (Pevsner), designed – no doubt with London inspiration – for James Brydges, Duke of Chandos, beginning in 1721. Holloway carried out most of the work and finished the last houses on the s side nearest the river after 1730.

North of the historic town is a fine and recently restored piece of 19th-century industrial archaeology, a complex of canal, dock, warehouse, glass cone, retractable railway bridge, and brick works. Glass manufacture was begun in the early 18th century by the Duke of Chandos; the dock and canal were built between 1837 and 1841, and the warehouse between 1840 and 1845. The bridge was built in 1871. The docks were closed in 1970, and Bridgwater's industry has moved to the outskirts, one product making visitors aware of its presence by a well-known and rather unpleasant aroma.

Two miles w of the town, towards the Quantocks and on the edge of DURLEIGH reservoir, stands the rather forlorn West Bower Farm, a converted 15th-century gatehouse probably built by a local lawyer Alexander Hody (d. 1461), whose initials, with those of his wife, are in glass quarries in the cusped window tracery. The church, at the other end of the reservoir, is essentially Norman, with a 14th-century gable-roofed tower.

Bristol Avon 5 B4 *(pop.* 426,657)
A city the size of Bristol cannot easily be understood, but the view from the top of the Cabot tower on Brandon Hill is a good beginning. Those names are significant in

themselves, for the hill was once topped by a chapel dedicated to St Brendan the Navigator, and the tower commemorates another explorer, John Cabot, discoverer of Newfoundland on an expedition promoted by Bristol merchants in 1497. Bristol's fame as a port, trading to the extremes of man's exploration, was achieved early in its history. The view sw from the tower also explains Bristol's success, for across the valley of the Avon, shared by roads and railways and occupied by docks and warehouses, is a skyline of green fields and a graceful village church; a hinterland rich in agricultural produce, wool, stone, and minerals, and a river giving access to the western seas. The hill on which the tower stands is demonstration enough of the city's strategic advantage, and the Royal Fort behind is another, both the sites of Civil War earthworks whose defence by Prince Rupert was for long the key to royal success in the West.

From Brandon Hill se, on a platform above the river, stands the Cathedral, but on a site which might have been chosen with deliberation by the founder, Robert Fitzharding, *c.* 1140. There may well in early times have been associations with St Augustine himself, and with his visit in 603 to meet the British bishops (see Aust). The foundation, significantly enough, was never known as Bristol Abbey when it was a monastery. Was this the 'stow' or 'holy place' which is one interpretation of the origin of the place-name of Bristol? (The ultimate 'l' on this and every other possible word in the language is a characteristic of local speech.) There are perhaps more surviving parts of this house than of any other house of canons in England, but extensive destruction in a riot of 1831 and later buildings make understanding them a complicated business. But clear enough is the late-Norman chapter house (1150–70) and the contemporary E cloister walk, the great gatehouse leading to the former conventual buildings, and two other archways there, one the entrance to the former abbot's lodgings. Next in date comes the Elder Lady Chapel on the N side of the choir, built *c.* 1210–20 with the help of the Wells masons. But the great triumph of the abbey was the next phase of building, 'superior to anything else . . . in England and indeed in Europe at the same time . . . (proving) incontrovertibly that English design surpassed that of all other countries during the first third of the C14' (Pevsner). An architectural historian's view, perhaps, but the simplicity of the choir, and the vaults of the aisles, and the Berkeley Chapel, have a balance and grace that masks the ingenuity of the master who designed the whole at the same height to make the most use of the space available.

Unusually, the beginning of this great work is known precisely – 21 August 1298; and the inspirer of it all was Edmund Knowle, subsequently Abbot 1306–32, who, according to a later roll of Abbots

> bilded the churche of the new fro the Fundamentes w^t the vestrary . . . He bilde also of the new from the Fundamentes the Kynges Hall And also the Kynges Chamber. Also he reparid And kevered the Freytoure w^t othir goode dedis.

This work continued until the 1330s. Next came the Newton Chapel and the beginnings of the S transept, but thereafter no new work seems to have been done until the late 15th century, the old Norman nave (consecrated 1148) presumably still standing. Abbot Newland (1481–1515) seems to have finished the tower and transepts and to have started a new nave, reaching sill height on the N side but completing more on the S. The last years of

Bristol Cathedral

the abbey were unhappy, and in 1539 the Abbot and only nine canons survived to surrender to the Crown. In 1542, however, there was a new beginning. The abbey church was elevated to the rank of Cathedral for the newly created bishopric of Bristol, and two former religious, Paul Bush and William Snowe, became the first Bishop and the first Dean. Poorly endowed from the first the Cathedral remained in its unfinished state, rather like the Abbey at Bath, until G. E. Street was given the difficult task of building a nave and w end. The result, achieved between 1868 and 1888, is sensible, harmonious, and restrained.

The monuments reflect the history of the building: abbots are to be expected, the best (artistically) in the Lady Chapel. Tombs of the Berkeleys recall the founder's family and their continued close association with the canons. Glass and the misericords of the stalls are some of the last survivals of the Abbey. After Paul Bush (d. 1558) Bishops are scarce, and the memorials are, on the whole, rather dull, hardly reflecting the life of the city. At least two treasures should be seen for their Bristol associations: the 15th-century candelabrum brought from the bombed Temple church, and the fragments of a screen from the Whitefriars in the city, rescued from an earlier age of destruction. And there is a pair of candlesticks given by a member of a semi-piratical expedition against the Spaniards which, incidentally, rescued Alexander Selkirk from San Juan Fernandes and thus gave birth to Robinson Crusoe.

The Cathedral stands on a step, as it were, down to the ancient heart of Bristol, facing across College Green the so-called Lord Mayor's Chapel, formerly the church of the Gaunts Hospital, founded in 1220. Dating in its fabric from the 13th century, with many additions from the 15th including a tower and the Poyntz Chapel, it has a fine collection of monuments including that of Bishop Miles Salley (d. 1516), successively almoner of Abingdon Abbey, Abbot of Eynsham, and Bishop of Llandaff. He claimed connection with the Berkeleys. There is also some interesting if entirely irrelevant glass, some bought at Beckford's sale at Fonthill, and coming from France and Flanders. The third side of the green is occupied by the massive screen of the Council House (1938–58), with a statue of Cabot in the central porch and stately gilded unicorns on the roof. Exploration and imagination might well be the twin Bristol themes.

Imagination is certainly needed to understand the core of Bristol, where changes have been both frequent and fundamental. The origin of the city hinges on its site, a narrow neck of land where the River Frome meandered to join the already curving Avon. In this narrow neck, in shape though not in height like the site of Durham, was almost certainly a mint producing coins between 1017 and 1023. Bristol was thus a *burh*, defended by nature and having a market centre, the prerequisites of burghal status. By 1051 its ships were travelling to Ireland; did they moor at jetties which (from the Norse

Interior, Bristol Cathedral

brygga rather than from the Saxon *brycg*, a bridge) gave the place the first part of its name? By 1067 the place was strongly defended and by 1086 its burgesses clearly had some independence. It was well known as a port, and in the early 12th century its trade with Ireland, Norway, 'and other overseas lands', largely in slaves, was commented on.

The *burh* may yet be traced in the heart of the old city, quartered by Corn, Wine (formerly Wynch), Broad, and High streets. To its E a strong motte-and-bailey castle was built, probably by Geoffrey, Bishop of Coutances. Robert, Earl of Gloucester (d. 1147), lord of Bristol, built its huge Caen-stone keep, 'the flower of all the keeps of

The cloisters, Bristol Cathedral

England', and the centre of the Empress Matilda's power against Stephen. Royal fortress, administrative headquarters, and prison, it was extended by Henry III, and last used significantly by Edward I. The site, bereft of its river, now makes little sense, though its remains have been skilfully excavated.

Bristol's reward for economic success was the charter of 1373 which gave her unique status as a county, acknowledgement that in the previous century and a half Bristol's merchants had achieved great things. In the late 13th century Bristol had been second only to London in the value of her imports, sometimes over three-quarters of a million gallons of wine a year. In the early 14th century she was in a position, near the Mendips, the Cotswolds, and Wales, to export cloth, and by the mid century had cornered some two-thirds of the whole of England's trade: wine from Bordeaux and Spain, and West Country cloth, the source of great mercantile profit. The 14th-century work at St Mary Redcliffe, so sensitively continued in the late 15th, is perhaps the best example of Bristol's prosperity, the result of the munificence and the trading success of two members of the same family, William Canynges, elder and younger (see Westbury on Trym). The church, founded by the 1150s,

rebuilt *c.* 1200, was transformed from the 1290s onwards, and its fantastic hexagonal outer N porch is a wonder in the city and beyond. Such were the tentacles of Bristol's trading links that the suggestion of oriental influence is not at all impossible. The 14th-century work is in the fine tradition of the abbey master mason, and its continuation into the late 15th century is a triumphant demonstration of artistic unity and mercantile success.

Wars and rumours of wars are not conducive to successful commerce, but the loss of Gascony did not completely sever the Bordeaux connexion, and the Bristol–Bordeaux link is a thriving civic and cultural affair. Nor did the later wars with Spain bring that connexion to an end, and Bristol Milk and Bristol Cream are the continuing results. But new trading links were essential, and Bristol merchants began to venture again across the western seas. Iceland was the first goal and then, after the Cabots, Newfoundland and the New World. Would that Bristol's Sheriff in John Cabot's day, Richard Ameryke, had given his name to the new continent!

The little town, gated and walled by the early 13th century if not earlier, had five parishes crammed within its walls, and five chapels over its gates (St John's survives); and already suburbs crossing the Frome to create the 'new borough of the meadow' (the origin of the Broadmead shopping centre), and clustering around St James's Priory (*c.* 1137) and St Michael's church. To the E was the market, now Old Market Street; and to the s across the marshes of the Avon, developed Temple Fee and Redcliffe, the latter round what came to be the most magnificent suburban church in the country. This phenomenal expansion was followed by and presumably dictated the diversion of the River Frome to create a complex of quays, 'backs', and docks to bring sea-going vessels into the heart of the town. Subsequent diversions followed this remarkable lead; and if today the docks are closed to commercial traffic, the basins, quays, and warehouses are a precious asset whose preservation is of cardinal importance.

These new works were a great achievement, only possible in a prosperous and organized town. Bristol had a mayor by 1216, and a guild merchant almost certainly before that time. And there were other signs, like the arrival of the friars, never far away when commerce was thriving (the Whitefriars are now commemorated in the name of a modern office building put up where their house used to stand on the edge of one of the quays so recently built), and hospitals for sick and poor. By the end of the Middle Ages there may have been as many as 26 religious houses, not to mention parish churches and chapels (see St Stephen, All Saints, and SS. Philip and Jacob, and St Nicholas's church museum). Parts of two of the religious houses at each end of Christmas Street are a valuable if rather shabby glimpse of medieval Bristol: the chapel of the Three Kings of Cologne (1504) at the top, and the doorway of St Bartholomew's Hospital (*c.* 1207) at the bottom.

By the late 17th century Bristol was again a principal port, this time for the growing Atlantic trade now added to the links its leading businessmen, the Merchant Venturers, had recently forged with the Baltic and the Medi-

North porch, St Mary Redcliffe

Colonnade, Hotwells

terranean. Ship-building and sugar-refining, tobacco processing, and metal industries like brass and gun-shot making, gave the city a new impetus. Bristol glass and Bristol Delft, chocolate and cocoa were soon to be added, though the most prosperous business of all was the notorious triangular trade in slaves between Africa, the West Indies, and North America. Bristol's merchants had returned to their evil ways.

In this context Bristol expanded as it had three centuries earlier. Queen's Square (begun in 1699 and enhanced by Rysbrack's equestrian William III) was Bristol's statement of intention, now not quite what it was before two sides were burnt in the riots of 1831 and modern traffic destroyed its intended quiet. But here, in this quarter, is mercantile and public-spirited Bristol: King Street, with the timber-framed Llandoger Trow (1669), St Nicholas's Almshouses (1652), the Coopers' Hall (1743–4), the Theatre Royal (1764–6), the former Public Library (1739–40), and the exposed remains of

the Merchant Venturers' almshouses (1696–9). There are, of course, glimpses elsewhere – Orchard Street (1716), for instance, or the Exchange in Corn Street (1740–3) by John Wood the Elder, with its famous brass 'nails'; or the Market (1745) in which Wood must, thinks Pevsner, have been involved. And glimpses, too, outside the city centre, as mansions, squares, and terraces climbed up the slopes of Kingsdown and the countryside to the west (e.g. Berkeley Square and Clifton Hill), and individual merchants took to living in the country (see Henbury, Westbury on Trym) as the Smythes of Long Ashton (q.v.) had done long since.

Undoubtedly the most spectacular development was at CLIFTON, not at all in the spirit of the Merchant Venturers but speculative in a way they would have understood. The Hotwells, near the entrance to the Avon Gorge, began in earnest as a spa after Catherine of Braganza visited in 1695. Dowry Square, a colonnade, parade, and gardens were developed during the 18th

The Paragon, Bristol

Christmas Steps, Bristol

Trade was not all, for the range of Bristol's manufactures expanded and developed. Joseph Fry acquired a patent for grinding chocolate in 1761; H. O. Wills came to join a tobacco business in 1786; E. S. Robinson began making paper bags for grocers in 1844: three names to conjure with. In 1818 John Loudon McAdam became Surveyor of Bristol's roads; in 1829 Isambard Kingdom Brunel won a competition to build a bridge across the gorge at Clifton (finished 1864); in 1833 that same I. K. Brunel became Engineer of the Great Western Railway Company, and his terminal building at Temple Meads Station still survives, though its present use as a car park is not worthy of a building half as good. The massive dock improvements of 1804–9 creating the Floating Harbour were as spectacular though in the end less useful than the diversion of the Frome in the 13th century, though the city's shipbuilders were able to cope with Brunel's steamships the *Great Western* (1837) and

A Bristol Nail

century, and terraces and crescents spread above the cliff on Clifton Hill. Clifton itself soon became a spa, too: 'the Montpelier of England' it was called, and could offer the dramatic natural beauties of the Avon Gorge and the Downs to add to the medicinal waters below. But it was never Bath, and its success after the turn of the 19th century with the Mall (1806–11, though terraces earlier), the magnificent Royal York Crescent (*c.* 1810–20), and the Paragon (1809–14) was less as a spa than as a Regency residential haven.

In other ways Clifton was hardly in the nonconforming Bristol spirit, the Bristol of the early Baptists of Broadmead and the Quakers of Quakers Friars. John Wesley's New Room in the Horsefair (1739, 1748), first of all Methodist churches, was the base from which he was to speak against the Theatre Royal, though most of his energies were devoted when in Bristol to the poorer quarters of the city and to Kingswood (q.v.). It was, if only for a time, the city of Edmund Burke and Henry Cruger, the orator and the American merchant, both anxious for peace with the American colonists. Burke's withdrawal as parliamentary candidate in 1780 was the beginning of tragedy: 'what shadows we are, and what shadows we pursue' he invited the electors of Bristol to consider; and the loss of the American colonies was a serious blow to the city's trade. Bristol became the home in exile of a number of loyalists.

Clifton

Roman Catholic Cathedral, Bristol

the *Great Britain* (1843), the latter brought back from the Falkland Islands in 1970 and now on show. Demands for a more efficient port in the end were inevitable, but Avonmouth (1877) and Portishead (1879) (q.v.) and the more modern facilities remain part of the Port of Bristol, able now to take the larger ocean-going shipping of the modern trade routes. Victorian warehouses and public buildings, new streets, the Colston Hall (façade 1867), West of England Academy (1857), Royal Infirmary (1906–11 but founded 1735), Clifton College (begun 1860), Municipal Library (1906) – all are elements of a prosperous provincial city, and survive despite the devastating bombing of the Second World War. Better preserved are the villas of Redland and Stoke Bishop and the terraces of Eastville and Bedminster. Dominant in the city centre now are tower blocks of business houses and the spreading buildings of the University, the last a product of Bristol's merchants, manufacturers, and medical school. The University's earlier buildings at the top of Park Street are marked by Sir George Oatley's great Gothic tower (1925), a fine piece of West-country remembrance. Only a short distance away is a building

ABOVE: *Berkeley Square, Bristol*

BELOW: *Redcliffe Parade, Bristol*

that owes nothing to Bristol and the West either in style or in materials; and yet the Roman Catholic Cathedral, boldly proclaiming its inspiring purpose in modern form and light-grey concrete, a stark contrast to the brown Edwardian villas that surround it, is another contribution to the variety that is Bristol.

'Ship shape and Bristol fashion' is a phrase from Bristol's past as a port; 'Blenheim', 'Beaufighter', 'Britannia', and 'Brabazon' were the products of a different age, for since 1910 Bristol has manufactured aeroplanes and aero engines, ships of the air and not now of the sea. The great complex at Filton so recently led the world with Concorde. Chemical works and zinc smelters, medical research, power-boat racing, and world wine fairs are examples of how Bristol advances and adapts. Its motorway and rail links make the city still an obvious regional centre with metropolitan character; and the Severn tides may yet be harnessed to national advantage, keeping the city as ever in the centre of technological advance.

Broadway Som. 2 B3
Broadway takes its name and the curious shape of its parish from the 'broad way' that led into the medieval forest of Neroche and once formed an ancient roadway between the Iron Age hillforts of Ham Hill and Castle Neroche. The church stands away from the village, the result it is said of the intervention of the Devil who, when the villagers were building it in the centre of the settlement, moved during the night what they had done during the day – the usual popular explanation for a change of village site actually caused by plague or economic factors. But there is no trace of a village near the church.

The church itself is dedicated jointly to St Aldhelm, the missionary of Somerset (see Doulting and Frome), and St Eadburga, probably Eadburga (d. 960), granddaughter of King Alfred and a nun of Winchester.

NEROCHE FOREST, a name spelt many ways and possibly derived from a word for hunting dog, stretched in the Middle Ages from Broadway to the Blackdowns, its western edge marked by Castle Neroche. This earthwork, now largely covered by trees, is a Norman motte-and-bailey castle which was owned in 1086 by the Count of Mortain, half-brother of William the Conqueror. The site and its surroundings now form part of a Forestry Commission nature trail. (The present Neroche Forest is a modern Forestry Commission creation.)

The countryside formerly within the medieval forest still bears many traces of its ancient status: rare species in hedges and surviving woodland, farms like Thickthorn, villages like Ashill, and the shapes of fields which reveal successive phases of enclosure. The village names Hatch and Donyatt ('Dunna's gate') mark its boundary, and the straight roads through it are not, as some assume, Roman in origin, but are routes laid out when the former common land was parcelled out, a process not complete until 1830.

Broomfield Som. *see* **The Quantock Hills**

Bruton Som. 3 E1
Bruton comes in two parts, divided by the River Brue which runs gently over stones and under a packhorse bridge. To the s, beneath and beyond the church, is oldest Bruton, a Saxon religious centre and borough which had two churches, one founded by St Aldhelm. There was a mint here in the 10th century and a small town by the 11th which probably lay beyond the River around a market place near the present Patwell and Quaperlake streets. Aldhelm's church probably became a religious house (founded by Algar, Earl of Cornwall, Leland believed), which William de Mohun of Dunster changed to a house of Augustinian canons between 1127 and 1135. It was from the first a rich house, with valuable estates in France until exchanged in 1260 for properties in Sussex and Gloucestershire.

William Gilbert (Prior from 1494/5) had his house converted into an Abbey in 1511, and then 'did great cost in the abbey … in building, almost reedifying it'. But after 1539 the monastery was sold, and all that remains is part of the heavily buttressed precinct wall in the street known mysteriously as Plox. The site was first occupied by a mansion built by the Berkeley family, and was later owned by the antiquarian and banker Sir Richard Colt Hoare. The wall now serves as part of the vicarage house, and the precinct was cut in two by the railway and is now the site of many of the buildings of King's School. The tower above is thought to be a dovecote (NT), though its date is not certain. King's School was endowed in 1519 by Bishop Richard Fitzjames of London who was born at nearby Redlynch, John his nephew, and John Edmundes, Chancellor of St Paul's, London, and another native. Old School, opposite the precinct wall, includes some original 16th-century work.

The parish church of St Mary is no earlier than the 14th century, but is remarkable for its two towers, one over the N porch of the later 14th century, the other at the w end late 15th. Before then the nave was rebuilt, but the clerestory was not added until the early 16th century, dated between 1506 and 1522 by shields on the parapets with the initials of Abbot Gilbert, Bishop Fitzjames, and Abbot Bere of Glastonbury. But even the magnificent roof will not be the first thing to catch the eye inside; that will be the chancel, entirely rebuilt in 1743 and happily retaining its original decoration and furnishings.

The regular form of High Street on the other side of the valley suggests medieval town planning. The street includes the former abbey court house of the mid 15th century and Sexey's Hospital (1638). There was much quality building in the 18th century, for Bruton was a prosperous clothing town. The Blue Ball Hotel, called the Unicorn in the 17th century and reckoned one of the seven best in Somerset, still has its Georgian Assembly Rooms, for the town was then something of a social centre. When

Packhorse bridge, Bruton

woollen-cloth manufacturing moved to the North of England, silk quickly took its place. In the 1790s up to 400 young people were employed reeling silk. In the 1830s, however, industry died; today Bruton is no longer the bustling local shopping centre of a few years ago. But this decline has notable conservation advantages: the developer is not interested, and Bruton is essentially preserved.

The Berkeleys who lived in the mansion on the abbey site were Anglican and Royalist. Three miles up Coombe Street and over the hills, where views over the countryside are among the very best in Somerset, lies BATCOMBE, where the prosperous clothiers in the 17th century were rich, rigid, and Roundhead. This was in fine contrast to their church, with its tower of *c.* 1540, sturdy and unpinnacled, but one of the most ornate and noble in the county. The Bisses were the leading family, donors of the s porch (1629) and no doubt of much else, and amply commemorated in the church. Richard Alleine, rector here, was one of the leaders of the Puritan movement in Somerset in the mid 17th century; and Royalist Bruton over the hill was the enemy. But when the attack came, Bruton was ready, as a verse in the parish register under 1642 records:

> All praise and thanks to God still give
> For our deliverance Matthias' Eve;
> By His great power we put to flight
> Our foes the raging Batcombeites.

Brympton D'Evercy Som. *see* **Odcombe**

Burnham on Sea Som. 4 G6
Until 1830 Burnham was a parish of scattered hamlets, cultivating its rich farmland and trying to ignore the sea. An enterprising curate, the Revd David Davies, built the first lighthouse on the Berrow road in 1800 to make the Parrett passage safer. Then in 1830 the spa known as Daviesville was established, centred on a bath house (now called Steart House) and two wells N of the church. Opinions about the efficacy of the water were not unanimous; some said it was extremely unpleasant. Terraces and an esplanade were developed with some pretension, and by 1836 a hotel boasted among its assets a fly and a bath chair. The railway brought more business: the Great Western came to HIGHBRIDGE in 1841 and a line was extended to Burnham Pier in 1858 for steamer trips to South Wales. But Burnham failed to attract business from the wharves at Highbridge and Bridgwater.

The 14th-century church marks the historic centre of the village, its leaning tower a reminder of the parable of building on the sand. It contains something both surprising and very foreign: the remains of the altarpiece commissioned by James II for the Royal Chapel at Whitehall Palace, to be part of a worthy setting for the revived services of the Roman Catholic faith. The overall design of the great altarpiece was the work of Sir Christopher Wren, but the sculpture was by Grinling Gibbons and Arnold Quellin. The two men were paid £1,875 1s. 8d. between them in 1686; and Evelyn, who saw it late in the year, wrote: 'Nothing can be finer than the magnificent marble work and architecture at the end . . . with all the carving and pillars of exquisite art and greate coste.' But Gibbons soon had to take it all down again; 'perhaps the greatest artistic production' of James II's reign was taken first to Hampton Court and then to Westminster Abbey, where it served, somewhat modified, until *c.* 1820.

It came to Burnham as some little recompense for the deficiencies of the Anglican Church in the early 19th century. Dr Walker King could quite legally be both Bishop of Rochester and vicar of Burnham; and it was he who brought it to Somerset. Subsequent restorers of the church have done nothing to make the work even mildly intelligible, but the exquisite quality of the work is still apparent. The figures of the child angels and the heads of the cherubs were clearly adapted from portrait studies of two children, possibly those of Gibbons himself.

North of Burnham the flat marshlands are protected from the sea by sand dunes; this is holiday camp and caravan country, and BERROW and BREAN are almost swamped by each summer's influx. St Mary's church at Berrow stands among the dunes from which the village took its name. It is a 13th-century building in essence, with some fine later details including a rescued 15th-century cross head and traces of an unusual 16th-century west gallery. St Bridget's at Brean, probably also of the 13th century, has a saddleback roof to its s porch tower, unusual in Somerset. But what is rare here is the dedication. St Bridget of Ireland, Abbess of Kildare, died *c.* 525; in Ireland and on the Continent her cult was second only in popularity to that of Patrick himself; her appearance here is because the founder was also owner of St Brides in Wales.

Burrowbridge   Som. *see* **Athelney**

Cadbury   Som.   2 D2

The little village of SOUTH CADBURY and much of the country to the change from a hamlet of the late Bronze Age to a N and w, is dominated by one of the most famous archaeological sites in the West Country. Cadbury Castle was known as early as Leland's time as the Camelot of Arthurian Legend;

> sumtyme a famose toun or castelle ... wunderfully enstrengtheid of nature ... Much gold, sylver and coper of the Romaine coynes hath be found ther yn plouing ... The people can telle nothing ther but that they have hard say that Arture much resorted to Camalat.

Between 1966 and 1970 this multi-vallate hillfort was excavated on a large scale, and there emerged the story of occupation from early Neolithic times (*c.* 4000 B.C.) to the early 13th century. Within that period there was a change from a hamlet of the late Bronze Age to a defended village for farming peasants of the early Iron Age; from there to an Iron Age town, with strong fortifications, wooden round houses, storage pits, and finds such as currency bars and iron implements which indicated both local industry and commerce. There were, too, several pieces of sophisticated metalwork – a bronze shield-mount and a bronze pendant among others – which may have been produced by craftsmen in the town.

The town came to an end after a battle at the gate and a massacre *c.* A.D. 70, perhaps as a result of its people's failure to conform in some way to Roman rule, and enforced evacuation of the survivors followed. But that was by no means the end; a temple or shrine was probably established there and the hill-top continued to be visited throughout the Roman period. After that comes a period of considerable uncertainty but of great significance: pottery imported from the Mediterranean found on the site shows that from *c.* 470 it was the centre of a community wealthy enough to engage in sophisticated trade. The defences discovered were also sophisticated, with earth and timber gateways; and within them was an aisled timber feasting hall. The settlement was clearly at the height of its importance when Arthur the *dux bellorum* was fighting against the invading Anglo-Saxons in southern England.

When the Saxons finally overwhelmed Somerset the hill-top was abandoned again until Ethelred II (the 'unready', but really meaning 'evil-' or 'no-counsel') faced a crisis at the beginning of the 11th century. As part of his defensive system against the Vikings, Ethelred, like Alfred before him, made fortified towns of which *Cadanbyrig* was one. It became for a time also a commercial and local government centre. Coins were minted here, and it is possible that a church was begun but never finished. The town seems to have been abandoned at the beginning of the reign of Cnut (*c.* 1016), though the repairs to 'the castle of Cadbury' in 1209 may perhaps have been made here. But that was the end; though the traditions survived in the village until Leland's time.

South Cadbury church, by the car park, was much restored in the 19th century, but in origin it must be earlier than the 14th when the s aisle was first built. Restoration uncovered the bishop, painted in the window splay in the aisle. A much finer church, perhaps the finest complete Perpendicular one in the county, is at NORTH CADBURY 1 mile N beyond the former medieval chapel at the cross-roads. The church, set at the edge of a pretty village beside the Tudor manor house, is notably plain outside, except for its porches, but its importance lies in its almost complete reconstruction *c.* 1422 by Elizabeth, Lady Botreaux (d. 1433) and her son Sir William. Almost complete, for the tower had only recently been built by John Feron (d. 1407), rector of the parish, whose tomb was damaged when a bell fell on it in 1567, destroying the inscription that he 'builded this tower at his owne proper coste'.

The chancel's high-silled windows leave room for stalls, for it was collegiate from 1427, the last parish rector becoming the first rector of the College of St Michael the Archangel with two chaplains (planned eventually to total seven members), who were to celebrate masses for the founders and their family and for the royal house. The College was not, apparently, a success, and did not survive until the end of the 15th century; the church was and is splendid, though it has suffered the removal of the collegiate stalls and the Hastings tombs from the chancel. The Botreaux monument has not been treated with the respect due to a foundress and her husband. And yet there are some rare and exciting survivals: black letter alphabets perhaps for teaching children in the (quite rare) 15th-century vestry; and the splendid series of carvings on the later benches – apparently all of 1538 and themselves adding to the unity of the building. Among these gems are a remarkably undamaged Madonna and Child; a post mill and millstone; a farmer driving his horse; a man's profile with obvious Renaissance feeling; a cat proving herself more adept than the trap below at catching a mouse; and a spirited flute-player.

The manor house was rebuilt and extended by Sir Francis Hastings (d. 1610, buried in the church). His brother the 3rd Earl of Huntingdon, granted him the property in 1586, and the house, which Sir Francis filled with heraldic glass to commemorate his illustrious family, was 'in good forwardnes' in 1592 and probably finished a year later. The w wing is of the early 16th century, and Hastings added the N front. Later alterations and additions were made in the 18th and early 19th centuries. Hastings himself was a Puritan pamphleteer, to whose pen is owed the 96-line epitaph to his first wife in the church, c. 1596. After his brother's gift of the patronage of the church to Emmanuel College, Cambridge, c. 1590 the parish became a centre of Puritanism in the early 17th century which clearly disapproved of much of the liveliness of local customs reflected in the bench-end carvings. So the parson was led to complain in 1634

> that on Midsomer day last in time of Morninge prayer and sermon a company from Gallington [Galhampton, hamlet 1 mile N] in the parish of North Cadbury, and other places [came] with a Morrice Daunce and with Fidlers and with a drume, and held on theire sports so neere unto the Church.

The kill-joy parson asked them at least twice 'to leafe makeinge such a noyse', but naturally to no avail.

Cameley Avon 5 B5

From the mid 18th century, when the Bristol road was turnpiked, the village of Cameley was threatened with extinction, and for several years after the Second World War the deserted church was actually closed. For good reason Sir John Betjeman described it as 'Rip-Van-Winkle's church', for restoration work in the 1960s led to almost fairy-tale discoveries, transforming a plain though charming Georgian interior into an art gallery of mural decoration reaching back perhaps to the 11th century.

The fabric of the church may be insignificant, as Pevsner says, but only the fact that it has not been altered since the 11th century has preserved what later generations put on its walls. The arms of Edward I and his Queen, Eleanor of Castile, face each other across the plain chancel arch, and in the nave fragments of a mid-14th-century jester, some 15th-century damask patterning, the foot of a huge St Christopher (accompanied by contemporary crab and fish and a row of 18th-century 'hat pins'), and the Royal Arms of James I are revealed as layers of Protestant whitewash are carefully removed.

The furnishings have the same fascinating variety: medieval pews, two-decker pulpit, and attached rectorial pew of 1637; 18th-century sanctuary woodwork and w gallery (1711); and the most modern addition of all, the s gallery of 1819 'for the free use of the inhabitants'. Only the existence of this last gallery could be guessed from the outside because of its stone stair; and the Bristol-type tower is of course an addition, partly given, if the arms over the door are to be believed, by one of the St Loes, though the coat of arms has not been positively dated. Inside the church are commemorated

the Moggs, local gentry in these parts in the 18th and 19th centuries; outside are some typical 18th-century gravestone cherubs, but also a rare companion, a coal truck, which presumably killed a 16-year-old miner in 1808.

Cannington Som. 2 B1

Cannington is a large village on a curious bend in the A39 between Bridgwater (q.v.) and Nether Stowey (q.v.). It lies in the flat Parrett Valley one and a quarter miles from the meandering river and the same from the beginnings of the dip slope of the Quantocks. Its ancient name was 'Quantock tun', and it was probably associated in some way with the ancient royal Saxon forest of Quantock. Land in Cannington was given by King Alfred to his son Edward the Elder.

But Cannington's history goes back further than that. At CANNINGTON PARK (1 mile NW) near the Iron Age hillfort is a huge cemetery, perhaps once containing 5,000 graves, largely Christian, dating between the 2nd and the 8th centuries. One of these graves, that of a young person, was marked out from the others – a young chieftain, perhaps, or a priestly figure? The bones now lie under an appropriate inscription before the screen in the parish church.

'A praty uplandisch towne', Leland called it, and noted the 'very fair and welle adornyd' church and, 'hard adnexid' to the E the nunnery. The church is very tall, its late-14th-century tower highly decorated, but from a distance seeming almost stark, perhaps because it lacks the expected pinnacles. Inside the height is striking; then the red sandstone walls, typical of Victorian restorers who removed colour-washed plaster wherever they found it, inside or out. The details are normal Somerset Perpendicular, including the screen based on Dunster's; and also the West Somerset windows, so tall that transoms are needed, but decorated with two sets of tracery, like the hall windows at Cleeve Abbey (q.v.).

North of the church is Cannington Priory, now part of the Somerset College of Agriculture and Horticulture. The Priory of Benedictine nuns was founded here c. 1138 by Robert de Courcy, and was given as its first endowment the manor and advowson of Cannington. The house was never very large but, like many houses of its kind, was popular with ladies as paying guests. The last Abbess, Cecilia de Vernay, came, like most of the sisters, from a local gentry family. She surrendered her house in 1536.

Leland says that 'Rogeres of the court' was given Cannington Priory. This was Sir Edward Rogers, a Devon man and a courtier, who built the Elizabethan house north of the church. How much, if any, of the nunnery survives has not yet been discovered. On the death of Henry Rogers in 1672 the property passed to the Catholic Thomas Clifford, Lord Clifford of Chudleigh, the 'C' of Charles II's Cabal. Under his grandson Thomas the house became a Catholic centre: a priest lived there

Castle Cary

from 1713 and the chapel was added *c.* 1730. From 1807 until 1836 a community of Benedictine nuns occupied the house, and from 1831 they opened their extended chapel to the public.

The village has some good Georgian houses and an almshouse dated 1672 but actually a conversion of that date. The building was formerly the church house or parish hall of the medieval parish and was erected *c.* 1500.

Carhampton   Som. *see* **Dunster**

Castle Cary   Som. 2 D2
Castle Cary is a bustling place, its small scale and friendly shops making it still a genuine and individual place of great charm. It has, curiously, little outstanding architecture: its castle, a motte-and-bailey structure, has virtually gone; its church was largely rebuilt in 1855; and its Market Hall, though retaining some 17th-century pillars, was also rebuilt in 1855. But there are some good houses including the 18th-century Post Office in Bailey Hill overlooking the delightful lock-up of 1779, delightful except to any Sunday-school children who found themselves inside for truancy.

The castle of the late 11th or early 12th century was built by the Lovel family; Ralph Lovel was besieged and had to surrender to King Stephen in 1138, but was relieved after another siege in 1148. The castle was probably abandoned *c.* 1153. A manor house took its place beside Fore Street near the pond; 'fine old arches ... [of] a stately edifice' were still there in the late 18th century. The pond is now much cleaner than when a Methodist preacher suffered a ducking in 1748. Not that the parish was staunchly Anglican, though among its vicars was Samuel Woodforde (d. 1771), who was also rector of ANSFORD (1 mile N), where he lived. His more famous son James, the diarist, acted as curate from 1765 to 1776, and records not only his visits to the Ansford Inn to read the newspapers, and the regular evenings with friends to dine or play cards, but notable events like the sermon at Castle Cary church in support of a fire engine (1762), the ringing of church bells to celebrate the victory of 'Wilkes and Liberty' in 1769, or the visits of strolling players to the court house. A century earlier another visit went carefully unrecorded at the time; Charles II stayed in the town for a night on his dangerous way from Abbots Leigh to Trent (Dorset) after the battle of Worcester.

Chapel Cleeve   Som. *see* **Cleeve Abbey**

Chard   Som.   2 B3

Some used to think, some still do, that a Saxon chieftain, Cerdic, gave his name to the town; but most likely the name refers to a settlement on rough common, still a feature of the rising ground E of the town until enclosure in the 19th century. The town lies in a hollow between Windwhistle and the Blackdowns, and seems to belong to Devon and Dorset with its flint buildings and thatch.

The wide main street is obviously for a market (founded here in 1253); until the 19th century it was interrupted by the inevitable market house and shambles standing in the middle of the road, the house so vandalized by 1835 that it could not be used in winter. But this is the second part of Chard; the first clusters around the church and Manor Farm, which belonged to the Bishops of Wells from Domesday onwards. Bishop Jocelin created a borough to the north in 1235, setting out a piece of land to be divided into 52 one-acre plots, let at a shilling each. Only a century later the town seemed strong enough to send representatives to Parliament, though the privilege was found to be too costly. The town's government under a Portreeve and burgesses

continued until the chief citizen became a Mayor in 1835. The bounds of the old borough, marked by a flint wall, can still be traced.

The 'grievous mishap' of a fire in 1578 destroyed the 'chiefest and greatest part' of the buildings connected with woollen-cloth-making, a business which had medieval origins here. The appeal for money after the fire claimed damage amounting to the huge sum of £9,000 and probably rightly said 'many a thousand' people for miles around were involved. Certainly coarse cloth was exported through Lyme Regis (Dorset) to France by the end of the 16th century; and more business came when the assizes were held here. The judges ceased to come after 1667. Until the early 19th century Chard's manufacturers continued to produce cloth, notably for the East India Company, and after its collapse it was replaced by lace-making, the factories still dominating the townscape. The town was the home of the manufacture of iron agricultural implements, made by the Dening family, which won awards as far afield as agricultural shows in New South Wales. It was also the home of John Stringfellow, the inventor and aircraft pioneer,

Chard

who lived in Chard from 1820 until his death in 1883. It was also the birthplace, in 1873, of Margaret Bondfield, the first British woman cabinet minister when she was appointed Minister of Labour in 1929.

Architecturally the main street of Chard is a pleasing mixture from the old Grammar School, the Court House, Godworthy House (the Chard Museum), and the Choughs Hotel, all of the late 16th century, showing the attractive use of flint and Ham stone, through Georgian and early Victorian houses, including the Town Hall with its portico (1834–5), to the lesser attractions of nonconformist building. Much older, of course, is the parish church; 'large, solid, stately', says Pevsner, and perhaps a surprise at first sight is its low tower, hardly a Somerset type at all and certainly not in the typical scale of the period. Inside it is truly Somerset, almost entirely Perpendicular, though a Norman arch may be seen in the s wall of the chancel.

CRICKET ST THOMAS, 3 miles E, has a Wild Life Park created in the grounds of Cricket House, the former home of Admiral Sir Alexander Hood, Viscount Bridport (d. 1814), and later of the chocolate manufacturer F. J. Fry (d. 1898). Part of the house was altered by Sir John Soane. The tiny church, very much part of the park complex, was probably built by the 2nd Lord Bridport (d. 1868). It contains enormous monuments to Viscount Bridport and to Nelson's nephew and heir, the Revd. William, Earl Nelson, and Duke of Brontë (d. 1835).

Charterhouse Som. *see* **The Mendips**

Cheddar Som. 5 A6
Cheddar means cheese and caves, but long before they were made or discovered its natural gorge, winding for more than a mile from the top of the Mendips to the village (the way the traffic comes), had a place in history. In 941 King Edmund, having just dismissed Dunstan from Court, went hunting in Mendip Forest. The 'flying stag' he was following came to the Gorge and fell in, followed by the hounds. The King's horse went out of control too, but a swift change of heart by Edmund brought him to a sudden and miraculous halt just in time; and Dunstan was reinstated.

The spectacular Gorge is outside the old village, which lies down on the lower ground nearer the River Yeo around the church and market cross. There, from Saxon times, was a royal palace, its standing remains only the ruined chapel of St Columbanus and the outline of the former wooden buildings marked out in the grounds of the Kings of Wessex School. The complex included a succession of halls in use from Alfred's time to the 14th century, a 10th-century corn mill, with attached grainstore and bakery, and at least two earlier chapels. Cheddar was then a place of importance, a 'famous town': the Witan met here, no doubt in one of the large halls, in 941, 956, and 968; Henry I was here in 1121 and 1130, and Henry II in 1158. King John spent money

on repairing the buildings in 1209–11 but soon afterwards the property was given to Wells Cathedral.

Columbanus (d. 615), to whom the palace chapel was dedicated, was an Irish monk who spent most of his days on the Continent trying vainly to maintain his own strict Celtic Rule and traditions at Luxeuil in the Vosges and later at Bobbio in the Apennines. He has been described as 'the most illustrious and influential of the adherents of the Celtic Order'. He had no known connexions with Britain, though Leland thought Culbone (q.v.) might have been named after him. But clearly enough Cheddar was an early religious centre: Alfred's will speaks of a 'community' here, probably a religious one, which had some rôle in the choice of his son as King, and its church was later called a minster. The present church of St Andrew is the result of a major rebuilding in the earlier 14th century with the addition of the tall tower, chancel chapels, and aisle windows from 1380 (the N chapel) onwards. The s chapel was dedicated to St Nectan, at least by 1493. He, like Columbanus, was Celtic, a 6th-century Welsh hermit who settled at Hartland (Devon) but who was commemorated at Wells Cathedral on 17 June each year, the date of his death.

The chancel contains the tomb and brass of Sir Thomas Cheddar (d. 1443) and his wife. Sir Thomas appears in armour, though his father was a rich Bristol merchant whose ancestors clearly came from here.

'A good husband tounelet' was how Leland saw Cheddar; its restored medieval market cross, the fame of its cheese and strawberries, and the few surviving farm houses in the old village show how the farming tradition continued. The cliffs in the Gorge have for long been the wonder of travellers and a point of interest for geologists and botanists, but the discovery of the first stalactite caves in 1838 marked the beginnings of Cheddar as a tourist resort and the gradual spread of the village in the form of restaurants, tea rooms, souvenir and gift shops up to the foot of the Gorge. The development of the caves themselves, both as museums of Ice Age and Old Stone Age remains, and of natural limestone phenomena, has come a long way since Francis Kilvert took an excursion train from Taunton in 1873. In one cave the guide was 'a ghastly old man, with his jaws bandaged white and an enormous nose ... almost entirely deaf', whom Kilvert christened 'the corpse'. 'Young Cox' showed them round another, 'the beautiful forest and fairyland of stalactites, one of the wonders of the world'.

The rocks of the Gorge, and more particularly the unique plants – Cheddar Pink and a variety of Hawkweed – are a temptation to the would-be climber which should be resisted; but so it has always been. As they walked up the Gorge Kilvert's party took shelter from the rain, while a number of the foolish excursionists insisted on climbing to the top of the cliffs, got wet through and saw nothing but rain. This was what they called 'doing Cheddar properly' and certainly they achieved it most completely, coming back hot, sulky, drenched with perspiration and rain, their shoes full of water, and having seen nothing but clouds, rain and mist. Every eating-house in the village was full to overflowing. . . . The problem of overflowing is now even greater.

Chew Magna   Avon   5 B5

There are still plenty of echoes of Leland's 'prety cloathing townelet'; around the triangular green at its centre are banks, shops, and pubs linked by raised pavements, most in the local red-brown conglomerate stone. At the top of the green, leading into the churchyard, was the townelet's social centre; the church house, built *c.* 1510, with ornate ogee gabled entrance to the ground floor, with the arms of St Loe, and two doors on the side entrance to the first floor alongside the churchyard wall. But what is St Michael doing, presiding over the building, when the church is St Andrew's? Elsewhere in the

main street Georgian houses proclaim a continuing prosperity which is declared most obviously in the magnificent parish church. The development of new routes south from Bristol isolated the village from the late 18th century, though its medieval bridges show how old and important the route had been formerly. Isolation is no problem in the age of the motor car, and Chew is again a busy commuter centre.

The parish church still has some Norman details and a Norman font; the s aisle was added *c.* 1300, but the general impression is of a largely 15th-century building, with nave and aisles slightly wider than their length. Sir John St Loe (d. 1448) left money for the N aisle; and the initials J.B. over the sw window of the s aisle may be those of vicar John Bubbe (1447–8). Inside, over the same window, are the arms and initials of another vicar, Thomas Cornish, in whose time the roof was probably

Cheddar Gorge

Hauteville monument, Chew Magna church

renewed. Cornish was both vicar of Chew Magna 1494–9 and 1505–13 and Bishop of Tenos, a see *in partibus infidelium*, and suffragan bishop in both Bath and Wells and Exeter dioceses. His initials, arms, and mitre are also on a rare reading desk, now used as the lectern. A fine screen, common enough in W Somerset but not here, stretches the whole width of the church.

Three outstanding tombs are those of Sir John St Loe, the typical medieval squire and his lady; Edward Baber, Elizabethan squire and Justice of the Peace, and his spouse; and Sir John de Hauteville, he who hurled the quoit (see Stanton Drew). Here is a real problem, a knight in 14th-century armour made (and this is a great rarity) in oak, reclining in an impossible posture with an equally uncomfortable lion. Pevsner thinks a late-16th century date 'most probable'. Kenneth Wickham describes the results of restoration in the 19th century, as 'an unhealthy state of coloured animation'.

The N chapel contains memorials of the Strachey family, successors of the St Loes at Sutton Court (2 miles SE). John Strachey was a great friend of the philosopher John Locke; his son was a notable scientist and antiquarian. Henry, the 1st Baronet, was secretary to Clive of India and Master of the Household to George III. John St Loe Strachey (d. 1927) of the *Spectator* and Giles Lytton Strachey (d. 1932), the critic and historian, are among many other members of the family commemorated there. The family home incorporates parts of a 14th-century fortified house of the St Loes, a 16th-century hall with a wing built by Sir William St Loe (d. 1558) and his famous wife Bess of Hardwick.

The medieval Bishops of Bath and Wells had an important estate here, worth nearly £130 in 1535, and then the favourite home of Bishop John Clerk (d. 1541), builder of Horton Court (q.v.). It was taken from Bishop Barlow in 1548. The house, now called Chew Court, stands at the E end of the church, and in the 19th century there still remained a gallery joining the two across the churchyard, from which, wrote John Strachey the antiquarian

thro' a hollow which is now shut up ... the Bishop or any of his family might see the Elevation ... without the trouble of coming into the Church.

Strachey also records a wing that contained another gallery and a library, taken down by one of the Baber family in 1698, leaving nothing of the medieval house but a gateway. The 'good appartment' of his time still remains, including an Elizabethan doorway.

The church at CHEW STOKE, 1½ miles SW, stands on a prominent and doubtless ancient site, though modern – to be accurate Victorian – restoration has festooned it with angels. Essentially it is a late-medieval building, and the ubiquitous arms of the St Loe family are over the SE chapel window. Down in the village is the remarkable Old Rectory, much altered from its original plan, but with its front wall still bearing a fantastic collection of carved panels including the St Loe arms, the name of the builder, John Barry (rector 1524–46), and the date, 1529, in arabic numerals. Further down still is a nice group of restored cottages beside a stream. The village was famous in the 18th century for its bell-founders, the Bilbie family.

The CHEW VALLEY LAKE lies just s. It covers 1,200 acres and was completed in 1955. Here the River Chew ran into a valley where once stood the small Domesday hamlet of Moreton, with a medieval chapel, a moated site, and a mill. Roman buildings and flints have also been found on the site, taking the origins of its settlement back into prehistory. The reservoir, with the nearby BLAGDON LAKE (1½ miles w) together supply the Bristol area with water, and provide fishing (the trout hatchery is at UBLEY between the two lakes), bird-watching, boating, and picnic areas.

The villages running w beneath the Mendip scarp include COMPTON MARTIN, 3 miles s of Chew Stoke, birthplace of St Wulfric of Haselbury, with 'perhaps the best Norman parish church in Somerset' (Pevsner). One pillar in the Norman arcade has a twisted design – like Durham Cathedral with a delicate touch. But this is southern, rural England, with early prosperity if on a different scale.

Chipping Sodbury　Avon　5 C3
Chipping Sodbury lies at the edge of Old Sodbury parish and, as its name indicates, it was a market centre planted on the main road between Bristol and London via Oxford. Planted and planned, a piece of 12th-century speculation, under which building plots were laid out in a regular pattern each side of the road (and the road itself was even diverted), with a church (a chapel, of course, of Old Sodbury) incorporated in the design. And the developer was William son of Stephen FitzOdo, otherwise William Crassus, William the fat.

The creation of this town is thought to have been complete by c. 1179, and a market was granted in 1227. Special attractions were offered to would-be settlers in the form of rights of title and self-government; by 1295 there were nearly 200 burgesses, though it was never to be even a major town. The 13th-century church fits well with these developments, although it is outwardly of two centuries later. The chancel arch, a pier in the N chancel chapel, and two capitals used as corbels indicate a substantial church to match the new town, and the later rebuilding is a fair reflection of continuing prosperity – a new aisled nave and enriched porch (doorway 1526), large, late-medieval tower, and interior details such as the pulpit.

And this prosperity was based on the market and on wool. 'A praty little market towne and thrwgh fayre to Brightstow', Leland called it, and used its other name, Sodbery Market. Richard Colmore (d. 1513) and his wife, buried in the parish church, were clearly prosperous, and a namesake who died in 1557 was in the weaving business. The old street names – Hatters Lane, Horse Street, Rouncival Street, Hounds Lane (and others now lost, Mortstreyte and Shoutinge Lane) – still have a medieval, almost Chaucerian, ring and indicate quite clearly how much a market town depended on its communications.

If new building is an indication of economic strength, then the 18th century was a time of prosperity, for the main street has good Georgian houses to add to the few of an earlier period, though perhaps the most interesting is the Tudor House in Hatters Lane, not Tudor at all, but essentially of the early 15th century.

But decline came. The corporation, which probably dated back to a guild of Henry VI's time and was supported by former chantry lands which financed a town hall and almshouses, acquired a new charter in 1681 and lost it in 1690. By the end of the 18th century the Tuesday market, according to Rudder, was 'very little frequented, being nothing more than a few neighbouring people assembled in the public houses'. Only one master clothier was left, and women and children took spinning work from outside the parish. But decline undoubtedly preserved this Cotswold town from 19th-century development; and although the population has greatly increased since the Second World War, it has not been greatly to the detriment of the town centre.

Christon　Avon　*see* **Banwell**

Churchill　Avon　*see* **Banwell**

Clapton in Gordano　Avon　5 A4
The church is perched rather perilously and remotely between the motorway and a steep drop, quite properly dedicated to St Michael, for its commands the Gordano valley and the Bristol Channel. But it is a remote site now, its only neighbour the former manor house, Clapton Court, which itself retains a late-medieval front wall and tower-porch; all in local red-brown stone. Even at a glance the church is much older: its site is one indication, and a narrow, blocked window with cusped Y-tracery on the N side continues the story. Here, now somewhat neglected, is a church with a complicated plan and some rare features. The Norman doorway with its plain tympanum (and later consecration cross) suggests a Norman nave, but might that not have come from what is now the N chapel opposite, whose windows may be of c. 1300 (Pevsner) but whose proportions suggest something older? Perhaps here is the original, one-cell church which, because of its position, could not be extended; the 13th-century expansion had to come s, and the consecration cross over the Norman door (and another in the chancel) belong to that period. So, too, does most of the tower and (though now re-used upside down) two Purbeck shafts with stiff-leaf capitals each side of the altar. The Perpendicular additions here are sparing and unusual: the chancel arch and the matching arch to the N chancel chapel, all indicating a rebuilding of the E end. The arms in the foliage are those of the Arthur family, owners of the manor from Stephen's reign until the 17th century.

Two other features of note are the wooden tower screen and the benches at the w end of the nave. The latter are probably the oldest benches in the diocese and perhaps belong to the early 14th century. What is the date of the screen? It came from the manor house in the 19th century and is claimed to be of the 13th; the arms – three sheaves of corn so delicately but unheraldically differentiated between three varieties – have not yet been identified.

Claverton Avon 5 C5

The 'clover farm' which belonged in the Middle Ages to the Bishops of Bath and Wells lies just off the A36 2 miles from the centre of Bath. The old manor house by the church, the site of the bishops' home, has gone, leaving behind only a series of impressive terraces with fine stonework, presumably the work of one of the Bassett family. The over-restored church contains a monument to one of them, William Bassett (d. 1613), and also a 14th-century stained-glass panel in the N transept. In the churchyard is the mausoleum of Ralph Allen (see Bath).

Claverton village commands a fine view of the Avon Valley and the woods beyond, a valley which is followed by both a railway and the Kennet and Avon Canal. Further up the hill is the newer manor house, built by Sir Jeffry Wyatville in 1819–20. It is famous, however, not for its architecture but for two other reasons. Here, on 26 July 1897, Winston Churchill made his first political speech. And here on 1 July 1961 was opened 'the only comprehensive museum of Americana in Europe'. In its rooms Classical Bath is forgotten as the visitor moves from the late-17th-century English Puritan settlers to the mid-19th-century Spanish colonists in New Mexico. Galleries of American craftsmanship in wood, metal, and textiles complement displays of American history, life, and culture. The old stables house a Folk Art collection, part of the grounds is planted as a reproduction of the garden of George Washington's home at Mount Vernon. The original garden included plants and seeds sent over from Somerset by the Fairfax family of Writhlington, near Radstock (q.v.).

Cleeve Abbey, Washford Som. 1 H1

Leland was not tempted to visit Cleeve Abbey, and for once this is no great loss for, apart from the church, the Abbey's buildings are still remarkably complete, standing in its large precinct in a beautiful valley. The Abbey of the Blessed Virgin in the Flower Valley (*vallis florida*) was founded by 1198 by William de Roumare. It is usually called Cleeve Abbey after the parish in which it lay, and which thereafter became Old Cleeve. Initially its site would have been isolated a mile from the village,

Cleeve Abbey

and the hamlet of Washford undoubtedly grew up as a result of the Abbey.

The early years of the Abbey were prosperous, and the first stone buildings were the E end of the church, followed by the E and S sides of the domestic buildings. All this took a century to complete, for the Abbey was never rich; though King Henry III gave oak for choir stalls in 1232, and Richard, Earl of Cornwall and King of the Romans (Henry's nephew), was an important benefactor, as his arms on the tiles declare. These early buildings contain a remarkable amount of painted wall decoration in the sacristy, chapter house, and dorter, and a fine collection of heraldic tiles. The later buildings – the S and W ranges – belong to the 15th and early 16th centuries when the monastic life had been considerably modified. The old ground-floor frater was turned to align with the S cloister and converted into a two-storeyed range with separate chambers below and magnificent rooms above; the hall was used both as the dining hall of the convent and as the great hall of the abbot's private quarters. The abbot's rooms themselves include a painted chamber, perhaps some kind of 'checker' or office; the decorations include figures of St Catherine and St Margaret each side of a bridge over a river full of fish. The gallery outside has a cartoon of a tonsured monk. A room above the painted chamber, not at present accessible, was once reached by a turret stair leading from the cloister.

The great hall is perhaps the most impressive single monastic building in Somerset. The roof is superb in a county of high-quality woodwork, with richly moulded arch braces, busts of crowned angels giving a hammer-beam effect, and moulded wall-plates with vine decoration. The hall is lit by large windows, those on the S in the typical West Somerset tradition of ogee cusping beneath the transoms. The E wall was until comparatively recently painted with a Crucifixion, and the outline has been added to the new plaster. The remains of the pulpit show that this hall was, until the Dissolution, used as the convent dining room; the fireplace was added in the early 17th century when the room was the hall of a secular house.

The W cloister range, built in the late 13th century when the nave of the church was also completed, was originally for the cellarer and the lay brethren. This, too, in the late 15th century was to become two-storeyed, and it was probably left unfinished at the Dissolution. Most of this rebuilding and reorganization, which also included the construction of separate cubicles in the once open dorter, was carried out by Cleeve's most famous Abbot, David Joyner, elected in 1435. William Dovell, the last Abbot, rebuilt the delightful gatehouse.

The Abbey was endowed from the first with a block of lands in the Brendons and elsewhere in Somerset, and also with property in Devon and Cornwall including the rectory of Lundy Island. A particularly valuable possession was the pilgrimage chapel of Our Lady on the shore of Blue Anchor Bay (the bay named after a 17th-century inn, not because of the colour of the water). Forty days' indulgence was granted in 1452 to all who would give to its rebuilding when the cliff fell on it after heavy rain and floods, leaving only the image of the Virgin and the altar unharmed. The new chapel was consecrated in 1455 at CHAPEL CLEEVE (2 miles NW of Cleeve Abbey), on a safer site, together with a large hospice for pilgrims. Much of this remains in Chapel Cleeve Manor. In 1536 the chapel possessed four bells, and a local gentlemen offered the large sun of £20 a year rent together with all offerings.

The Abbey fell in the first wave of the Dissolution, although the hospitality it offered was important in these remote parts. There were 15 monks when the house surrendered in 1536, among whom was one John Hooper, later to become the Protestant Bishop of Gloucester who was burnt as a heretic by Queen Mary in 1555.

The church at OLD CLEEVE (1 mile NW of Cleeve Abbey) has much 15th-century work by the masons and tile-makers of the abbey; the building of its notable tower was helped in 1533 by the bequest of a pair of tucker's shears.

Clevedon Avon 4 H4

The story of Clevedon as a seaside resort is eloquently told by its buildings. The simple Grecian-style Adelaide, Clarence, and Brunswick houses, part of the terrace above the beach, mark the tentative beginnings c. 1820. The same terrace includes a 'Sunset Restaurant' and faces the broken pier; that is what Clevedon has come to. Coleridge's honeymoon cottage or the visits of Southey and Lamb, and later of Thackeray and Tennyson were as nothing in its development compared with the foresight of the Revd Sir Abraham Elton (d. 1842), whose inclosure of the commons made land available for building on a large scale. During the 1820s the population nearly doubled, nearly doubled again by 1851, and was up to 5,900 in 1901, 10 times its size 80 years before. But here, as the *Bristol Mirror* declared, was 'not a smoky, hurry, skurry sort of Brightonian affair', but with substantial if not always elegant Italianate, Tudoresque, and even Jacobean villas, spreading up the wooded slopes above the beach; here was the 'Hastings of the West'. Sir Arthur Hallam Elton designed villas, planned streets, built a lending library and a cottage hospital, sponsored coffee houses, and guided the pier company. By 1880 the town had the largest swimming bath in the West and the largest skating rink outside London. In 1897 it celebrated the Diamond Jubilee with a clock-tower decorated with a local product, the colourful earthenware called Elton Ware, the invention of Sir Edmund Elton. So Clevedon at the turn of the century was at the height of its popularity: gentlemen's bathing at Ladye Bay, steamer trips from the pier, and in the evenings music from the bandstand for those thronging the Esplanade.

Clevedon remains a residential, rather than a holiday resort, and is now expanding rapidly over the adjoining moors since the motorway has brought Bristol and work so much nearer. Old Clevedon, the pre-19th-century village, is hard to find: a few cottages in Old Church Road seem to be the only link between the ancient parish church of St Andrew at the extreme w end of the town and Clevedon Court on the E. Modern blocks of flats are taking the place of expensive villas; and the pier, which suffered damage in 1970, is now to be demolished. G. N. Abernethy's pavilion (1892) is now cut off from J. W. Gower's ingenious construction of 1869, much of it made of rails bought cheap after the failure of one of Brunel's schemes.

The 'obscure and solitary' late-Norman church is intriguing, for it stands in a dip on what may have been an island, hardly the beacon it has sometimes been claimed, at least until its tower was raised in the 17th century. It is a church rich in Norman carving not only on the *pointed* chancel arch but on the corbel table of the chancel; rich, too, in modern woodwork. The raising of the roof of the aisle has left more corbels exposed, and also a 'green man'. The s transept has memorials to the Eltons and their relatives the Hallams, including Henry Hallam the historian (d. 1859). More famous still is the one to Arthur Henry Hallam (d. 1833), whose death in Vienna caused Tennyson's spiritual crisis and evoked *In Memoriam*. The poet only came to Clevedon many years afterwards, when he was obliged, it is said, to change the words of one of the verses from chancel to 'dark church', for the position of his friend's memorial tablet.

Clevedon Court (NT) was built by Sir John de Clevedon *c.* 1320 within a defensive shield of earlier battlemented walls and towers. The Old Kitchen, at an angle to the rest, has been dated to the 13th century. Perhaps the most remarkable feature of the house is the chapel, lit by two square-headed windows with reticulated tracery. Here, when it must have been still new, Bishop Drokensford tonsured 10 clerks in September 1323. The house passed to the Wake family of Northamptonshire, who owned it until the mid 17th century and who considerably altered and extended the house and also built a tower on the hill above. The Eltons, a Bristol merchant family, bought Clevedon Court and estate in 1709. A fire in 1882 destroyed some of the 16th-century work, but it was rebuilt in the original style. The house contains collections of Nailsea glass and Elton Ware.

Walton Castle, on the top of the hill E of the town, is an almost convincing folly built *c.* 1620.

Clifton Avon *see* **Bristol**

Combe Florey Som. *see* **Crowcombe**

Combwich Som. *see* **Stogursey**

Compton Dando Avon *see* **Pensford**

Compton Dundon Som. *see* **Somerton**

Compton Martin Avon *see* **Chew Magna**

Congresbury Avon 5 A5 (*pron.* Coomsbury)
On a hilltop above the village, known to archaeologists as Cadbury–Congresbury, there is a site that bears all the marks of occupation both in the Roman period and in the Dark Ages, and where finds have included pottery and glass similar to those found at Tintagel and on Glastonbury Tor. Were there Christians here then? For it is certain that the place, either hilltop or valley site, was the burying place of St Congar, a 6th-century Celtic missionary, probably from Pembrokeshire. A monastery was established here before 880, when it was given by King Alfred to Asser; 11th- and 14th-century pilgrim guides listed Congar's shrine, and late-medieval wills referred to lights before it. But there is now no trace in the church or elsewhere, evidence enough of the completeness of Reformation destruction.

Indeed, for an English parish church St Andrew's at Congresbury is, despite the obvious wealth of the parish in the Middle Ages, remarkably bare. It stands at the edge of the moors and away from the village, noticeable at once for its spire, and then for its fine but now hardly used s porch, a tall, Perpendicular building from the outside, though the outer doorway is a clue to an earlier building. Inside the story becomes clear: a Norman church was given aisles in two stages in the 13th century, with workmanship of high quality, for the arcades have unusual shafts, those on the s in Purbeck marble, attached to the circular piers, a quality perhaps to be expected from the church's ownership by the Bishops of Bath and Wells. In the 15th century the clerestory and porch were added and the whole was given new windows; and the screens and probably the side chapels came too.

At about the same time more building was going on a few yards away. The vicarage house is partly of the early 19th century, but partly the work of the executors of Bishop Thomas Bekynton (d. 1465), a rare survival of a medieval clergy house in the county. The village itself doubled in size in the 1960s, for it is within the Bristol commuter area. It retains, however, many traces of its past, including a fine market cross at the end of a wide street. Its new estates, a busy main road, and the embanked River Yeo, tidal to this point, are evidence of a continuing prosperity, seen in the 14th century in the bishop's manor here, when rents were worth over £45 and two windmills – not unusual on these level lands – were worth together 20 shillings.

Cotham Avon *see* **Westbury on Trym**

Cothay Som. *see* **Wellington**

Cothelstone Som. *see* **Bishops Lydeard**

Cranmore Som. *see* **Doulting**

Crewkerne Som. 2 C3
Crewkerne lies under Windwhistle hill looking into Dorset; 'sette under the rootes of an hille', says Leland, and this is what the place-name means. The church was a Saxon minster and the large estate, royal at least from Alfred's time, had an urban centre: there was a mint here in the 10th century and a market later mentioned in Domesday. St Bartholomew's fair began in the 1270s, and still each year the centre of the town is taken over by stalls, sideshows, and roundabouts: the continuity of history. But all in the Middle Ages was agricultural.

The little town had, however, one great asset: it was on the main road from London to Exeter. Catherine of Aragon stayed a night on her way from Plymouth to marry Prince Arthur in 1501. By 1580 the town was a regular post stage, and between 1619 and 1631 Thomas Hutchins its Postmaster ran the first profitable postal system between London and Plymouth. Troops from both sides in the Civil War stayed too long and returned too soon for comfort, attracted no doubt by the numerous inns (most of them belonging to the rectory) which in the late 17th century could offer 54 guest beds and stabling for 130 horses. But by this time Crewkerne was more truly urban, with a wide range of trades connected with the cloth-making industry including webbing and, by the 19th century, sailcloth, hair-seating, and shirts. The elegant proportions of houses and shop-fronts in the town centre, especially in Church Street and Abbey Street, are evidence both of the prosperity these manufacturers brought to the town, and of the fortunate immunity from modern development that decline in trade was to bring. Older buildings in the heart of the town add a satisfying variation in size and style; Crewkerne is a place of character, heavy traffic, and bustle; and yet with oases of quiet at its very heart.

The crowning glory is the church, set apart above the town and overlooking a green valley. It is almost a cathedral in miniature, a declaration of prosperity which has more than a touch of ostentation. John Harvey thinks it might be the work of the Wells mason William Smyth c. 1475–90, but several of the rectors (there were three at a time in Crewkerne) were royal chaplains. The twin turrets at the w end, a reminder of the Tudor royal chapels as well as of Bath Abbey, might have come from further afield. The heavy crossing piers and traces of a late-13th-century arch in the E wall of the s transept show that already there was a cruciform building of the same size; and earlier evidence still is the magnificent Purbeck marble font with Norman pillared design. The great rebuilding seems to have begun at the crossing in the early 15th century but the rest, presumably including the E sacristy, of which only the ornate entrance doors remain each side of the high altar, belongs to the

end of the century. The six-light windows in the nave and the succession of chapels on the N side make the church perhaps the most lavish in the county.

Outside is one great curiosity, the covered seat at the SE corner. Two medieval hermits lived near the church, but both outside the w end. There was also a chantry of Our Lady in the churchyard; perhaps the seat was linked with that? North of the church is the Old Grammar School (1636), a foundation that dates back at least to the 14th century and boasted Captain Thomas Masterman Hardy and Charles James Brooke, Rajah of Sarawak, among its pupils. The Abbey, the last of the three rectory houses that circled the churchyard in the Middle Ages, was rebuilt in the 19th century. Its access road used to be called Carter Street, but that would not do for a new mansion; so Abbey Street it has since been. Elsewhere in the town Oxen Road, Court Barton (site of the manor house of the Courtenays), and Market Street have retained their country origins.

Cricket St Thomas Som. *see* **Chard**

Croscombe Som. 5 B6
In a valley between the medieval clothing centres of Shepton Mallet and Wells, Croscombe still bears many marks of its prosperity as a weaving village especially in three medieval houses, one the Manor House, the others inaccurately named so, and the glorious parish church. The church is uncommonly well documented, for although only a few manorial records survive, church-wardens' accounts dating from 1475 were still in the parish chest at the turn of the century, when many were fortunately printed. The manorial accounts of the 15th century all refer to racks, where newly woven cloth was stretched and bleached, and to tucking mills where it was finished. The wardens recorded the gifts of the villagers to their church, much of it cash raised by their social and craft guilds – the archers, the hogglers (labourers), the young men, the maidens, the wives, and, most significant of all, the weavers or webbers and the tuckers or fullers. Local benefactors such as John Toker, a master fuller, and village events like Christmas and Robin Hood's revels helped to swell the funds.

The efforts of generations of Croscombe villagers are splendidly witnessed in the glory of their parish church. Already by the end of the 13th century it had an aisled nave, for the s porch dates from that time, and two corbels in the s aisle are almost certainly of Richard II and his Queen. Sir William Palton, the last of his family to be lord of the manor, probably built the clerestory and the roof, and left money for the s chancel chapel. But the most remarkable additions are the Vestry or Treasury on the sw of the church, with its ground-floor room strongly barred for safe custody of valuables, finished in 1509, and the chapel on the N side of the chancel, now the clergy vestry. It was also completed in 1509 (though not paid for until 1512!) and included a painted statue of St George. The new work was done by John Carter, a mason from Exeter, and cost the parish at least £37.

Even more striking initially are the Jacobean furnishings, dated 1616, and associated with the then lords of the manor, the Fortescue family. There is a tall and rather exotic screen, topped by the royal arms, replacing the medieval rood, a pulpit and tester, readers' desks, and box pews, the whole a rare example of Anglican woodwork. Notice, in the churchyard on the N of the church, the church house, a common medieval West Country feature (see Chew Magna and Crowcombe). It was built in 1480–1 and served as a parish hall where money-raising revels were held.

By 1448 Sir William Palton let the manor house, just N of the church. The main house was divided and a detached kitchen was also let. Remarkably, much has survived, including the hall with its fine arch-braced roof with Sir William's arms, preserved by being a Baptist Chapel from the early 18th century and recently restored. The 'Old Manor House' at the E end of the village boasts a rare oriel window, often mistaken for a porch, which bears initials that have been interpreted as those of the ubiquitous John Selwood, Abbot of Glastonbury.

Crowcombe Som. 2 A1

Nestling under the Quantocks just off the A358, it was once, as its medieval market cross shows, a place of some importance at the junction of a hill crossing and a road from Taunton to the coast. The church, curiously, though only recently, dedicated to the Holy Ghost, has a sumptuous s aisle and porch of the early 16th century, and inside are equally splendid bench ends including one with the date 1534. The naturalistic subjects of the carvings – green man, merman, and men fighting a dragon – are finely reflected in a wrought iron chandelier by a local 20th-century blacksmith. Unusual features of this light and graceful church are the family pew of the Carews (1655) in the N transept, complete with hatchments, and the 18th-century screen (1729), pulpit, communion rails, and altar, all by Thomas Parker, the designer of Crowcombe Court. Outside, in the sloping churchyard, the top of the spire has suffered a comedown, for it crashed through the roof in 1725 (hence the new woodwork). Outside the Carew N transept are some monuments to their estate and household servants.

Opposite the church, between the road and a car park, and only a few yards from the old market place, is another rarity, the church house, built in 1515. Here, as in most late-medieval parishes, the holy bread was baked and the holy ale was brewed, to be sold and consumed at the 'church ale' or parish revel for the benefit of church funds. The building survived the displeasure of 17th-century Puritans even if the jollifications ceased, and it was converted; the upper floor into a school, the lower to almshouses.

Not surviving so well is Crowcombe Court, a large brick mansion begun c. 1725 by Thomas Parker of Gittisham (Devon), and completed between 1734 and 1739 by the Wincanton builder Nathaniel Ireson for Thomas Carew. Parker was discharged from employment after being found guilty of stealing coins discovered hidden in the previous house on the site and declared to be Treasure Trove. The park contains a romantic ruin which Dorothy Wordsworth was glad to see being overtaken by Nature.

Four miles s, just w of the same A358, is COMBE FLOREY; remarkable enough for its delightful little red sandstone church dating from c. 1300 in its oldest part, the N aisle. The Norman-French inscription recording the heart burial of Dame Maud de Meriet, a nun of Cannington (q.v.), and the adjoining tomb of a knight and two ladies has produced a local story that she was the wife of Sir John de Meriet of Hestercombe (q.v.) (d. 1327), and that his attempt to secure at least the heart for burial outside the nunnery had resulted in his excommunication. Certainly he suffered such a sentence for, as it was said, disembowelling the body of his late wife, and was only absolved in 1314 when he returned her heart; but his wife was called Mary, not Maud, which makes the story of the nun not quite accurate, though it leaves the Meriets with a penchant for heart burials. Notice in the church, too, the Poor Box, dated 1634 and inscribed 'Remember the Poore', put there by obedient churchwardens after orders at the Bishop's visitation.

Combe Florey is remarkable enough, too, for its sandstone gatehouse (1593), all that is left of the medieval manor house complex; though the later house of c. 1675 and 1730 stands higher up the hill. But Combe Florey is remarkable even more for two literary giants: the rector from 1829 to 1845 was the great Sydney Smith who, though he feared the country as 'a kind of healthy grave', was 'extremely pleased' with his parish, 'a very pretty place in a very beautiful country'. And the second manor house – 'cosy, sequestered, with great possibilities' he wrote in his diary – was the home from 1956 until his death in 1966 of the no less witty Evelyn Waugh.

Three miles w of Combe Florey is GAULDEN or GOLDEN MANOR, in Tolland, a 17th-century manor house with unusual plaster ceiling and fine fireplace, the whole with a slightly odd plan, for it has a room behind the hall fireplace. Romantic traditions, that it was the retreat of the deprived Marian Bishop of Exeter, James Turberville, and that it was also the home of the Woolcotts, later to settle in America, have no foundation in fact, though the Woolcotts certainly lived on the estate. The house was the work of a later Turberville, John, a London lawyer, who settled and built here from 1642, though a detachment of Parliamentary soldiers was sharing it with him in 1647 and drank so much, so John wrote,

that a barrell of good beare trembles at the sight of them, and the whole house nothing but a rendesvous of tobacco and spittings.

Culbone Som. *see* **Oare**

Dillington Som. *see* **Ilminster**

Dodington Avon 5 C3

The Codringtons have been in the neighbourhood since at least 1300, and at Dodington since the end of Elizabeth's reign, though much of their fortune was built many miles away. Three brothers, John, Robert, and Christopher, went their several ways: John (d. 1670) was for the King; Robert was for Cromwell; Christopher was for adventure, and in 1628 sailed for the West Indies, to make his fortune in Barbados. Christopher's son, also Christopher (1640–99), became Governor of the Leeward Islands, moved to a plantation on Antigua, and leased the shipwrecking island of Barbuda. His even more remarkable son, yet another Christopher (1668–1710), was poet, wit, and soldier. He succeeded his father in the Leewards, but gave up the post when the Navy failed to take Guadeloupe from the French. On his death he left £10,000 to his old college of All Souls, Oxford, whose library is named after him; and some estates in the West Indies to found a college in Georgetown, Barbados, still called Codrington College.

Dodington descended to this last Christopher, and on his death it passed to a cousin, Sir William. The house, the 'large and handsome' building known to Rudder in the 1770s, was 'not in the modern taste', though 'Capability' Brown had in 1744 improved the park, now stretching to some 700 acres, forming the lakes and building the Gothic cascade buildings. In this setting Christopher Bethell Codrington (1764–1839) and his friend, architect James Wyatt, between them built the present house between 1796 and Wyatt's death in 1813.

It is a building in the Classical style, but (especially inside) with the stamp of Wyatt's genius. The three fronts of the house differ in design: the entrance front is largely a huge *porte cochère*, with a curving conservatory to one side; the terrace front facing up the lake has a central section of attached pilasters and columns; the E front is plainer still, with bows at each end. The demolished service wing lay to the N behind the church, itself also Classical in style, a Doric porch leading to a cruciform plan under a dome.

Inside the house is Wyatt magnificence and ingenuity: a hall with lavish gilding, porphyry scagliola columns, black marble, Cotswold stone, and brass inlay floors; a library with hidden doors and retractable writing desk; a staircase with divided second flight incorporating earlier iron-work which Wyatt (who was at the same time working on the Gothic palace at Fonthill (Wilts.)) saved from Beckford's earlier house there. Details throughout the house include several cast-iron and brass fireplaces by Wyatt, and curious early gasoliers. At the entrance to and exit from the park are lodges, both by Wyatt.

Doulting Som. 5 B6

The typically English tree-shrouded spire of the church stands sentinel on the brow of the hill up from Shepton. A spire is not common in Somerset, and this one dates from the 15th century above a 13th-century octagonal tower. The beautiful S porch of *c.* 1500 is also worth a careful look, a splendid example of delicate work in local stone. It has two storeys, an elegant, concave-sided gable, decorated panels, and an intricate ogee-headed doorway. The vaulting inside includes a splendid green man. But there is grave disappointment inside the church, dark and vastly over-restored; so can the porch be genuine or is it a skilful reconstruction?

But beneath the 19th-century restoration is a late-12th-century cruciform church which was of more than local importance. Its extensive parish included the Cranmores and Stoke St Michael, and was in part bounded by the Fosse Way – it was probably an earlier, secular estate, even a Roman one. St Aldhelm, the great missionary saint of Wessex, died in the little wooden church here in 709, and the route along which they carried his body back to Malmesbury was marked every seven miles by a stone cross. He had been Abbot of Malmesbury since *c.* 675, and in 705 became the first Bishop of Sherborne. He founded religious communities at Frome (q.v.) and Bradford on Avon (Wilts., where part of his church still survives), and built churches at Sherborne and other places in Dorset. A spring behind the former Georgian vicarage at Doulting and the dedication of the church recalls the saint's last visit.

The 'estate-style' cottages and terrace near the church bear dates between 1881 and 1901 and the arms of the Paget family of Cranmore Hall (2 miles E), the last owners. A former, and more dominating, owner was Glastonbury Abbey. Its 15th-century barn, on the S side of the village, has two porches on each long side and a fine timber roof. Barn, church, and houses are, of course, in stone from the famous local quarry (see Introduction).

WEST CRANMORE, 1 mile E, has a church tower modelled on Shepton Mallet and curious memorials inside the church to the Bisse family, local clothiers. Its railway station and, at present, only a few yards of track on the former East Somerset Railway (Witham to Shepton Mallet, 1858) are the focus of a collection of steam locomotives and an art gallery, the property and inspiration of the artist David Shepherd.

Downend Avon *see* **Kingswood**

Downside Som. *see* **Stratton on the Fosse**

Dulverton Som. 1 G2

Almost in Devon and on the s of Exmoor, Dulverton stands by the delightful River Barle just above its junction with the Exe. 'A little market towne', said Gerard in the 1630s; Leland never reached there, for it was ever a small place. A market and three-day fair were established in 1306, and fulling mills on the surrounding streams treated woollen cloth produced from sheep on the moor. But fairs had to be refounded in 1488, and again in 1555, in the last year quite clearly to stimulate business in the 'town and borough . . . very populous and in decay'. The market's profits were to be controlled by local trustees and any profits were for public benefit. A fire engine was bought from the fund in 1732. Coarse woollens and blanketings were still produced in the late 18th century.

The town became the centre of the county's remotest Poor Law union in 1836, but this was West Somerset; no workhouse was built until 1855, and then it was a delightful-looking building in a beautiful setting by the river. It is now called Exmoor House, and is the administrative centre of the Exmoor National Park.

The 13th-century church was rebuilt and extended in 1855, leaving the tower looking rather more squat than its medieval designers intended. The town's buildings are also largely of the 19th century, but irregular shapes and local stone combine to create an ageless look. The market house was built in 1866, and converted in 1930 by Sir Albert Richardson.

Two 19th-century figures have Dulverton links. Dr Charles Palk Collyns, the author of the famous *Chase of Wild Red Deer*, was the local doctor until his death in 1846. More famous was Sir George Williams, born at Ashway Farm in 1821; in 1844 he founded the YMCA, and was buried in St Paul's Cathedral in 1905.

One mile NE in a farmyard beside the Exe are the remains of the small Augustinian priory of BARLINCH, founded in the late 12th century and dissolved in 1536. East of Dulverton, in the valley of the River Haddeo, WIMBLEBALL RESERVOIR was begun in 1974 and opened in 1979. It cost some £11 million, and holds 892 million gallons of water. The landscaping has been designed by Dame Sylvia Crowe, and the lake is stocked with some 40,000 trout. Below the dam, the road beside the river, originally from Upton through Hartford and Bury to the entrance to Pixton Park, is known as Lady Harriet's Drive. In the defeat of the British at Saratoga in 1777 during the American War of Independence, Major John Dyke Acland of Pixton was wounded and taken prisoner. His wife Lady Harriet, daughter of the Earl of Ilchester, crossed the Hudson river to nurse him in the enemy camp, an exploit which gave her instant fame. The Major returned home soon after, but died in the following year as the result, it is said, of a duel at Bampton Down (Devon) with a fellow officer who accused him

of disloyalty for praising the Americans who had released him. The Bampton version of the story says that the Major was run through and that his wife thereupon gave chase after the victor.

Dunster Som. 4 E6

The view of Dunster from the A39 is almost fairy-tale: a turreted pile rising above trees and a flat meadow, with higher ground and a ruined tower behind. And if the Castle owes much to the genius of Anthony Salvin, the Victorian architect; if the tower on Conygar Hill is an 18th-century folly; and the flat meadow is the silted valley of the River Avill, which was once wide and deep enough to make Dunster a port; still the Castle stands over the village, together the supreme example of the triumph of English feudalism and the survival of medieval England.

Undoubtedly the Castle is the key to Dunster. It was built on a natural hill by the Norman family of Mohun before 1086, and the family remained there, at the centre of their estates and of their feudal connexion called the Honor of Dunster, until the death of Joan, Lady Mohun, in 1404. She was then succeeded by Sir Hugh Luttrell, whose mother had bought the reversion of the property in 1376 for the huge sum of 5,000 marks or £3,334. The Luttrells continued the old feudal traditions until the 17th century and members of the family lived in the Castle until it was made over to the National Trust in 1976.

The Castle itself has had, like most, a chequered history. William de Mohun's fortification was probably on the levelled top of the 'tor' which gave the place its name. Probably at first of wood, it was certainly built in stone by 1138, and then comprised a higher and a lower ward. Its defences at the time, when William de Mohun II was supporting the Empress Matilda against King Stephen, were on one side towers and walls, a rampart and earthworks, and on the other a tidal river – too strong for a successful assault, and thus only to be taken by blockade. For his services to her cause, the Empress made William an Earl. The thick walls still remaining in the NE angle of the Castle may perhaps date from this period.

To the mid 13th century belongs the gateway to the lower ward with its semi-circular towers – work paid for, it was claimed, by castle tenants contributing cash instead of their feudal obligation of repair. Reynold de Mohun's work left the Castle in 1266 having in its upper ward a hall, with adjoining buttery, pantry, kitchen, and bakehouse, a chapel, a knights' hall, three towers with rooms inside, and a prison. There were three towers in the lower ward. More building in the next century included a bell turret, chambers for the children and the knights, more towers and turrets, and buildings roofed in lead or shingle.

Sir Hugh Luttrell in the 1420s built the present gatehouse over the entrance from the town, which involved the destruction of part of a hall and the purchase of free-

Staircase, Dunster Castle

74

stone from Bristol. During the later years of the 15th century the Luttrells were in disgrace because of Sir James's support for the Lancastrians. He fought at Wakefield against the Duke of York in 1460 and was knighted on the battlefield. Soon afterwards he was mortally wounded at the second battle of St Albans, and the victorious Yorkists condemned him for high treason. His family estates were given to the grasping Herberts, and were only recovered when Henry VII succeeded to the throne in 1485. Already the Castle must have gone out of repair, and by Leland's time there was only a chapel 'in good case', evidently then the most prominent building on the top of the tor. Lower down there were still parts in a good state, but all still, quite clearly, a medieval castle.

The great transformation came under George Luttrell (d. 1629), when the buildings in the lower ward became the mansion which is the core of the castle today. It took several years: the date 1589 is in the hall, but George signed a contract with William Arnold, designer of Wadham College, Oxford, and probably of Montacute (q.v.), to build what appears to be the centre of the main façade, as late as 1617.

The castle was obviously damaged during the Civil War. Thomas Luttrell held it for Parliament, but was somehow persuaded to give it up to the Royalists in 1643, together with the sum of £1,000; and after his death in the following year, his widow and sons had to find a further £1,500. The young Prince of Wales, later Charles II, stayed with the Royalist garrison for a short time in 1645, despite the outbreak of plague in the town; but soon after he left the Royalists found themselves with Dunster as their only strongpoint in the county. It was merely a nuisance to the Parliamentary forces, but in November 1645 Robert Blake began a siege. Part of a wall was destroyed by mines, but little other damage was done, and the garrison finally surrendered through exhaustion after 160 days. The castle was garrisoned for the next five years, and was then slighted: the chapel on the tor, and two towers and part of the curtain wall of the lower ward were demolished. The rest was saved just in time, and later owners added their contributions to George Luttrell's mansion.

The magnificent staircase, fitted into a medieval tower, and the decorations in the Dining Room (1681) – one of the most gorgeous plaster ceilings in sw England, judges Pevsner – were the work of Francis and Mary Luttrell in Charles II's time. The staircase is perhaps the mansion's most notable feature, with oak handrail, elm flowers and scrolls, and panels with cherubs, hounds chasing stag and fox, and military trophies; together they make an example of woodwork 'without doubt a match of Grinling Gibbons's' (Pevsner).

A new chapel was built in 1723–4 by Sir James Thornhill, and various landscaping alterations obliterated the medieval stronghold, but these alterations were minor compared with those by Anthony Salvin for Mr G. F.

Luttrell from 1867, which ingeniously added accommodation on the limited site by means of new or larger towers and internal changes. The demands of 19th-century living gave Salvin the chance to make Dunster Castle more like a medieval fortress than it had been since the 16th.

Below the Castle lies the town of Dunster: wide High Street with the Yarn Market near its far end, and Church and West streets curving beneath the walls. The 11th-century village had become a market town by 1100 and a borough by 1197. By the 13th century it had become a clothing centre, and its surviving medieval houses are as much a reflection of the town's prosperity as of Mohun and Luttrell influence. Most notable are the Luttrell Arms Hotel, an inn by 1651 but built in the early 16th century and including a fine hall, and plasterwork of the time of George Luttrell, transformer of the castle in the early 17th century; and the large, slate-hung building in Church Street called the Nunnery, partly of the 14th century and not a nunnery at all, but owned by the Abbots of Cleeve (q.v.). Most of the houses in the town centre, occupied now by shops catering for the tourists who flock to the place, are of the 17th and 18th centuries.

Dunster church was in existence by 1100, for then or a little before (since the charter is not dated but must be between 1090 and 1100) it was given to Bath Abbey with the tithes of the Mohun home estates. Soon afterwards the monks certainly set about rebuilding. Before 1177, and perhaps long before, a group of Bath monks took up permanent residence at Dunster, and the present church and its outbuildings bear witness to the existence of a community there which lasted until 1539. The large chancel was occupied by the monks for their services, and a settlement between monks and parishioners in 1357 not only illustrates the rivalry between them, but clearly defines the responsibilities of each party in the maintenance of the fabric: the monks repaired the roof of the tower with the help of specified contributions from the parish, and were solely responsible for the Lady Chapel and the 'dorter aisle'. The parish was to support the chapel of St Leonard and the aisle between the chapel of St Lawrence and the tower.

Another agreement, dated 1442, gives Dunster an important place in the history of architecture in the county and beyond. John Marys of Stogursey (q.v.) contracted with the parishioners to build the tower 100 ft high at 13s. 4d. a ft, with an extra 20s. for the pinnacles, the whole to be completed within three years. This tower, and the screen stretching across both nave and aisles, are outstanding features of the church. The fabric is largely of the 15th and 16th centuries, but Norman work survives, as one might expect, in the massive piers of the central tower, and a fragment in the otherwise 19th-century w doorway. The chancel is basically of the 13th century. The remodelling of the nave, and the insertion of the screen resulted in part from another dispute between

Nave and screen, Carhampton church

the monks and parishioners in 1498. The agreement between them involved a new choir established for the layfolk in the nave, and regulations about processions at festivals when

> the little band of monks 'coming through the middle of their own choir' was to be met by the rest of the congregation as they began to come through 'the door on the north side' of the new parochial choir. Then the bearer of the monks' cross and the bearer of the parish cross were to walk side by side, followed by the clerks, the Vicar, the monks, the Prior and the layfolk.
> (Maxwell-Lyte, *History of Dunster*)

Monuments in the church date from *c.* 1300 and include the tombs of Sir Hugh Luttrell (d. 1428), first of his family to live in the Castle, and George Luttrell (d. 1629), the great builder. A painting of the Brazen Serpent, originally from the castle chapel, is thought to be by Thornhill, the chapel's designer.

Not much survives of the priory buildings – a house w of the church, a barn, and a circular dovecot, still containing its movable ladder.

One and a half miles SE is CARHAMPTON, surrounded by orchards where the ceremony of wassailing is still a serious matter. The restored church has a fine screen of the Dunster type, not in the usual dark stain but gleaming in the colours of its prime. The parish is associated with the Celtic St Carantoc who, according to legend, arrived from across the Channel having thrown his altar in the sea and simply followed it. A church was named after him here which survived until the mid 16th century. A less pleasant legend is associated with Sandhill Manor, where the ghost of Madame Carne (d. 1612), a witch supposed to have killed three husbands, returned home to fry eggs and bacon for the mourners after her own funeral. The Manor was pillaged by the Roundheads in the Civil War, but Col. Francis Wyndham (whose initials are on the gable) rode out from Dunster and with 30 men routed a force of 250 at Nettlecombe.

Durleigh Som. *see* **Bridgwater**

Dyrham Avon 5 C4
The name Dyrham means 'deer enclosure', and it is a fine acknowledgement that deer once again roam the

parkland which runs down so dramatically from the Cotswold scarp almost to the doors of the Baroque mansion Dyrham Park (NT). But the site has another early claim to fame, for here in 577 Cuthwine and Ceawlin, two Saxon leaders, fought against the Britons, killed three of their kings, and captured their cities of Cirencester, Gloucester, and Bath. The Saxon penetration into north Somerset had begun.

Dyrham Park is the result of foreign influence of a much later period, and completely replaced a late-medieval house of the Denys family. The new house is the work of two architects, William Talman, Comptroller of the Royal Works and deputy to Wren; and a Huguenot, Samuel Hauduroy; and it was built on a modest and charming scale for a curious man, William Blathwayt, who had married the heiress to the property in 1686.

Blathwayt was an influential diplomat and civil servant who began his career at the Hague in 1668 and progressed via the Plantations Office, the Privy Council, and the Board of Trade to be Secretary at War and acting Secretary of State to William III. He spoke Dutch and during his active life spent much time abroad. Many of the decorations in the house, including paintings, Delftware and leather hangings, plainly recall his tastes.

Hauduroy built the w front which now faces the formal garden as an addition to the medieval house, and

it was probably finished by 1696. The stable block followed, probably by Talman and his general foreman Edward Wilcox. Much more radical was the addition of the E front, in pure if slightly old-fashioned Baroque, which took the place of the older house. This was Talman's work, begun in 1698 and finished in 1705. The monumental orangery, which continues the main front and cleverly hides the stables and offices, is also probably by Talman. The classical advice on its frieze to 'observe moderation, keep the end in view, follow the law of nature' is as appropriate for its original function as for its present rôle as a National Trust tearoom.

On a terrace overlooking the garden and so close by the house is the delightful parish church, a light and delicate structure, at first sight late medieval, but only its superficial details. Its core could be Norman, like the font; the N aisle is mid 13th century. The s aisle is two centuries later, after the tower and porch. The glass in the E window of the chancel is a fine example of late-medieval work, and remarkable too is the brass of Sir Maurice Russell (d. 1416) and his wife, former owners of the estate. Monuments to their successors, the Wynters and the Blathwayts, tell the remarkable story of the link between great house and church which is the epitome of English rural history.

East Brent Som. *see* **Brent Knoll**

Dyrham

East Coker Som. 2 D3
Approach from the w, via North Coker, and there is
T. S. Eliot's

> deep lane
> Shuttered with branches, dark in the afternoon,
> Where you lean against a bank while a van passes,
> And the deep lane insists on the direction
> Into the village . . .

(Four Quartets: East Coker)

There has been much new commuter building to add
to the former industry of linen cloth and rope, but Coker
remains essentially a delightful residential centre, especially the village beyond the church; but before that is
Hymerford House, the medieval birthplace of William
Dampier (1651–1715) 'buccaneer, explorer, hydro-
grapher' as the memorial in the church declares, who
circumnavigated the world three times and first explored
and described the coast of Australia. Other restless spirits
from the village included Nicholas Dodge who founded
Block Island, and Andrew Elliott, who was baptised in
the church in 1627 and who similarly settled in America.
So it was to his ancestor's birthplace that T. S. Eliot
returned, and here his ashes were by his wish buried in
1965.

The church, Coker Court, and the Helyar almshouses
(c. 1640) form an outstanding group up the drive under
the trees. The church was altered in the mid 18th century
when the central tower, found to be unsafe, was replaced
by the present one. The house, once owned by the Courtenays, and from 1616 by the Helyars, has a 15th-century
hall, early-17th-century additions, and an E front and
s wing in the style of Sir William Chambers.

The rest of the village is as picturesque as any in
Somerset, with irregular thatched cottages and substantial farm houses, some like Slades Farm dating possibly
from the late 14th century. Then, a walk of a mile SE
through Sandy Lane or a slightly longer drive to the tiny
church of SUTTON BINGHAM on the edge of the reservoir
(boating, fishing). Here is a Norman church with some
later alterations in the windows but nothing after c.
1300: the surprise is not simply the sumptuous chancel
arch, but the wall paintings of c. 1300 – the Coronation
of the Virgin, the Death of the Virgin, bishops and saints.

East Quantoxhead Som. 1 H1
In the rich narrow coastal strip between the headland
of the Quantock Hills and the sea is one of Somerset's
most picturesque and untouched villages. The Court
House, on a bluff above the village and overlooking the
sea, has been the home of Luttrells since long before they
went to Dunster. Andrew Luttrell inherited the manor
in 1232 through his grandmother, and she could trace
her ancestry directly to Ralph Pagnell, who owned the
property when Domesday Book was compiled in 1086.
The house has a medieval core and was probably fortified, with at least one tower, but much of the present
house dates from the time of Sir Hugh Luttrell (d. 1522);

and the E and s sides were the work of George Luttrell
(d. 1629). George's coat of arms, with that of his second
wife Silvestra (Capps), occurs with the date 1628. After
George's death the lady, who still lived in the house,
married Sir Edmund Skory. He bitterly regretted the
match, for in his will in 1632 he left money to his servant
Giles Baker 'who hath lived under the tyranny of my
wife, to the danger of his life, during the space of two
years'. To Silvestra, whom he 'hartely' forgave 'all her
wicked attempts' against him, he gave 'a praier booke
called The Practice of Piety, desiring that she better love
and affect the same than hitherto she hath done'. Sir
Edmund died soon afterwards, and incredibly his widow
found another husband. The lady lived at the Court
House until 1655.

The church clinging to the side of the house demonstrates its manorial origin. The building dates from the
early 14th century, though there were many alterations
a century later. The rood screen seems to be of the 14th
century, a rare case in Somerset, and the pulpit, reader's
desk, communion rail, and benches are of the early 16th
century and later. On the N side of the chancel, originally
forming an Easter sepulchre before the vestry took the
place of an earlier chapel, is a tomb chest commemorating two Luttrells, Hugh (d. 1522) and his son Andrew
(d. 1538). Hugh fought on the King's side against Perkin
Warbeck in 1497, and in 1501 was one of the Somerset
gentry who met the young Catherine of Aragon at Plymouth and conducted her to London when she came as
a bride for Prince Arthur. Andrew quarrelled with his
stepmother for possession of East Quantoxhead and their
servants had a pitched battle in the park. At his death
he left a silver cup to Thomas Cromwell to induce the
powerful minister to be 'good lord' to his widow and
children.

The millpond with its ducks, the gardens beyond, and
the church and Court House make a haunting and very
English picture, and the irregular thatched cottages in
the village behind seem almost changeless. The footpath
beside the pond passes the mill and leads to KILVE, either
directly across the fields (½ mile) or along the top of the
low cliffs. The ivy-covered ruins by the church there, the
so-called Chantry, is one half of the medieval manor
house, given in the 14th century by the last of the Fur-
neaux family as home for a college of chantry priests,
whose chapel stood on the N side of the church (see the
arcade in the vestry). The church tower is a puzzle, looking very squat and medieval, but apparently of the 17th
century, for until 1636 the bells were hung in a wooden
cage in the churchyard, and proved too tempting for the
village boys. Kilve Court in PUTSHAM, the present centre
of population on the A39, was built between 1782 and
1785, and now serves as the Somerset County Council's
Residential Youth Centre. Kilve beach, which so
charmed Wordsworth (see Introduction), bears traces of
industry in the form of a ruined limekiln at the head of
the abandoned creek, and a brick building, relic of an

attempt to extract shale oil *c.* 1914.

The old village of WEST QUANTOXHEAD or ST AUDRIES, 2 miles W of Putsham, disappeared in the 19th century. All that remains on the site are the church of St Etheldreda (hence the village name) and, at the far end of the drive that was once the village street, the mansion. The church is a splendid example of the estate variety, built in 1854–6 by John Norton for Sir Peregrine Acland and his son-in-law Sir Alexander Acland-Hood, as part of a grand scheme of emparkment which at the same time provided much-needed local employment. Armorial tiles on the chancel floor and initials in the tower parapet proclaim the family proudly; the lodges, the village school, a farm by the coast (charge for admission to the beach), even a Gothick gas works, and above all the Tudor-style mansion, declare the taste and opulence of the 1850s. The house was, in fact, not finished until 1872, and is now a girls' school; its lakes and drives, even the beautiful cast-iron gates and fencing, are the epitome of mid-Victorian taste. Washington Irving was impressed by the lawns 'like sheets of vivid green' and the trees 'heaping up rich piles of foliage'. The heaping, especially on the hill above the church, once the deer park, is now part of the Forestry Commission's Quantock State Forest.

Exmoor Som.

At the western edge of Somerset and stretching into Devon is the wild and magnificent country that is Exmoor, a rich landscape of open moorland and wooded valleys rising to 1,705 ft at Dunkery, its highest point, with Lype Hill on the adjoining Brendons to the E, reaching 1,390 ft. The high ground is gouged out by the rivers Barle and Exe, flowing S to Dulverton, and is broken up by the rich vale around Porlock, a contrast to the much less fertile high ground of Devonian and Old Red Sandstone rocks.

At the core of Exmoor was the ancient royal forest, probably Saxon in origin and protected by the savage laws of Norman kings. By the end of the Middle Ages the forest proper extended hardly beyond the present parishes of Exmoor and Oare (q.v.), and Crown-appointed Wardens protected the royal deer, controlled grazing of cattle, horses and sheep at the Swainmote courts held at Landacre Bridge, Hawkridge churchyard or Simonsbath, and generally oversaw the rights of the local 'Suitors', as they were called, who were allowed to cut turf, heath, and fern. By the end of the 16th century some 30,000 sheep were grazed between March and October and an unknown number of ponies; and between them the open ground and the valleys provided

Exmoor

Tarr Steps on the R. Barle

heather, gorse, rush, fern, reeds, nuts, willows, and charcoal.

The system continued (with a break after the Civil War when the forest was sold to a man who *c.* 1654 built a house and established an enclosed farm at Simonsbath) until 1819. To the casual visitor the moor was bleak and unproductive: 'forest, baren, and morisch ground, wher ys store and breading of yong catelle, but litle or no corne or habitation', wrote Leland; 'filthy, barren ground', said Camden; and Defoe agreed with him. By 1814 there were, remarkably, only 37 trees on the moor, and those mostly around Simonsbath. But for John Knight, a Worcestershire ironmaster, it had possibilities, and when Exmoor was enclosed and allotted to various claimants, he was by far the highest bidder for the 10,000 acres sold by the Crown, and he later bought up other estates as well, by 1820 possessing some 15,500 acres, three-quarters of the old royal forest. From the 1840s John Knight's son Frederic encouraged the establishment of tenant farms, improved the land, planted hedges and trees, and built roads, establishing the present basic pattern of stock raising, mainly of sheep. Less successful were the attempts both on Exmoor and the Brendons to establish mining for copper and iron, though the remarkable remains at BRENDON HILL above Treborough, 1 mile E of Raleigh's Cross, represent much more successful investment. The work of the Knights may be said to have culminated in the establishment in 1856 of a new parish, the parish of Exmoor, based on Simonsbath and the focus of a new community created, like villages 1,000 years earlier, out

of unpromising land by the initiative of a local landowner.

The Knights sold their property to Devon neighbours in 1897, but not until the late 1920s did the pattern of holdings change greatly. The NT began to lease moorland in 1918 and now, in the whole of the moor, owns over 16,000 acres (mostly from the former Aclands' Holnicote estate); the Forestry Commission has over 3,000 acres, and the Somerset County Council a little more, including the famous PINKERY POND. The greater change, however, has come with the establishment of the Exmoor National Park (1974), whose authority covers 170,000 acres, two-thirds in Somerset.

The maintenance of the delicate balance of interests is the prime concern of the Park Authority. Farmers and visitors are only two aspects of Exmoor life. The archaeology and the natural history are two others. The high ground has yielded Palaeolithic and Neolithic tools, Bronze Age barrows like Black Barrow, Iron Age hillforts like Cow Castle, enclosures like Berry Castle above Porlock, ditches, and the well-known clapper bridge over the Barle a mile N of Hawkridge, TARR STEPS. It is a packhorse and foot bridge *c.* 5 ft wide, and *c.* 180 ft long, with 17 spans. Its date has been the subject of much controversy, though flooding has certainly caused the replacement of some of the original stones in recent times if not earlier. Seventy years ago it was thought to be of Bronze Age origin, but is now considered to be medieval.

The wild life of Exmoor is dominated in the popular mind by the wild Red Deer and the Exmoor pony, both indigenous. The moor is the home, either temporary or permanent, of some 245 species of birds, and some 800 varieties of plants; some of extreme rarity grow in the wide range of terrain.

The enjoyment of the variety of Exmoor life, with its characteristic scattered settlements, humble churches, red stone buildings, and wild open spaces, is enhanced by the products of the Exmoor Press and the protective and stimulating work of the Exmoor Society. Without both the visitor to Exmoor would be the poorer.

See also Culbone, Dulverton, Dunster, Oare, Porlock, Selworthy.

Fairfield   Som. *see* **Stogursey**

Farleigh Hungerford   Som.   5 C5
'On a rokky hill', says Leland, overlooking the valley of the river Frome, Farleigh Castle (DoE) was built by Sir Thomas Hungerford, Speaker of the House of Commons in 1377, in succession to, and no doubt incorporating, an earlier manor house. From the reign of William Rufus until 1337 Farleigh had belonged to the Montfort family and bore their name. It passed to the family of Lord Burghersh, a colleague of Hungerford and friend of the Black Prince, and in 1369 Burghersh sold it to Hungerford. Building of the castle probably began in the next decade, and in 1383 Hungerford was given licence, very likely retrospective, to have fortifications. It formed a rectangular structure with circular towers at its corners and a large gatehouse in one long side, enclosing buildings including hall, great dining room, and kitchen. Leland called this gatehouse 'fair', describing the 'richly made' arms of the family carved in stone.

Sir Thomas died in 1397 and was buried in the parish church of St Leonard just outside his castle, where his wife Joan later joined him. His son Walter, Speaker of the Commons in 1414, High Treasurer of England under Henry VI, and Baron Hungerford, extended the castle southwards to form an outer courtyard, with stables and guard rooms, entered by a square gateway with a drawbridge. The sickle, the badge of the Hungerfords, appears below their arms and the initials of Sir Edward Hungerford (*c.* 1520). This new work was added *c.* 1425, and the parish church thus found itself within the castle. It became the private chapel of the family and the centre of two chantries founded by Sir Walter Hungerford in 1430 and 1443. The house of the chantry priests stands behind the chapel.

Walter, Lord Hungerford of Heytesbury, was executed in 1540 alongside Thomas Cromwell. At his death the castle was described as

portly and very strongly buylded, havyng inward and outward wardes, and in the inward wardes many fayre chambers, a fayre large hall, on the hedde of which hall iij or iiij goodly great chambers, with fayre and strong roffes, and dyvers other fayre lodginges, with

all manner howses of offices.
(Jackson, *Farleigh Hungerford*)

The castle was garrisoned by the Royalists in 1644, but it was taken by Parliament in the following year without a fight, and it survived as a substantial building until the 18th century, though it was said to be 'very ruinous' in 1701.

Sir Walter Hungerford's extension of the castle left the parish without a church. The present building was consecrated in 1443 by James, Bishop of Achonry (Ireland), suffragan to the then new Bishop of Bath and Wells, Thomas Bekynton. It includes an inscription on the porch which appears to be earlier, and a portrait of Sir Thomas Hungerford in a nave window, recognized by his initials and the Hungerford sickle, which belongs to the 14th century and was probably brought to the new church from the castle chapel. The castle chapel, rebuilt 1380–90 by Sir Thomas, with an early-16th-century porch, has the founder's massive tomb between chancel and N chapel, and other family monuments of the 16th and 17th centuries, both in the chapel and the vault, the whole forming a fascinating collection in its own right, and a fine addition to a most attractive site.

Fishponds   Avon *see* **Kingswood**

Frampton Cotterell   Avon *see* **Winterbourne**

Frome   Som.   5 C6   (*pron.* Froom)
Frome has had a bad press in the past. John Wesley, who for once had a poor reception, called it a 'dry, barren, uncomfortable place', and a local Baptist minister thought it 'a large and surpassingly ugly town'. Cobbett, visiting in 1826, saw it as 'a sort of little Manchester. A very small Manchester indeed ... all the *flash* of a Manchester, and the innkeepers and their people look and behave like the Manchester fellows'. Cobbett made no secret of his delight in finding 'proofs of the irretrievable decay of the place' in the heavy unemployment and half-finished houses. But this decay was undoubtedly the town's salvation, for in the previous century or so its growth had been phenomenal: it was said in 1720 to be bigger than Bath or Salisbury, and by 1801, although overtaken by Bath, had 8,748 inhabitants. Within 20 years the number had risen to 12,411. But its economy was based almost entirely on the manufacture of woollen cloth, the 'Spanish medleys' which Defoe mentioned in the 1720s. The decline noted by Cobbett was halted by diversification, but until the 1960s Frome's population remained almost static, though the town has expanded away from the crowded historic centre.

And there is no doubt about its history. The full and official name of Frome Selwood is a reminder that it stood near the ancient royal forest of Selwood on the Wiltshire border. Its sloping site near the River Frome (much less attractive though less prone to flood since it was canalized) was chosen for a monastery planted by

Catherine Hill, Frome

St Aldhelm (d. 709). By Domesday the settlement around it had a substantial market, probably stretching down the hill between the church and the river, a market which was still 'metly good' in Leland's time and which continues (in a much smaller area) at the end of Cheap Street and on a new site beyond the river.

But what Leland mentioned particularly were the church and the 'dyvers fayre stone howsys in the toune that standythe moste by clothinge'. Many still stand for the observant walker who will climb the narrow streets and look above shop-fronts. The streets are certainly narrow and steep, and wind their way from the river to the top of the town, offering fascinating views of mellow tiles and irregular gables. The cobbled Gentle Street, and Cheap Street with its water channel and ancient 'market' name, both near the church, are the best known, but recently the 'Trinity' area to the NW of the town has been fortunately preserved from wholesale destruction after it was discovered to be a remarkable 17th-century housing estate for artisans, the speculation of a single family. The names of the streets themselves – Stony Street, Blindhouse Lane, Sheppards Barton (the Sheppards were clothiers), Catherine Hill and Street (after a 13th-century chapel), Button Street, Twattle Alley, Pudding-Bag Lane, Palmer Street, Rook Lane – give an impression of quaintness fully borne out by high pavements, mellow, irregular buildings, and a general lack of Victorian imposition. Only Bath Street (after the Marquess, lord of the manor) in the town centre, sweeps through so grandly; and that indeed was intended, a 'development' of 1810–11.

To Wesley Frome was full of nonconformist sects: 'Anabaptists, Quakers, Presbyterians, Arians, Antinomians, Moravians, and whatnot', sects so often associated with clothing towns. Cobbett noted the 'new gingerbread "places of worship"', many of which are now closed, though they still stand high and bulky above the surrounding houses. Notable are the former Rook Lane Chapel in Bath Street with a huge Classical front of 1707, though the cause itself was founded in 1662 when John Humfry was ejected from the Anglican vicarage. At the top of the hill the Methodists built a tabernacle more graceful inside than out, and later demonstrated their strength with a complex of schools and manses.

Anglicanism remained on the defensive until later in the 19th century (Christ Church (rebuilt 1844), Holy Trinity 1837–8, St Mary's, Innox Hill, 1863–4), but the incumbency at St John's of W. J. E. Bennett (1852–66) put an end to that. 'No restoration of any church in England [is] to be compared with it', said Archdeacon Denison at Bennett's funeral; 'the C19 did much altogether to alter and confuse', admits Pevsner, defeated. Between 1862 and 1865 Bennett, John Giles his architect, and the expenditure of some £40,000 destroyed, virtually unrecorded, a large early church, undoubtedly Saxon in origin if not in surviving structure, and re-

placed it with a bold declaration of Tractarianism. There are clearly details of a late 12th-century church in places, and even fragments of Saxon carving (under the tower). Chantry chapels were added in some profusion and splendour from the late 14th century and the tower and spire were finished in the 15th. The chancel was totally rebuilt in 1847–9, but the surviving spirit of the whole is 19th-century Anglicanism at its grandest.

The grandeur is not continued outside; the w front, which faces Wyatville's screen across a courtyard, is a disappointment, though the *Via Crucis* and the steps to the street continue the Tractarian theme.

At the E end, under a Victorian tomb (1844) which he would have found over-ornate, but with the inscription which he himself composed added so long after his death, lies Bishop Ken. Simple and saintly in his life, and a conservative by inclination, Ken was among the Seven Bishops imprisoned for their opposition to James II in 1688. But he believed in the principle of hereditary monarchy, and could not take the oath of allegiance to William III while James was still alive. He was therefore deprived of his see of Bath and Wells and retired to Longleat, just outside its borders. At his death in 1711 he was, at his own wish, buried in the nearest parish of his former diocese, and he gave to its church his paten and chalice, relics still preciously preserved.

Gaulden Som. *see* **Crowcombe**

Glastonbury Som. 2 C1
History and legend, mystery and imagination have made of Glastonbury more than a feast for any visitor. Perhaps the earliest Christian shrine in the country, certainly the site of the richest monastery, and still a place of pilgrimage, Glastonbury is unique. The Glastonbury Legends have many strands and developed over many centuries. They tell of Christ coming here as a child with his merchant uncle, Joseph of Arimathea; they tell of Joseph coming here with the Holy Grail, the cup of the Last Supper; they tell of the apostle Philip sending missionaries from Gaul to establish a church, and of those missionaries finding a church already here, dedicated by Christ Himself. The undoubted Irish influence here is traced back to St Patrick who came here as first Abbot, and of his follower St Benignus, the second Abbot, to whom the lower church in Glastonbury is dedicated; and of the visit of the Irish St Bridget of Kildare, who left behind at Beckery (1 mile SW; but does that mean Little Ireland?) a bell and a wallet and other objects of veneration.

Archaeology has yet to substantiate these claims, though the Tor was evidently occupied in the Dark Ages by someone with taste and the means to enjoy imported wine or oil from the Mediterranean, a liking for meat (which seems to rule out a Celtic religious site), and an ability to work metal. The tradition that it was the stronghold of Melwas, King of Somerset, he who

Glastonbury Abbey

abducted Guinevere and kept King Arthur at bay, is at least borne out by these traces on the Tor.

The abbey site itself cannot yet be pushed back so far. Its earliest feature is a long-hidden boundary ditch, going back no earlier (as yet) than the 7th century. Whatever more ancient stood within, the Vetusta Ecclesia, the Old Church of Wattles, was destroyed by fire in 1184, and its successor was deliberately built over the holy spot; and when, at the end of the Middle Ages, a crypt was formed, all archaeological evidence was destroyed for ever.

By 1184, of course, there was more than just a church of wattles. Tradition said that St David had come with seven bishops but found that the church had already been consecrated by Christ himself; so he built another church and consecrated that. And there is evidence enough of Welsh interest in Glastonbury which has more historical support in the likely presence of SS. Gildas, Kea (see Street), and Rumon there. King Ine (d. 726) built a new church, as an appendix to the old, and it was dedicated to the Apostles Peter and Paul. This church, at the E end of the Lady Chapel, was replaced by another built by Abbot Herlwin before 1125. The foundations of both have been discovered by archaeologists. Conventual buildings, a cloister and chapel represent the general reform which began at Glastonbury under St Dunstan (Abbot 946–57) and which laid the foundations of its spiritual and economic power. Three English Kings, Edmund, Edgar, and Edmund Ironside were buried here, and Edgar was later moved to the E end

of the abbey church to a magnificent fan-vaulted chapel built by the last two Abbots, Richard Bere and Richard Whiting.

By the time of Domesday, Glastonbury owned an eighth of the county of Somerset, its estates occupying much of the Levels, large parts of which were soon to be drained and made profitable. The Norman Abbots Thurstin and Herlwin continued to add to the buildings, but most was done by the influential Henry of Blois, grandson of Henry I (Abbot 1126–71, Bishop of Winchester 1129–71). He built separate lodgings for himself on such a scale that the buildings seemed like a castle or palace. The huge foundations of this building were recently uncovered. Abbot Henry also built a bell-tower, chapter house, cloister, and other buildings for the monks, and a great gatehouse. And it was Abbot Henry who at the beginning of his reign invited the historian William of Malmesbury to write the history of the house, a history which is of the greatest importance in understanding the growth of the legends of Glastonbury. But on St Urban's Day 1184 everything but Abbot Henry's bell-tower, a chamber, and a chapel was destroyed by fire.

Rebuilding started immediately, beginning with the Lady Chapel on the site of the old church, and now the most complete part of the abbey church. Everything at first was under the control of Ralph FitzStephen, the King's agent, but after Henry II's death in 1189 royal finance dried up and the monks were thrown back on their own resources. And they achieved a master stroke.

In 1191 in digging a grave for a monk (as one source says) or in searching in the old monks' graveyard following what a bard had told Henry II years before – there, between the shafts of two ancient crosses, 16 ft down in a wooden sarcophagus, were found the bones of a large man and a delicate woman (her golden tresses still preserved until an over-eager monk touched them and they turned to dust). A leaden cross found in the grave left the monks in no doubt that here were King Arthur and Queen Guinevere. But there are doubts. The cross has disappeared, but we know from drawings that it did not name Guinevere, even though the chroniclers claimed it did! And even more suspicious, William of Malmesbury in his *History of Glastonbury*, first written 60 years before, did not even mention Arthur, let alone say he was buried there. The monks' acute need for money and the discovery of the bones of the greatest figure in Romance, was, to say the least, timely.

And, of course, successful. By 1278, when Edward I and his Queen came to attend the final placing of Arthur in a great tomb in the choir, the main part of the Abbey had been completed. By 1291 the Galilee which linked the church to St Mary's Chapel was finished; and when the Edgar Chapel was added by Abbot Bere the whole magnificent building was 562 ft long, with a central bell-tower and twin towers at the w end of the nave. Inside there were shrines, tombs of kings and abbots, a famous clock, decorations of all kinds, and even histories of the abbey for pilgrims. Only a small part of this magnificence survives in the abbey museum. At the Dissolution in 1539 the monastery was still thriving, with over 50 monks. After the mock trial and horrible execution of Abbot Whiting and two monks on the Tor, the buildings were soon used as a quarry, though occasional visitors recorded what they saw, and the 'original' Glastonbury Thorn remained until cut down by a Puritan fanatic in the 17th century. The Abbot's Kitchen was used in the 16th century by weavers and in the 17th as a temporary Quaker Meeting House. In the 18th and 19th centuries it was regarded as a romantic ruin in the grounds of Abbey House, and visitors like Francis Kilvert had some difficulty in finding the site. And when he found it a 'kindly woman' showed him a holly staff from the coffin of one of the abbots, a Glastonbury chair (the original in the Palace at Wells), St Joseph's well, and the Holy Thorn. In 1909 the site was bought by the Church of England and excavations over a long period thereafter have retrieved much of the layout. The site now includes, besides the abbey itself, a museum, the chapel of St Patrick formerly part of a group of almshouses, the

Glastonbury – the Barn

Abbot's Kitchen, now including an exhibition outlining the history of the Abbey, and an estate with a large variety of trees, a picnic orchard, and a fish pond.

Kilvert thought of Glastonbury as a 'bright clean cheerful-looking town'. The Abbey owned it until the Dissolution including its hostelry, the sumptuous 15th-century George and Pilgrim Hotel, rebuilt by Abbot John Selwood for visiting pilgrims, in High Street. St Mary's almshouses in Magdalen Street, or rather part of them, were originally a single 13th-century building with two rows of dwellings facing each other and a chapel at the end, all under a single roof. The two parish churches are something of a contrast. St Benignus, in the lower part of the town, is of c. 1520, plain and simple inside. St John the Baptist's, in the centre, is more elaborate, though much of it was a rebuilding of necessity, when the central tower started to collapse in the mid 15th century. The w tower is one of the most splendid in Somerset, its delicate crown rising high above the town. Beyond the abbey estate at the end of Bere Lane is the Abbey Barn, a 14th-century manor barn which forms part of the Somerset Rural Life Museum established by the County Council. Further se is Chalice Well and the Tor. The Well, which has a masonry structure that may be of the 13th century, played a vital rôle in the Abbey's water system, and has since acquired legendary connotations. The Tor, topped by the tower of the 13th-century church of St Michael, is a stiff climb but worth all the effort: a most magnificent, and often almost mystical view of Somerset.

Great Badminton　Avon　5 C3

Surrounded by rolling acres of the high Cotswolds and a park famed for its annual Horse Trials and guarded by ornate lodges, Badminton House is still hardly visible even from the village and not open to the public. The great mansion of the Dukes of Beaufort still has many secrets to yield, including the name of its original designer.

Thomas Somerset, Viscount Somerset of Cashel, bought the estate from the Botelet family in 1608, and through his daughter it passed to Henry Somerset, Lord Herbert. In consideration of his noble descent from Edward III through John de Beaufort, eldest son of John of Gaunt and Catherine Swynford, Henry was created Duke of Beaufort in 1682. But there is more to the family than that. Beauforts played a vital if unpopular part in the Wars of the Roses. Charles (d. 1526), son of Henry Beaufort, Duke of Somerset, was a supporter of Henry VII and married the Herbert heiress who brought Raglan and other Welsh estates to the family. He was created Earl of Worcester in 1514. Henry (d. 1646), the 5th Earl, supported the Crown in the Civil War, gallantly defended Raglan Castle, and was

Glastonbury Tor

created Marquess of Worcester. His son Edward (d. 1667), was sentenced to death by the House of Commons for his Royalism, but was later imprisoned in the Tower and pensioned by Cromwell who held some of his confiscated estates. Charles I once wrote to the Duke of Ormonde that Edward's honesty or affection to Royal service would not deceive him, but that he would not answer for Edward's judgement. As if to prove the point Edward once produced forged papers creating him Duke of Somerset and Beaufort. He also produced a 'water-commanding engine' which worked at Vauxhall until 1670 and was involved in publishing a book of inventions.

Henry, 3rd Marquess of Worcester and 1st Duke of Beaufort (d. 1699), refused to swear the oath to William III after his years as a faithful supporter of the Stuarts. The oldest part of Badminton House is the work of Henry and his father, for when they recovered their estates at the Restoration, their house at Raglan was no longer habitable. It began with the central block with wings on each side. Further, single-storeyed wings were added in the early 18th century, linked to pavilions; and these pavilions and the cupolas and pediment on the central block were designed by William Kent. Kent also designed buildings in the park including the impressive Worcester Lodge, which later in the century was altered by Capability Brown. Inside there is work by Grinling Gibbons and Wyatville.

The church of St Michael, attached to the house, was built as a simple rectangle with tower in 1785 and replaced the medieval church. The chancel and apse were added in 1875. Eighteenth-century box pews and pulpit blend with other early-20th-century fittings. The church is dominated by Beaufort memorials, that to the 1st Duke by Gibbons having been moved from St George's Chapel, Windsor, in the 19th century. Monuments to the next three dukes are by Rysbrack.

The village is a fine collection of estate houses in wide streets, including a pedimented terrace c. 1714 for retired servants, and interesting late-18th and 19th-century houses and cottages in charming variety, including *cottages ornés*, with rustic verandas and diamond window panes.

LITTLE BADMINTON, 1 mile N, lies round a green with a dovecot at its centre. The little church, 'gone to decay' in the 1770s, is probably Norman in origin, but its earliest datable feature is the late-12th-century arcade, still bearing traces of wall painting. The church had new windows in the 14th century but those on the N side are now are of the 19th.

Greenham Barton　Som. *see* **Wellington**

Ham Hill　Som.　2 C3

An outcrop of golden shelly limestone, often confused with sandstone, Ham Hill often looks gaunt against the skyline. It is only c. 400 ft above sea-level but rises

Badminton

abruptly above the flat Parrett and Yeo valleys to give vantage points to the Mendips, the Quantocks, and the Dorset hills. Evidence of occupation starts with the Stone Age, but the earliest settlement was during the Iron Age, when ramparts were raised around a huge L-shaped area. The camp was later occupied by the Romans, whose Fosse Way could be controlled from the hill-top. But the Romans also recognized the hill as a source of high-quality building stone, and from that time the hill became covered in small quarry workings, to which its present surface bears witness. Parts have always been used for arable farming; one area in the 14th century was a rabbit warren; and much was grazed with sheep. There was probably a small village on the summit in the 14th century and the quarrymen and masons in the 17th century were said to have created for themselves 'a pretty kind of commonwealth' with their own courts, and made their quarries, according to Thomas Gerard,

> seeme rather little parishes than quarryes, soe many buildings have they under the vast workes to shelter them selves in wet weather, and their wrought stones in winter.

The product of these quarries can be seen in buildings all over s Somerset and well beyond: the abbeys at Forde (Dorset) and Muchelney, or country houses like Barrington Court, Montacute, and Brympton D'Evercy as prestige buildings might be expected to use such high-quality material; but the golden Ham stone and its locally quarried near relatives are found in the humblest cottage, the standard patterns for doors, windows, and other mouldings were for sale at the quarry to anyone who could afford the high cost of transport. Barring-

ton Court, not far away, is covered with the trademarks of the 16th-century freemasons who produced fine ashlar on the hill for walling which lesser clients could not afford; but Ham stone dressings are found on buildings at a considerable distance.

The hill has also been a place of recreation: 'I will desire your company to the topp of it', says Gerard in the 17th century, 'where besides the pleasure of the prospect, I hope to find something that may countervaile your pains'. The hill is now officially a country park. Its soil, thrown up into curious forms by generations of quarrymen, gives home to some rare plants, its wooded slopes welcome early migrants, and its irregular hollows have hidden generations of picnickers.

Hawkesbury Avon 5 C3

Nestling in a wooded combe below the Cotswold scarp, Hawkesbury church, old parsonage, and derelict farm buildings have been deserted by its village; Hawkesbury Upton is a mile away on the hill, and has been at least since the 18th century and probably for much longer. Pershore Abbey acquired the church and estate by the 11th century and one of its abbots, Thomas Upton (d. 1413), may have been buried in the sanctuary under a stone now bereft of its elaborate brass. Does his name and his burial not suggest that he was brought back to his native parish for burial? Another ecclesiastical native was Gilbert Ironside (1588–1671), who was Bishop of Bristol during the last 10 years of his life. He was a man of wealth, able to maintain the episcopal dignity even though his see was so poor; and is remembered for a confrontation with John Wesley, incumbent of Winterborne

Whitchurch (Dorset), grandfather of the founder of Methodism, who refused to use the Book of Common Prayer. 'The bishop (it was recalled) was more civil to him than he to the bishop'.

The large medieval parish, which included Hillesley, Tresham, Wast, Little Badminton, and Alderley, was prosperous if the size of its magnificent church is any indication; Pershore had a weekly market and fairs there in 1252; and there were clothworkers there by the 14th century. But the church's expansion came later: a six-stage 14th-century tower, a Perpendicular arcade when the s aisle was formed, then the clerestory over the nave, the noble N porch, and then a raised roof above the 13th-century chancel. The height is what strikes one first, and then the unplastered walls, adorned, though, with plenty of interesting monuments. In the chancel Jenkinsons from 1766 to 1964 are recorded, including the 1st and 2nd Earls of Liverpool, the 2nd the Prime Minister from 1812 to 1827. Another of the family, John Banks Jenkinson, was vicar here 1805–15, and later became Bishop of St David's and Dean of Durham. Another vicar is

recorded near the font: the Revd Potter Cole died in 1802 at the age of 97 after 'constant practice of every Christian duty' as vicar of the parish for 73 years.

Visitors are still warned as they enter the splendid Norman N doorway, that

It is desired that all persons that come to this Church would be Careful to leave their Dogs at home and that the Women would not walk in with their Pattens on.

And a pair of pattens still hangs there, too.

Henbury Avon 5 B4

North from Bristol, beyond Westbury on Trym (q.v.), Henbury Hill leads to what is still at heart a village. The name means 'high or chief fortification', the Saxon word for the Iron Age hillfort, later occupied by the Romans, on the Blaise Castle estate. Henbury church is largely the work of two periods in the 13th century, the first c. 1200, when the walls of the simple nave of an earlier church were pierced by the fine six-bay arcade – work of the first order, according to Pevsner, and not in the Somerset style. But why should it be so? Henbury had

Blaise Hamlet

belonged to the Bishops of Worcester since (according to a probably forged charter) 692; and certainly since 1093 it had belonged to the monastery of Westbury on Trym. These were more exalted connexions, and a different sphere of influence.

Later in the 13th century the curiously-formed clerestory was added above the nave, the tower was built or replaced an earlier one, the chancel was extended and given a large s chapel, the latter with characteristic stepped lancets. Very little save the aisle windows and perhaps some details of the tower belong to the usually flourishing period of rebuilding in the late Middle Ages – was all Westbury's money spent on the new buildings of the College? A succession of Victorian restorers, Rickman in 1836 and Street in 1875, altered the E end, Rickman certainly adding the N chapel and altering the chancel. The black marble font was bought in Bridgwater (q.v.) in 1806.

Henbury was clearly a genteel place: the monument in the church to Sir Robert Southwell (by Grinling Gibbons) stands beside others commemorating occupiers of some of the elegant Georgian houses in Henbury Road. Such gentility contrasts nicely with the inscription on the tomb outside the N door, to the Earl of Suffolk's 18-year-old negro servant Scipio (d. 1720). It was hardly his fault to be born 'a pagan and a slave' but still, despite the claim on his grave that he sleeps sweetly as a Christian, his name does not appear in the church's burial register, and his place of burial was probably then unconsecrated. So much for the Christianity of 18th-century Anglicanism.

Over the wall at the w end of the churchyard is the BLAISE CASTLE estate, some 400 acres bought by Bristol Corporation in 1926. The house, now the home of a fine Folk Museum, was built in 1796 by William Paty for the Quaker banker J. S. Harford. It is a plain building, as might be expected for such a client, but its original plan was altered by Nash's curved orangery, and by a picture gallery added by C. R. Cockerell in 1832. Nash also contributed in 1802, on the site of an earlier house, the romantic little thatched dairy, which fits well with the grounds laid out by Repton in 1796. These grounds, making good use of the natural gorge of the Hazel Brook (gouged out by the Giant Goram whose chair is a rock above), have the usual caves and Lovers' Leap and, since 1952, a mill, brought from Stratford in West Harptree (Avon). The whole park sweeps upwards to its highest point, Blaise Castle itself, so called after a nearby medieval chapel of St Blaise, patron saint of woolcombers. The three-towered sham was built in 1766 by a former owner of the estate, another Bristol merchant, Thomas Farr.

Nash was also responsible in 1811 for the group of 10 cottages for Mr Harford's estate retainers, known as Blaise Hamlet (NT). Here is variety for its own sake, windows in all sorts of places, thatch, stone slate, and tile for roofs of almost incredible shape. The little green,

the gardens, the fantastic skyline have been the inspiration for similar groups, such as the cottages at Selworthy (q.v.); less tasteful descendants appeared in porcelain and celluloid.

Hestercombe Som. *see* **Kingston St Mary**

High Ham Som. 2 C2
Standing at the end of a picturesque green, this church is something of a rarity, for its age is almost exactly known, thanks to the memories of villagers, written in the parish register by a 16th-century rector. The tower was earlier than they could recall (early 14th century at its base), but the nave was the work of a group of local notables led by Abbot John Selwood of Glastonbury (the Abbey owned the manor), and all was completed in one year, 1476. The chancel came a little later, paid for principally by the rector, John Dyer, who died in 1499. Both parts are embattled and have big gargoyles. Inside, the slender piers lead the eye to a splendid nave roof and tall rood-screen. Notice the lectern, rare in form and possibly Jacobean in date.

High Ham is only relatively high, occupying a ridge overlooking King's Sedgemoor. The whole ridge from Aller to Somerton (qq.v.) was from medieval times dotted thickly with windmills, but only one now stands, in High Ham (NT), dating back in this case only to the early years of the 19th century but in use until 1910. The NT also owns Turn Hill ($\frac{1}{2}$ mile NW), which forms a magnificent viewpoint over Sedgemoor to the coast.

LOW HAM, 1 mile s, is a small hamlet with a remarkable church, in the middle of a field where only terraces remain, the ghost of a great house. The notice on the church door bids the visitor close it with care to prevent the entry of animals, for there is no fence or churchyard. This was, in effect, a private chapel for the big house; and the big house has gone. The church is at first sight conservative Somerset Perpendicular; it is still pre-Reformation in plan and style, even to the rood-screen, or rather to screen without rood. For there on the screen is the clue, even if its details had not given it away; the words from Proverbs 24:21

My sonne, feare God and the Kinge and meddle not
    with them that are given to change,

the sentiments of an Anglican and a Royalist; the philosophy of George Stawell, who finished in 1668 what his grandfather Sir Edward Hext had begun. The house remained unfinished (though its gateway now stands in Sparkford) because of the severe treatment meted out to his father Sir John Stawell (d. 1662) (see Cothelstone); the church is a triumphant statement of the Restoration.

The monuments are to Sir Edward Hext (d. 1623) and his wife, and to Sir Ralph Stawell, George's brother and heir, created Lord Stawell as a belated recognition of his father's support of the Royalist cause. Pulpit and benches, even the plate, are contemporary; so, too, the

Hinton Charterhouse

heavy velvet altar frontal, dated 1670 and until recently still in place.

Low Ham was, long before the Stawells, the home of a substantial Roman family of the 2nd century. The most important feature of their villa was the bath block; and the mosaic floor of the cold room, showing Dido and Aeneas and other scenes from the Aeneid, is on view in the County Museum in Taunton (q.v.).

Hinkley Point   Som.   *see* **Stogursey**

Hinton Charterhouse   Avon   5 C5
Hinton Priory, on the A36 s of Bath, was the second Carthusian monastery in England. It was founded here by Ela, Countess of Salisbury; in one day in 1232 she attended the consecration of the Abbey at Lacock (Wilts.) and then rode over to attend the same ceremonies here. Unlike the Charterhouse at Witham, the ruins s of Hinton Priory are of the monastic site. The undercroft of the refectory, the chapter house with library above, the sacristy, and parts of the guest house survive, and excavations in the 1950s revealed the outlines of the simple church and of the great cloister, with 14 little houses around it, each in its walled garden, to give the monks the solitude for which they had joined the Order.

Not all the monks found the quiet life to their taste. Brother Stephen of Hinton at the end of the 15th century was famous as an ecstatic visionary; and Nicholas Hopkins, spiritual director of the 3rd Duke of Buckingham, predicted that the Duke would succeed to the throne. In 1521 Hopkins found himself in the Tower for his unwise words and Buckingham was executed. Shakespeare's *Henry VIII* recalls the event:
SURVEYOR: He was brought to this
By a vain prophecy of Nicholas Hopkins.
KING: What was that Hopkins?
SURVEYOR: Sir, a Chartreux friar,
His confessor, who fed him every minute
With words of sovereignty.
There was some opposition from the monks of Hinton when the house was dissolved in 1539, but like many other sites it was soon converted to a mansion, the present house incorporating the 15th-century gatehouse, but being essentially the work of the Hungerfords in the later 16th.

The parish church, 1 mile sw, just outside the village of Hinton, came before the monastery, and much of that date remains: the s doorway, the tower, and the font were already there when the monks came, though details in the porch look like work at the Priory, and the chancel and s chapel belong to the same period. The N aisle is 19th-century.

Half a mile E by the river in Friary Wood are remains of what are thought to have been the lay brothers' quarters.

91

Hinton St George Som. 2 C3

Hinton St George is an estate village with a difference; a village that until recent years was entirely owned by the Earls Poulett, but one that has, with an important exception, been left largely untouched by succeeding owners until now when restoration and protection are the order of the day. The important exception is not apparent to the visitor, but involved at the time (the late 18th century) the stopping of the village street where it ran too close to the big house, and its diversion in a wide sweep N of the church. Lord Poulett's kitchen gardens could then be laid out to accommodate a new hot-house and the traffic on the road could be kept at a more seemly distance.

The Pouletts came to Hinton in the 15th century and Sir Amias (d. 1538) built a new house which included 'two goodly high towers'. This house lies at the core of the present mansion and grew to include a new s front (c. 1636), very like wings at Brympton and Long Ashton (qq.v.). Further additions were made in the next two centuries with work by Matthew Brettingham, Soane, Wyatt, and Wyatville to create the present mansion which, with its service and stable blocks, and porte cochère, is now divided into various dwellings. A characteristic of Soane's work is the stone facing of the western side of the house to resemble cobbling. The 18th-century plans for the park stretching away from the lawns to the Windwhistle ridge included to the w a statue of Diana surrounded by a double circle of limes; Diana alone remains. Large lakes and belts of trees suggested by Kent were never established.

The church is a gem, showing Ham stone work at its very best. Someone left money for the tower in 1486, a noble work on a prominent site, with a splendid crown of pinnacles. The body of the church belongs to the same period though the font is of the 13th century, recut to go with the rebuilding. What makes the church of particular interest is the wealth of memorials, mostly to the Poulett family or their retainers; and especially the family pew and chapel (entered from outside), the pew remodelled c. 1814 by James Wyatt. Here Pouletts are assembled: Sir Amias, the builder of the house; Sir Hugh (d. 1573), Governor of Jersey; Sir Amias (d. 1588), stern keeper of Mary Queen of Scots at Tutbury; John, 1st Baron Poulett (d. 1649), heavily fined for his loyalty to the Crown in the Civil War; John, 1st Earl Poulett (d. 1745), First Lord of the Treasury to Queen Anne (monument by Rysbrack). A memorial in the nave to his child Anne (d. 1765) recalls the family's close personal connexion with Queen Anne, who, standing sponsor, gave her name to the boy!

Notice in the village the Priory, a Victorian name for the oldest house in Hinton, which includes a 14th-century window in the chapel at its E end. The house itself is no earlier than the 16th century, but may represent a property of Monkton Farleigh Priory (Wilts.).

Horton Court

Holcombe Som. 5 B6 1 mile E of Stratton-on-the-Fosse

Down in the valley, the deep ravine N of the village, is where Holcombe began, as a name and as a place. The old church of St Andrew has an inscribed stone built upside down by the Normans into the s doorway, which records in a rare and remarkable way the beginnings of the church here. The inscription is not complete, but it seems to declare that a church was consecrated by one Wrotard; and this Wrotard was almost certainly Archbishop of York. And what was he doing here, and when? Archbishop Wrotard of York attended a Church Council at Exeter in the spring of 928; so he may well have come to Holcombe on his way there or back.

The Saxon church was rebuilt by the Normans, and again in the later Middle Ages. Its remote setting close to Georgian rectory and farm is part of its charm, its interior adds more. So although it has been closed for regular worship since the 1880s when a new church in the village was opened, the key is worth searching for. Jacobean pulpit, early-19th-century gallery and box pews are united by simplicity and white paint. In the churchyard, among the graves of the Scott family is a memorial to Capt. Robert Falcon Scott 'translated by a glorious death, March 1912'.

The village on the hill is a curious mixture of suburban and industrial, though its move to a new site was almost certainly the result not of the inevitable Black Death but to be nearer an important trade route. A brewery and collieries were its life-blood in the 19th century, and quarries and a cement works dominate in the 20th.

Holford Som. *see* **Nether Stowey**

Horton Avon 5 C3

Manor house, church, and farm make a truly English group, nestling under the Iron Age hillfort called the Castles. And yet, on closer examination, the house has details that are far from English; the local Cotswold stone walls and gables, and the stone tiled roofs hide one of the most fascinating buildings in the county. The church, by contrast, seems quite ordinary; essentially a 14th-century building, or rather a building with a 14th-century N arcade, but with all the details of the Perpendicular period, the best being the two-storeyed porch with a vaulted roof and carved capitals to the jambs, one with a man playing pipes. The font is the only clear relic of the Norman church on the site, though it, too, has suffered a transformation, carved into an octagon in the 17th century. There are several tablets to members of the Paston family (formerly of Norfolk), who lived in the house next door from the early 17th century.

Horton Court (NT) has preserved more of its early stages than the church, and has a more fascinating history. About 1125 Agnes and Hubert de la Rye gave the property to the Cathedral at Salisbury, and it became one of the prebendal estates, its owner for the time being a senior ecclesiastic, and a member of the Chapter of Salisbury. The first known prebendary, Robert de Beaufeu, has the distinction of being the author of a poem in praise of ale, and perhaps it was he who built the Norman hall *c.* 1140. The value of the estate may be guessed by its nickname of the Golden Prebend, and its holders in the later Middle Ages are a catalogue of distinguished clergy: Roger Walden (1392–7), Archbishop of Canterbury; Henry Beaufort (1397–8), Cardinal, Bishop of Winchester; John Russell (1462–76), Bishop of Rochester; John Morton (1476–8), Cardinal, Archbishop of Canterbury; Christopher Bainbridge (1486–8), Cardinal, Archbishop of York.

There is little indication that these, and the others who held the prebend during the Middle Ages, personally came to the house, though the arms of Robert Neville, Bishop of Salisbury 1427–38, who did not hold the estate, have been recognized on the timber roof of the hall. But one prebendary certainly left more than his arms. William Knight was prebendary of Horton from 1517 until his appointment as Bishop of Bath and Wells in 1541; and despite his frequent absences abroad on diplomatic missions, he left a most particular mark on the house, in a style that was the direct result of his education and his career. Knight was a Scholar of Winchester, but in 1501 he went to Ferrara to study law, and by 1507 was a Doctor of Law, probably of some Italian university, and was staying at the English College in Rome (where Cardinal Bainbridge was later to be buried). After diplomatic missions in Spain, the Low Countries, Switzerland, and France, he went back to Italy in 1527 on a secret mission to the Pope concerning the King's divorce and was nearly murdered in the attempt. By then the house bore the marks of Knight's Italian and English tastes, the magnificent front door with Renaissance arabesques, a Tudor fireplace with Renaissance frieze and classical pilasters, and the famous ambulatory with four-centred arches and stucco heads of Roman emperors. And Knight's own, fabricated coat of arms is there, over the front door and a chimney piece, the arms of a diplomat to be sure, with the rose of Lancaster, the sun of York and the eagle of the Emperor Charles V, though the Emperor would not accept him as ambassador because of his low birth. Above the arms is the tasselled hat of a protonotary apostolic, and, over the chimney piece in the living room, his name and title and the date 1521.

Knight's house, with all this magnificence, swept away all but the hall of its predecssor, and that hall, now the N wing, is remarkable, for it dates from *c.* 1140, although its roof is of the early 15th century. In the 18th century it was divided into two storeys to create an upper floor for a Roman Catholic chapel, but it was restored at the end of the 19th.

Huish Episcopi Som. *see* **Langport**

Ilchester Som. 2 C2

Modern road-builders have done their best to make what was once a busy (in summer far too busy) town a place all too easy to miss. And at first glance there is not much to see. But this place was once a Roman town, the 'chester' on the River Yeo or Ivel, but known to the Romans as *Lendinis*. It was founded where the great Fosse Way from Lincoln to Axmouth (Devon) was joined by a road from the Bristol Channel to Dorchester (*Durnovaria*) at a ford.

Lendinis was a town of importance. It lay on routes that took Mendip lead south to a major port; it housed a garrison which had been transferred from an old native strongpoint on Ham Hill (q.v.); it was the centre of local administration; and it lay in a rich plain where Roman farmsteads are common. The first (native) settlement was here in the 1st century A.D., probably surrounded by ditch-and-bank defences. Soon afterwards it was replanned on Roman lines and extended, so that by the 4th century the town was walled, though buildings and graves are found well outside the line of the wall whenever new houses or roads are built. Little of these remains can now be seen, only the basic street pattern, though museums at Taunton and Yeovil have many finds in their custody, and few inhabitants have not found Roman coins in their gardens.

The Dark Ages in Ilchester are as dark as anywhere. The place was still Romanized in the early 5th century; its defences were strong enough to shield a mint in the 10th century and to withstand a siege in the 11th, though walls and gates were forcibly dismantled in John's reign. There were four gates in the later Middle Ages but the last, West Gate, only survived until 1605. All this implies some continuing importance, and so there was, for the county gaol was established here by 1166, and the consequent regular visits of Sheriff and circuit judges made Ilchester the county town of Somerset. The town already had a valuable market by 1086 and was given a midsummer fair about 1183. By about 1250, at the height of its prosperity, it had at least six parish churches, a Dominican friary, a hospital (later converted to a nunnery), and at least one chapel. And from 1298 it sent two representatives to Parliament.

Only one of these churches, the early-13th-century St Mary Major, is left, but worth a visit, for its E window is a primitive form of plate tracery, and its slightly later octagonal tower was the pattern for several in the neighbourhood (including Barrington and South Petherton, qq.v.). The pillar base outside was discovered in the 19th century when the church was extended again to its original size after contraction in the 15th (when the N chapel was built to rehouse a chantry).

Ilchester could not live up to its 13th-century prosperity. For 100 years it had to yield its county town status to neighbouring Somerton, and it was crippled by the loss of valuable grazing rights and by heavy taxation. From 1361 it ceased to send representatives to Parliament, and by 1502 its three remaining parishes were united. But some prosperity returned with inclosures in the 16th century, and the county gaol had returned, bringing business of a sort. And business of a sort returned when representatives were again chosen from 1621, at the request of Sir Robert Phelips of Montacute (q.v.).

The medieval gaol stood on an island in the middle of Ilchester Bridge (which although superficially modern is of *c.* 1200). It was replaced by one just over the river in NORTHOVER, which was fortified during the Civil War and was so overcrowded with Quakers, other nonconformists, and Monmouth rebels in the late 17th century that prisoners had to be lodged in the town. The prison buildings were extended in 1789 and later included 'refractory' and 'misdemeanour' wards constructed with prison labour. The brutality of William Bridle, the Governor, was exposed by Henry Hunt, the radical politician imprisoned there after the Peterloo demonstrations of 1819 and resulted in a Parliamentary inquiry and Bridle's dismissal. Public executions were held in a field by the Yeovil road until the new drop over the main entrance was built in 1811. The gaol was closed in 1843 and only part of its laundry and bakehouse survive, the rest having been made into a private garden.

Much of the town's physical appearance, notably the regular early-19th-century houses, derives from its Parliamentary history. Between 1621 and 1832 there were at least 19 disputed elections, and the electors were said to be 'poor and corrupt, without honour, morals, or attachment to any man or party'. Hence the price of a vote rose from £5 in 1702 to £30 in 1784, and rival borough-mongers spent enormous sums for control, Richard Troward £40,000 in 1790 and Sir William Manners £53,000 in 1802. Even such sums did not guarantee success. Manners, a Tory whose 'insane intolerance' was well known, cajoled by offering his (successful) support for the proposed new route of the London road through the town, and then threatened. Indeed, after elections in 1802, 1812, and 1818 he demolished many houses (100 in 1812), putting the occupants in rented tenements and inns, thus taking away their votes. Then enter Lord Darlington, a Whig, who built two blocks of houses in the town and leased land at the Mead, just outside the town (seen from the A303 to Ilminster) to build yet more. His candidates won the next two elections. But small wonder that the Reform Bill removed Ilchester's franchise, though among its MPs had been the poet Edmund Waller (1624–5) and the playwright Richard Brinsley Sheridan (1807).

One of the oldest houses in the town, the so-called 'Manor House', dates from the mid 17th century, and cannot therefore have been the birthplace of Roger Bacon (b. *c.* 1214).

In NORTHOVER, over the river, stands the 18th-century Darlington House, recalling Ilchester's borough-monger. The church of St Andrew, on its hill-top site, is largely a rebuilding of 1821 but represents a minster church which in the 11th century was the religious centre of a wide area. One and a half miles NE at the Royal Naval Air Station at YEOVILTON, established in 1940, is the Fleet Air Arm Museum housing a fine collection of aircraft including Concorde 002.

Ilminster Som. 2 B3

As its name implies this was a Saxon missionary centre, the minster on the River Isle; and it is said that the church was founded by King Ine (d. 726). That, at least, was the claim made by its later owners, the monks of Muchelney, in a charter in their archives – forged, almost certainly, but probably true all the same. The town was at the centre of a large agricultural parish and had three mills and a market by 1086.

The A303 is not a bypass, although it takes most of the through traffic from the town centre; it was, in fact, one of two parallel streets on the hill slope which marked out the medieval town, and a house on Strawberry Bank has a late-medieval wall painting. Further down the valley is the charming market place and shopping centre, the minster and Court Barton. The open-sided market hall (rebuilt *c.* 1813), the George Hotel (where Princess Victoria stayed with her mother just before she became Queen), and the Georgian houses in Court Barton nicely demonstrate the 18th-century prosperity of the town which for a century had been an important cloth-making and gloving centre. But the minster suggests great prosperity in the later Middle Ages.

The superb crossing tower so reminiscent of the central tower at Wells Cathedral with battlements and pinnacles, rich Somerset tracery in the bell openings, and the delicately finished stair turret, stands over a N transept that rivals Crewkerne's attempt to create a building of glass. The Wadham chapel was probably built after a bequest from Sir William Wadham (d. 1452) of Merrifield, who lies there with his wife under a splendid brass.

Near William lie another couple, Nicholas (d. 1618) and Dorothy Wadham. Their tomb was already needing attention only 15 years after they were buried; Thomas Gerard noticed when writing his *Particular Description of Somerset*. It was, most appropriately, restored in 1899 by the eminent Oxford architect Sir Thomas G. Jackson, for Jackson was both a former Fellow and the historian of the College that Nicholas and Dorothy founded, Wadham College.

Behind the church in Court Barton is a 15th-century chantry house, partly Georgianized, and the former grammar school, founded by Humphrey Walrond in 1549 but successor to a school at least a century older.

WHITELACKINGTON (1 mile NE) and DILLINGTON HOUSE (1 mile N) are both associated with the Speke family. John Hanning Speke (d. 1864), the explorer of Africa is buried at another Speke home, DOWLISHWAKE,

(2 miles SE). Whitelackington was their main home in the 17th century, where they were visited by the Duke of Monmouth on his Western Progress in 1680. For years they showed a tree in the park under which he sat to touch people for the King's Evil. In return for their friendship, the unfortunate Charles Speke, the only member of the family Judge Jeffreys could lay hands on, was condemned for shaking the Duke's hand.

The church, dating from the 13th century, includes monuments to the family of a former vicar; the most notable is Charles James Brooke, Rajah of Sarawak.

The last Speke heiress, Mary, married Frederick, Lord North, Prime Minister under George III 1770–82, under whom the American Colonies were lost. He was, nevertheless, a man without a personal enemy. Dillington, then a small house, was one of his country retreats. The present house, is largely a 19th-century

St Mary's Ilminster

remodelling. When the North family was in residence they certainly kept up style: the 'head' servants for an ordinary dinner managed to consume

a dish of fish, a sirloin of beef roasted, a loin of veal with cauliflower, carrots etc., for the first course, and for the second a roast turkey, a hare, pigeon pie, fried oysters, chicken tarts, laver etc.

The house later became the home of the Vaughan-Lee family, who built the imposing stables and created the gardens and arboretum. The whole is now the Somerset County Council's Dillington House College, and the stable block has been converted into a theatre complex.

Iron Acton   Avon   5 B3

'The farmstead by the oak trees' is what Acton means; and by the late 13th century iron stone had been dug for long enough to give the additional name. Samuel Rudder in the late 18th century referred to the heaps of cinders still to be seen in the neighbourhood, but they may have been related to the local coal workings in and around ENGINE COMMON ($\frac{1}{2}$ mile NE). Iron Acton stood on a main route to Bristol and its narrow curving main street with irregular dark-brown stone houses in local Pennant leads to its splendid church on a raised site well above even the causewayed pavement. What strikes first is the tower, with its blind arcade and ogee arches, thought to have been completed c. 1439, on the grounds that a tomb in the church declares 'Here lyeth Robert Poyntz Lord of Iron Acton and this stepyl here maked'. But is it likely that the figure of a knight on the 15th-century parapet of the tower is Sir John Poyntz (d. 1376)?; and the damaged w door looks early 14th century. So is the 'stepyl' the unusual churchyard cross of the early 15th century, but almost with an air of the 18th? The actual cross has disappeared, but its surrounding shafts and arches are undoubtedly pre-Reformation, and include shields with symbols of the Passion and the arms of Acton and FitzNicoll, indicating a direct connexion with Robert Poyntz.

Another feature of the church most noticeable from the outside is its short but lofty nave lit with very late, square-topped windows. The whole building is Perpendicular, though not of one build. The SE chapel contains tombs of the Poyntz family dating from 1376, and of later local gentry. Notice, on the wall above, a 17th-century funeral helm, a spur, and a piece of leather surcoat.

The old Poyntz home, Iron Acton Court, N of the village on the B4059, probably dates from the 15th century, and is approached under an elaborate archway with Renaissance details.

Kelston   Avon   see Bitton

Keynsham   Avon   5 B4   (pop. 19,018)

Keynsham has suffered from its position on a main road between Bristol and Bath, and although now bypassed, the rebuilding of its centre and its rapidly increased size since the Second Word War make old Keynsham difficult to find. In Leland's day it was 'a poore market town, and ruinus', for it had depended upon the Abbey here, and this had been dissolved in 1539 and rapidly destroyed.

The Abbey, a Victorine house like Bristol, was founded c. 1167 by William, Earl of Gloucester. Leland, in fact, says there was a small priory at Keynsham already, and that both William and his son Robert were buried in the Abbey; there may well be truth in the statement, for certainly there was a Saxon minster here whose 'parish' stretched as far s as Chew Stoke and Publow (qq.v.). The monastery was well endowed, but its standards were not always high, the canons being told in 1350 not to keep sporting dogs, and in 1451, among many other orders, not to go out at night, not to invite women into the monastery, and not to employ their own washerwomen.

The Abbey buildings lay on the sloping ground between the parish church and the River Chew, in the middle of a precinct whose boundary ran down the E side of the old High Street. It has never been fully excavated, and most of the cloister, the w end of the nave, and some of the conventual buildings now lie under the bypass. The railway cut through a graveyard c. 1835. Norman and later fragments and a fine collection of encaustic tiles have been found on the site, and some now decorate rockeries in Station Road, near the imposing entrance to a mansion which the Bridges family built. The history of the abbey church is thus not clearly known, though a new Lady Chapel was built c. 1314, when Sir John Bitton left money for the project, and late-15th-century piers and other details suggest that it follows the pattern of most religious houses in the West Country which spent large sums on rebuilding in the last few years of their existence.

The parish church now dominates the scene, its tower a bold piece of Somerset Gothic, but built in 1634 to replace a N transeptal tower which collapsed two years earlier in a storm. Eighteenth-century neglect, followed by 19th-century restoration, has left the interior over-Victorian, though the lancets in the chancel are of the 13th century and the rest outwardly Perpendicular. The pulpit is of the 17th century, the font dated 1725. The Bridges family, owners of the abbey site, ensured their prominence in death by two large tombs, one a chest, the other a vast hanging monument.

The Abbey had a market and annual fair from 1307, and by the 1530s owned two fulling mills on the Chew at the edge of the precinct, the site of one now topped by a bandstand. Water power brought quite different business to Keynsham in 1706 when Abraham Darby opened two brass mills, one on the Avon and one on the Chew. He moved to Coalbrookdale (Salop) a few years later to develop iron-smelting, and the Keynsham mills were taken over by Nehemiah Champion, whose complex of mills in the area around Bristol produced copper, brass and iron plates, wire, pans, and many kinds of vessels. The Chew mill at Keynsham closed in the 1890s, but the Avon mill, working until 1927, produced brass plate for shells in the First World War.

Two miles SE towards Bath is SALTFORD, where the church seems to be largely of the early 19th century with an earlier tower and a fine font. The porch contains a tombstone recording the burial of the feet of Frances Flood on 1 April 1723 after what appears to have been a terrible case of smallpox:

> Stop, Reader, and a wonder see
> As strange as e'er was known;
> My feet fell off from my body
> In the midst of the bone.
> I had no surgeon for my help,
> But God Almighty's aid
> On Whom I always will rely
> And never be afraid.
> Though here beneath interr'd they lie
> Destruction for to see
> Yet they shall live and reunite
> To all Eternity.

West of the church stands the manor house, one of the oldest inhabited houses in the country, for its 17th-century front masks a two-storeyed Norman house with a first-floor hall, traces of wall painting of c. 1300, and evidence of an early-Tudor screen.

Kilve   Som. *see* **East Quantoxhead**

Kingston St Mary   Som.   2 A2
The red sandstone of the tower at Kingston, standing above the village against the slope of the Quantocks, is nothing short of memorable. A. K. Wickham calls it the 'perfected model' of a group of three Somerset towers (the others are Staple Fitzpaine and Isle Abbots) which are 'among the great masterpieces of English architecture', and dates it to c. 1480–90, part of a scheme which outwardly was a complete rebuilding. But inside, the 13th-century arcade shows that here was an important church at an early date, possibly boasting a central tower. Even after the expense of the tower, more money was forthcoming for the benches, a large set, one dated 1522 and another with a weaver's shuttle; cloth was again providing the funds. The benches around the font are a piece of history in themselves, carved with symbols of the Passion and defaced in an age when enthusiasm had priority over taste. The fan-vaulted porch is of c. 1520.

The huge tomb in the s chapel is thought to be of John de la Warre of HESTERCOMBE (2 miles SE), who fought at Poitiers (1356) with the Black Prince and somehow acquired the sword of King John of France. Hestercombe House, now the headquarters of the Somerset Fire Brigade, is outwardly a rather monstrous creation of 1875 for the Portman family. The view from its terraces, however, is superb, and so are the terraces themselves, part of a garden created by Lutyens and Gertrude Jekyll, and including water-channels for irises set in a square parterre flanked on one side by a long pergola. The garden is open by appointment with the Chief Fire Officer.

Kingsweston   Avon *see* **Westbury on Trym**

Kingswood   Avon   5 B4
It is difficult to discern Kingswood's origin from its present semi-industrial landscape, but its name (as so often) provides the key; though the area E and SE of Bristol including Oldland and Hanham was known in the early 13th century as the Wood of Furches and was, with the barton (hence Barton Hill) and the Forest and Chace of Keynsham (q.v.), part of the land that went with the office of Constable of Bristol Castle. It became known as the Forest or Chace of Kingswood by Edward I's reign. Like all medieval forest areas it was not completely wooded, but the Crown had absolute control within its boundaries under Forest Law, and frequently sold licences to others to hunt or cut or dig. Thus in 1276 Petronilla de Vivonia was allowed to dig coal within the Forest, and Thomas de Berkeley in 1283 was permitted to hunt fox, hare, badger, and cat, but was to take no deer nor chase rabbits in the royal warrens.

Over the years the royal claims were whittled away by coal-miners, hunters, and local landowners: one of the keepers' lodges was turned into an ale house; goats and sheep ruined the young trees and barked the old ones; miners cut down hollies for pit props. In theory some 4,298 acres of forest existed, but by the early 17th century much of the woodland had disappeared. A map of the forest made at the time shows that it began just E of Bristol at Lawford's Gate, at the end of Old Market. From there it stretched away to Barton Hill, the 'barley farm' of Bristol castle, and thence to MANGOTSFIELD. Its N boundary was vaguely marked by the River Frome, interrupted by a succession of water mills, but had clearly retreated S, to the road to Westerleigh (q.v.), which then passed a few country houses and by the 'quarrs' and the 'new pools', the flooded quarry workings which became FISHPONDS. DOWNEND, further out, occurs by 1573, and is famous as the birthplace in 1848 of Dr W. G. Grace. He made his cricket debut in 1857 at Mangotsfield.

'If you have a mind to convert Indians', someone remarked to George Whitefield in 1739, 'there are colliers enough at Kingswood.' He and John Wesley saw the miners as a challenge, and after only two months in 1739 Wesley had begun a school in Kingswood and was preaching regularly throughout the area – Connam, on the s side, Hanham Mount, Rose Green, near the fishponds, and at the school itself to crowds of 5,000 miners at a time. In 1748 he also founded Kingswood School for the sons of ministers, which in later years was transferred to Bath.

Coal mining in the Kingswood area continued until 1949, but it was by no means the only, or even the most important industry. From the 19th century boots and shoes took on a significant rôle after the development of the riveting process. Brass wire, pins, iron ore, and zinc have all been manufactured in the area of the old royal forest and have left their traces on the landscape, less now in the form of surviving factories and mine workings, but still clear in the prominent chapels of nonconformity and in rarer traces of workers' housing like the terraces around the cotton factory at Barton Hill.

Langport Som. 2 C2

There are two parts to Langport: the residential hill-top and the commercial centre below; the Hill and Beneathcliff, as they used to say. The oldest part is on the hill, where the church stands beside what was once a market place, of which only the pump remains to tell the tale. The hill is a promontory overlooking the moors and the Langport Gap, where the Parrett passes through an easily flooded valley. The place was defended by earthworks in Saxon times and again during the Civil War, and the most obvious survival is the Hanging Chapel, a barrel-vaulted gateway with a former chapel above, probably dating from the 15th century.

Cheapside and Bow Street, the present main shopping streets, run along an artificial causeway to the river, a piece of civil engineering which probably gave the town its name – long market. An old tradition, accepted on philological grounds, makes it the site of the battle of Llongborth in the later 6th century. Langport had a mint by c. 930, a sure sign of defensive strength and commercial life; but it was only a small parish, carved out of the older and more important Huish Episcopi. In fact Langport's church was therefore only a chapelry of Huish, a cause of bitter jealousy for many years. The two churches were said in 1548 to be only 'a bird-bolt shot' apart, but the townsmen of Langport made sure that threatened demolition never came about.

At the end of Bow Street the road crosses the Parrett and the course of the old railway. At least one early-19th-century warehouse indicates that the river was still used for transport (mostly coal, lime, and stone) until the 1850s. In the 15th and 16th centuries Langport had been an important distribution centre: woad for dyeing cloth came from Spain through Southampton and then by road; along the Parrett from Bridgwater came Atlantic herrings, Cheshire salt, and other commodities. The railway (from Yeovil to Taunton) came in 1853, but Langport West Station (there was another at the other end of the town on the main London line) has now given place to a trading estate and road transport.

But 'port' means market first of all, a market held both on the hill and at Cheapside at its foot. In the 17th century eels and duck were a speciality:

well furnished with fowle in the winter time, and full of pect eles as they call them, because they take them in those waters by pecking an eale speare on them where they lye in their beds but I cannot comend the goodness of them; marry the fowle is fetched hence farr and neere, but the waters being abroad such as are sent for it many times missing the Cawsway goe a fishing instead of getting fowle.   (Gerard)

In the early 19th century there was another gruesome product remembered by William Quekett (d. 1888), one of a remarkable family of brothers: the moors covered with geese, kept and each year plucked bare for their feathers.

From the later 18th century Langport depended for most of its business on the firm of Stuckey and Bagehot, who began as merchants and maltsters and then turned bankers. By the turn of the century they were trading as far afield as Manchester and Liverpool. By 1866 they owned 14 East Indiamen and 19 barges. When the bank was taken over in 1909 (later absorbed into the National Westminster) its banknote circulation was second only to that of the Bank of England. Walter Bagehot (1826–77), the economist, gained his early experience in the family bank. Some Georgian houses at the foot of the hill, the Guildhall (1733) and the Langport Arms (formerly the Swan, and dating back as an inn to the early 16th century) are reminders of Langport's past prosperity. Nineteenth-century elegance, even opulence, is up on the hill.

Langport church, in grey lias with Ham stone dressings, is largely a rebuilding of the late Middle Ages, but the rare 12th-century carved lintel over the s doorway presumably comes from an earlier building on the site which, from details in the N aisle, was as long as the present nave. The new work, at least partly the gift of John Heyron (d. 1501), includes an eastern vestry. The portcullis on the E face of the tower may refer to Margaret Beaufort, lady of the manor, or be a statement of loyalty to her son Henry VII or her grandson Henry VIII. The E window has a remarkable collection of medieval glass including the figure of Joseph of Arimathea carrying his two 'cruets', the one containing Christ's blood, the other His sweat.

Langport was garrisoned for the King during the Civil War, and a rampart then built is still on the NE side of the hill. It availed them nothing on 10 July 1645, for a battle took place further E along the Somerton road, where Goring's men were completely swept aside by Fairfax and the Parliamentary forces. Cromwell described the victory as the Long Sutton Mercy (the troops had marched from there), and compared it to Naseby in importance. A 50-gun ship in the Commonwealth navy was called Langport to commemorate the event.

Half a mile E at HUISH EPISCOPI is one of Somerset's most famous views, the church tower seen through the orchards. The grey-and-golden tower shows the local 16th-century masons at their best, though the s door is equally elaborate work of the 12th century reddened by a fire which seems to have destroyed much of an earlier

Huish Episcopi church

church in the early 13th century. In the 14th century its chancel was rebuilt and the transepts erected each side of a central tower. A century or more later the s transept was rebuilt in two stages as a short aisle when the new tower was built, topped with fine pierced parapets and finials, its lights flanked by elaborate niches and divided by traceried bands. Inside, the light and grace of Somerset Perpendicular are seen at their best in a church full of light and free from overwhelming furniture. The E window of the s chapel, the Adoration of the Magi, is a late Burne-Jones design by Morris & Co. The church was depicted on a postage stamp in 1972.

Lansdown　Avon *see* **Bath**

Leigh on Mendip　Som. *see* **Mells**

Little Badminton　Avon *see* **Great Badminton**

Little Sodbury　Avon *see* **Old Sodbury**

Long Ashton　Avon　5 B4

Long Ashton – 'long', of course, because the village stretches for more than a mile – enshrines in its largest house, Ashton Court, the peculiarly English phenomenon of the creation of a gentry family. The Smyths, who came to Bristol from the Forest of Dean *c.* 1500, one as a hooper, the other as a merchant, in the next generation made money and invested in land. John Smyth, son of the merchant, died in 1556 the proud possessor of goods and money worth well over £2,000 including cash and plate worth more than half that sum; and he had land and houses in various parts of Bristol and Somerset, including a manor house and its lands at Long Ashton bought in 1545 for £920. His wealth was made (so his surviving accounts interestingly reveal) by exporting Somerset and Wiltshire wool, Welsh leather, wheat, and Mendip lead to France and Spain, and importing wine, oil, iron, and dyestuffs, much of which reached the local clothiers.

John's medieval house is still there, at least in part, surrounded by additions of the late 16th century, to which was added in 1633–5 a remarkable sw wing, in just the same spirit (and from the same pattern books) as the additions that Smyth relatives put up at Brympton D'Evercy and Hinton St George (qq.v.). Further extensions were made, notably the N wing, in 1805. Smyths lived there continuously from 1553 until 1946, no longer, after the great John's death, content to be merchants and mayors of Bristol but, with Sir Hugh (1575–1627) one of the most considerable landowners in Somerset, member of an embassy to the Archduke of Austria; with his son Thomas (1609–42) allied to the Pouletts and with a seat in Parliament; or with later members of the family whose mining interests in Bedminster and Ashton Vale enabled them to diversify their wealth and position. Ashton Court, owned by Bristol Corporation since 1959, is

not at present open to the public, though its extensive walled park, the work of several generations in the 16th and 17th centuries, who concerned themselves with stocking it with deer and bringing cattle from Wales to fatten on its rich grassland, is open.

The creation of the park evidently involved the destruction of some of the medieval settlement, for the parish church would not otherwise have stood so awkwardly at the end of the village. It is a fine, late-14th-century church, the tower built, as the coat of arms indicates, by the Lyon family (one of several families who were lords of manors here until the Smyths came along and bought them all up). One of the chapels in the church belonged to the Chokke family, and in it stands the ornate tomb of Sir Richard Chokke (d. 1483) and his wife (d. 1484). Sir Richard was a Judge of the Common Pleas under Edward IV, and would have served Richard III too, but died the day before the coronation, when he would have received the King's gift of 7 yd of red cloth. His English will established a chantry for his family and gave away a large collection of plate and possessions, after requiring a funeral 'honestly wᵗoute pompe or bost after the sadde discrecion' of his executors. He did not specify the tomb he was to occupy, for his wife was still alive, only

　　that there be made a scuptur making mencion of the
　　day moneth and yer of my decesse.

The church also possesses a screen of the general Midlands type, but certainly the best in this area. Near the church, and forming with it a delightful group of houses and a farm, is a 15th-century barn, and the early-19th-century schoolroom.

Low Ham　Som. *see* **High Ham**

Luccombe　Som. *see* **Selworthy**

Lullington　Som. *see* **Beckington**

Lyng　Som. *see* **Athelney**

Lytes Cary　Som.　2 D2　(NT)

In the flat and almost treeless country 3½ miles N of Ilchester, just off the Fosse Way in the parish of Charlton Mackrell, stands a house of great charm and national associations. It seems to have been begun in the mid 14th century by Peter le Lyte (d. 1348), whose great-grandfather William le Lyte had held an estate called Cary here in the 1280s, but who only then, when he built the house, added his name to the property, to distinguish it from the farm he had left, now called Cooks Cary, on the other side of Cary Lane. The move took place *c.* 1343, and included the transfer of his private chaplain, to serve in the chapel, the oldest surviving part of the house.

Peter le Lyte's house with its additions by Thomas Lyte (d. *c.* 1469) and John Lyte (d. 1566) formed a rectangle around a small courtyard, and until the 15th century the chapel stood unconnected at its E corner.

Thomas Lyte rebuilt Peter's house, now represented by the hall and screens passage, but once having service rooms at the NW end. John Lyte probably completed the courtyard buildings, but all that survives is the charming solar wing, including the great parlour below and the great chamber above, lit by the superb oriel bay dated 1533. The roof of the hall is original work of the 15th century, having arch-braced collar-beam trusses, three rows of cusped windbraces, and quatrefoils and carved angels on the cornices. The fireplace, too, is original, but the screen and other features are part of John Lyte's improvements – perhaps at the instigation of his wife Elizabeth Horsey, for his arms and hers can be seen in many places. Yet his own additions were later to be themselves improved, notably by the Jacobean panelling and the chimney piece in the great parlour.

The chapel was restored in 1631 by the third Thomas Lyte, the antiquarian, who began the series of coats of arms on the frieze to commemorate his family's marriages and who put up the two tablets, one to record his work and the other a copy of a window once in Charlton Mackrell parish church showing his earliest known ancestor.

The Lytes lived in the house with hardly a break from its beginning until 1755. Apart from the builders the family produced Henry (c. 1529–1607) who translated and edited Dodoens' *Cruydeboeck*, ever after to be known as *Lyte's Herbal*, first published in 1578. Lyte's own additions included information on the 'Cary Bridge Pear' and the 'Somerton Pear'. His son Thomas (c. 1568–1638), the antiquarian, compiled a pedigree for James I, flattering the King by tracing his descent from Brutus the Trojan. The King presented him with a jewel containing a royal miniature, evidently the work of Nicholas Hilliard, and a painting of Thomas wearing the jewel is in the Somerset County Museum at Taunton.

The Dickinsons of Kingweston owned the house for a century until it was bought in 1907 by Sir Walter Jenner. The NW range had already been rebuilt as a farmhouse, and Jenner built the SW range in a late-17th-century style with internal fittings including carving from a Wren church in London. Jenner also restored the surviving medieval and Tudor house and laid out the gardens with entirely appropriate yew and grass. Even the essential modern water tower is marvellously disguised as a dovecote. The NT acquired the house by gift of Sir Walter in 1948.

Mangotsfield Avon *see* **Kingswood**

Marshfield Avon 5 C4
There is no marsh here on this high, open ground; the name refers to the nearby mere or boundary between the ancient counties of Wiltshire and Gloucestershire. This is corn-growing country on the top of the Cotswolds, which in the 17th and early 18th centuries produced malt for Bristol and Bath, and has left behind large malthouses in the town. The town, however, owed its obvious prosperity to the inevitable Cotswold wool. To a village clustered around its Norman church a piece of urban development was added c. 1265 along what is now High Street. Marshfield became a borough, with a regular Tuesday market and two fairs a year, all for the benefit of its lords, the canons of Keynsham Abbey. By the mid 14th century it was the fourth most prosperous town in Gloucestershire, and it continued to expand with an eastward extension of the built-up area and to show its prosperity in a rebuilt church.

Most of the prominent houses in the town reflect the wealth of the 17th and 18th centuries, notably the Crispe almshouses (1619), the Tolzey Hall (1690, rebuilt 1793), and several distinguished inns taking advantage of Marshfield's position on a main road. The bypass now mercifully takes most of the 20th-century traffic away.

All that is left of the Norman church is a blocked arch on the S side of the arcade which implies a central tower. The rest is mostly Perpendicular, and includes two choir chapels and traces of a chantry, presumably the site of the two chantries of Jesus and St Clement, and possibly also a chapel for the guild which existed just before the Reformation. The furnishings are contemporary, and include two pillar piscinae and very late sedilia. The 17th- and 18th-century monuments declare in death the prosperity of Marshfield's people as eloquently as the Cotswold ashlar in the streets outside.

Less sophisticated, but of much more ancient origin, are the Marshfield Mummers, whose play is performed on Boxing Day each year. The play is the traditional conflict between Good and Evil, and the players disguise themselves with makeshift costumes of strips of newspaper.

Marston Bigot Som. *see* **Nunney**

Martock Som. 2 C3
Take a Martock man by the collar and shake him, recommended Defoe, and beans will rattle in his belly. A century earlier Thomas Gerard had noted that Martock was 'seated in the fattest place of the earth of this county, especially for arable, which makes the inhabitants so fat in their purses'. The quality of even the small houses in Martock itself, and in the surrounding hamlets of Hurst, Bower Hinton, Coat, Stapleton, and Witcombe, certainly bears witness to agricultural prosperity in the 17th and 18th centuries, and Martock itself expanded considerably in the 19th. Its centre, with market house (c. 1753) and obelisk, has something of an urban air which a carefully hidden modern shopping precinct has encouraged.

But Martock has two earlier gems, its church and the Treasurer's House (NT). The church, possibly in origin a minster, was certainly in existence in 1156 when it belonged to the Abbey of Mont St Michel. About 1190 it was somehow acquired by Bishop Reginald of Bath;

The Marshfield mummers

one of his successors, Bishop Jocelin, in 1226 divided the income, giving half, and the patronage of the living, to the Treasurers of Wells Cathedral. How many Treasurers lived in the house is not known, though John de Langton certainly did. Whilst he was Chancellor of England under Edward I, he left the Great Seal here when he went abroad in 1297, and came back in person to fetch it. Other Treasurers included figures of national importance like Simon Langham, who held the office from 1368 to 1376 after resigning the archbishopric of Canterbury on being appointed Cardinal. Three hundred years later the Cathedral Treasurer was the famous Headmaster of Westminster, Dr Richard Busby (Treasurer 1660–95), though in his time the house and estate were let, and he probably never darkened its doors; he hardly ever went to Wells, either.

The Treasurer's House comprises a medieval hall and cross wing; the wing has a window of the later 13th century and the hall was probably rebuilt *c.* 1290. A kitchen wing was added beside the hall in the late 15th or early 16th century, when the whole was remodelled, with a fireplace and new windows. The gateway belongs to this same period, replacing a more elaborate structure with a chamber over the entrance.

Opposite stands the church, almost, but not quite, a work of the early 16th century; not quite, because the E window of the chancel is a classic five-light lancet of the 13th century; and on the s side of the building are the remains of a 14th-century transept, suggesting a central tower which a 13th-century church almost certainly possessed. The tower's removal and replacement at the w end was probably accompanied by the new nave, aisles, chapels, and clerestory, covered so magnificently by the richly carved and painted roof (though most of the original paint can only be seen close to!) made in 1513, and at least since the 18th century a drain on parish finances. The latest restoration is only recently complete. A curiosity on the N side of the church is a buttress with footholds, cut in the 18th century to allow the recovery of fives balls from the leads.

Just w of the churchyard is the site of the manor house of Martock. At the end of the 16th century the property was held by William Stanley, Lord Monteagle (d. 1581), from whom it passed to his son-in-law Edward Parker, Lord Morley, who lost the estate to the Crown in 1592 because of his debts. Edward's son William has a particular place in national history, for it was he whom Guy Fawkes warned not to attend Parliament on the night the Gunpowder Plot was to be carried out. Monteagle's report to the government brought him a reward of £200 in land and a pension of £500. The return of his forfeited family holding was part of the deal.

A few yards sw of the church is the Old Court House, formerly the parish house, where a grammar school was held from 1662 to 1862. An earlier grammar school had been started in the 16th century, and from 1605 was under Thomas Farnaby or Bainrafe (an anagram of his name). He later founded the first great private school in London and acquired a European reputation as an educationalist.

Martock's prosperity was not exclusively agricultural; clothing, gloving, canvas-making, poultry appliances, and engineering have now given way to tent-making and the production of prefabricated wooden buildings. During the agricultural crisis of the 1840s some paupers were assisted by the parish to emigrate to Tasmania. At least one other, Robert Patten Adams (b. 1831), from a prosperous local family of solicitors and wine merchants,

also went there, and later became Solicitor-general of the colony. The present Lord of the manor of Martock lives in Florida.

Meare Som. *see* **Somerset Levels**

Mells Som. 5 C6
'Melles stondith clyving, and hath bene a praty townelet of clothing': so Leland. And he went on to tell how it had belonged to Glastonbury Abbey and that Abbot John Selwood (1456–92) 'seing the welthines there of the people' planned to rebuild the village in the form of an Anthony cross (i.e. with arms of equal length). Only one arm of the cross was completed, still known as New Street; each house there has an unusual plan, having two rooms on the ground floor one each side of a door, with a spiral stair at the rear.

The wealth of the people was evidently based on clothmaking. Fulling had begun by the end of the 13th century and the Abbot of Glastonbury alone had a flock of

Martock

South porch, Mells church

300 sheep in the 15th. Among the prosperous families were the Horners, gentleman farmers under the Abbots for at least a century before 'Little Jack' put in his thumb. And despite the stories of misappropriation of title-deeds on their way to London after the Dissolution of Glastonbury, all was quite legal. John Horner the younger managed to find the huge sum of £1,831 19s. 11¼d. in 1543, and the Glastonbury manors of Mells, Leigh on Mendip, and Nunney (q.v.) were his. And Horners stayed at Mells, living where Abbot Selwood had built his 'praty Maner Place of stone', until Mrs Raymond Asquith, the last of the family, died over 400 years later. The house has, of course, been altered, and Elizabethan gables peep over the high churchyard wall.

The church, and especially its tower, is a fine example of Somerset Perpendicular. The tower was under construction in 1446 and the whole was finished, so Leland said, 'yn tyme of mynde . . . by the hole paroche'. A London draper called Garlande paid for the remarkable two-storeyed, polygonal vestry; the whole richly decorated building is a striking demonstration of Somerset's wealth in the later Middle Ages.

What makes Mells even more remarkable is that it contains examples of the work of most of the leading artists of the early 20th century, brought together too often by family tragedy and by the influence of Lady Horner. It is a vignette of the politics and social life of England in the years before and during the First World War. Eric Gill designed the inscriptions on the memorials to Raymond Asquith, eldest son of H. H. Asquith, the Prime Minister, who was killed in the War, and to Mark Horner (d. 1908). Gill also designed the tablets on the water taps in the village which stand as a lasting and practical memorial to Mark Horner. Burne-Jones contributed the memorial to Laura Lyttleton; Munnings and Lutyens to the Edward Horner memorial (1917); Nicholson the window in the Horner Chapel. Lutyens also designed the village War Memorial, parts of the manor house, and Mells Park House. And in the churchyard there are memorials to Reginald McKenna, successively First Lord of the Admiralty, Home Secretary, and Chancellor of the Exchequer under Asquith; Siegfried Sassoon; and Mgr Ronald Knox, the latter spending his last years at the manor house.

Mells is a place of curious contrasts, for from 1744 until 1844 it was an industrial centre. Water in the Wadbury Valley which had powered fulling mills in the Middle Ages now drove the Fussell edge-tool works. When Napoleon threatened invasion in 1804 an inventory of the goods of James and John Fussell was taken in case of loss. Between them they had 1,700 dozen scythes, 500 dozen reaphooks, 160 dozen spades and shovels, 12 dozen hooks and axes in stock; and their works included water-wheels, forges, hammers, anvils, and bellows. Nature managed to conceal the site, but industrial archaeologists are trying to recover what remains of this remarkable local industry.

LEIGH (*pron.* lie) ON MENDIP, 3 miles sw, was linked with Mells in several ways. It was part of the medieval manor of Mells and also part of the parish. The tower of the church was undoubtedly copied from that of the mother church, but the Norman font shows how much earlier the church's origin may be traced. The simple benches give the interior a unity with the rest of the fabric, all dating, of course, from the late 15th century. The roofs of nave and chancel are, as Pevsner says, 'excellent'.

The village also contributed to the Mells industrial scene, producing most of the handles for spades and shovels at least until the end of the 19th century.

Three miles NW at the end of a beech avenue is a perfect 18th-century composition, Babington House and, across the lawn, its church – all that remains of the medieval village of BABINGTON. The house dates from *c.* 1700, with a wing of 1790. St Margaret's church is one of Somerset's rarities, built in 1750 and virtually unchanged, with the original box pews and panelling. The apsidal east end with its blue dome balances perfectly the cupola at the west end above the small tower.

The Mendips Som./Avon

The first part of the name means hill – Celtic in origin; the second part seems to mean valley, which sounds like a contradiction. But although from the w the Mendips appear as a great scarp that stretches from Crook Peak to Pen Hill (1,002 ft) above Wells (q.v.), behind is a country of ridges and valleys with a character all its own. The scarp, most of which has been declared an area of outstanding natural beauty, is the real Mendip, in landscape unlike anything elsewhere in Somerset. The roads and fields are lined with stone walls, like the Cotswolds; but this is different country, higher at its peaks, rising to 1,065 ft on Black Down above Burrington; somehow with wider horizons, broken by belts of trees planted as windbreaks by improving landowners in the 18th century; and scattered settlement of isolated farms and one main village, PRIDDY (5 A6).

For some the fascination of Mendip is underground, the limestone caverns which insinuate their way into the bowels of the earth and reveal the earliest traces of man and beast, washed down from the surface or lying where they sheltered in life. Worked flints found in a fissure at WESTBURY SUB MENDIP (5 A6) were left by Man (or more likely *Homo erectus*) living on Mendip nearly half a million years ago; and the caves at Cheddar and Wookey Hole (qq.v) have produced remains of rhinoceros and cat, reindeer, wolf, and arctic fox, which point to an age of glaciation here some 35,000 years ago. Then, about 7,000 B.C., as the ice receded, Man returned, 'Cheddar Man' of Gough's Cave. Flints and monuments fill in the story, notably at Priddy where the four Neolithic circles were constructed for some religious purpose *c.* 2,500 B.C. There are only a few long barrows, the contemporary burial cairns, but in the next millenium the

The hurdle pile, Priddy

Beaker people left their dead here in great numbers, nine round barrows forming the largest group, also near Priddy, and eight more on Ashen Hill nearby.

And then the Romans came for the lead that lay at CHARTERHOUSE (5 A5), constructing their roads along the ridge and providing both a theatre and a fort, to entertain and to protect the workers in the mining town. The name Charterhouse comes from the Carthusian monks of Witham who later owned the property (q.v.), one of the four 'Liberties' into which Mendip was divided by the lead miners by the 16th century. Mining continued at Priddy until 1908, and the landscape still contains its fascinating scars: the 'gruffy' ground where the old pits have collapsed, five tunnels at Charterhouse, overgrown buddle pits, silted reservoirs, and slag heaps. It is an industrial landscape more than 1,000 years old.

Priddy, lone on Mendip height, has a haunting quality. The wide skies are mirrored in its huge church-yard surrounding a church whose fascination is endless: a 13th-century building already with a tower and N aisle, so what was there earlier? And did it, too, have a N tower or N transept? And what is that stone structure by the chancel arch? Surely not a pulpit, for its steps seem to have continued higher; is it an unfinished stone rood-screen? There clearly was money here, if the 15th-century altar frontal is anything to go by; for Priddy was a place of considerable importance.

Down on the green is a pile of hurdles, thatched to protect it from the weather, for if the hurdles should ever disappear, so too will Priddy. Ever since the plague drove one of Wells's fairs up to the healthy heights in 1348, an annual sheep fair has been held each August. Here was a great medieval market centre, where Mendip

wool was collected for the clothiers of the valleys and Mendip sheep bought and sold.

Below Priddy is Ebbor Gorge (NT), impressive and refreshingly uncommercial. The view from the scarp over the mysterious Somerset Levels to the Quantocks (qq.v.) is the best introduction to the mystery that is Somerset.

Midsomer Norton Avon 5 B5
The town began as an offshoot of Stratton-on-the-Fosse (q.v.) – hence Norton for north *tun*; and because there are so many Nortons in the county it was usually known as Norton Canonicorum in the Middle Ages, for the canons of the Augustinian Priory of Merton (Surrey) owned the rectory estate. The 'Midsomer' came later, after the priory had been dissolved, and is a reminder of the annual midsummer fair held on the patronal fes-tival of the parish church of St John. John Wesley had another explanation which he entered in his *Journal* after his first visit in 1767: that midsummer was the only time when the place was accessible.

Despite its coal Midsomer Norton is not industrial-ized, and even its public buildings, save for the Italianate Town Hall (1860), were formerly private houses. The original village can still be seen in the older houses around the church, which is itself rather a newcomer. Its tower is of the 17th century and bears a statue of Charles II; the rest of the church was rebuilt in 1830, and the chancel and Lady Chapel belong to the 20th. Wesley called the old church a neat and cheerful build-ing when he came in 1784, but then, he had always been made welcome: the rector once stayed to hear him preach, and the curate actually read prayers for him in 1785 and, said Wesley, read them well.

So, unusually, the Roman Catholic church is prob-ably the oldest building in the town, created by Sir Giles Gilbert Scott from a 15th-century barn and consecrated in 1913. If it is, indeed, a tithe barn, it was presumably built for the owners of the tithe, the canons of Merton. The outstanding decorations and fittings, dating from the 16th century and of foreign as well as of English ori-gin, are an indication of the interest Downside Abbey has for many years shown in the parish.

Milborne Port Som. 3 E3
Milborne Port had impressive beginnings: this far inland the 'port' means market, of course, and there was a mint here between 997 and 1007, though the moneyers took refuge on South Cadbury (q.v.) when times became un-safe. By 1086 the place was a borough, with a prosperous market and at least the foundations of its later industry – cloth-making – in six recorded mills. The prosperity and importance of the town is clear enough from its church, a very fine building of late-Saxon and early-Nor-man date remarkably undamaged by later alterations. Characteristic late-Saxon work is best seen on the s wall of the chancel and in the triangular-topped windows of the (rebuilt) w front, now in the mortuary chapel. When

the nave, N aisle and N transept were rebuilt and enlarged the 18th-centuries galleries and decoration were removed, doubtless to aesthetic advantage, but the embattled parapet on the s side with the names of two wardens and the date 1517 were lost.

Milborne Port sent representatives to three Parliaments in Edward I's time and then from 1640 until, as a typical rotten borough, it was disenfranchised in 1832. Corruption in elections was inevitable when control of the vote belonged to whoever owned nine pieces of land in the borough. The last sitting member, Sir William Coles Medlycott of Ven (see below), actually bought control from the Marquess of Anglesey, after intervention by the Whig borough-monger, the Earl of Darlington, had resulted in the creation of the suburb of New Town to house potential new voters and a fantastic rise in the cost of a vote.

The little town still has traces of past glories: the 18th-century town hall, the guildhall with its reused Norman doorway, the Pump House, a tannery (c. 1800), and a brick-built glove factory (c. 1850). Ven House, on the SE outskirts beside the main road, was built c. 1725 by Nathaniel Ireson, probably for James Medlycott (d. 1731). The grounds were laid out for Thomas Medlycott by Richard Grange in the 1730s. The building is of brick with stone dressings; a large square block, three storeys high, with pilasters and a balustrade. Decimus Burton c. 1835–6 added offices and a conservatory each side of the central block.

The little church at TEMPLE COMBE, 3 miles NE, shown by its name to have once been a possession of the Knights Templar, has a wooden panel painted with the face of Christ, which bears a remarkable resemblance to the face on the Turin Shroud.

Capitals on transept arch, Milborne Port

Milverton　Som.　2 A2

The regular grid pattern of the streets in this large village, and its position around a prominent church on a spur commanding the road through the Vale of Taunton, suggests a Saxon market centre. For long a possession of the Royal House, it was sometimes called a borough in the Middle Ages, though it was hardly a commercial success. Its market was only 'ordinary' in the 17th century, but a prosperous trade in serges and other coarse woollen cloths created a revival in the 18th.

This period was perhaps Milverton's most prosperous, and the Georgian houses in North Street, now happily bereft of the heavy traffic by the bypass, are a delight. Two other houses hold more of the village's elusive history. The Fort or Forts, formerly called Lancasters after the occupiers (see monument in church), was held in the 16th century with land called 'Old Halls'; was this a manor house? The Parsonage or Old House, E of the church, was the residence of the Archdeacons of Taunton, holders of one of the two prebendal estates here. It was built in the late 15th century, and subsequent holders of the estate (though not necessarily occupiers of the house) have included the two main protagonists of the English Reformation, Stephen Gardiner and Thomas Cranmer. One remarkable native was Thomas Young (1773–1829), an accomplished linguist at 14, a doctor, editor of the *Nautical Almanac*, co-decipherer of the Rosetta Stone, and originator of the wave theory of light.

The dark-red sandstone church of St Michael has a Norman font with cross and cable designs, and possessed a tower by c. 1200. The rest is late 14th century and later, the tower unusually plain. The rood-screen includes a dated panel (1540) contemporary with the many bench ends (see the splendid drinker and the Arms of Henry VIII); the stalls are earlier, and bear the 12 Apostles (possibly recut) on their fronts.

Minehead　Som.　1 G1

> The fairest part of the toun standith in the botom of an hille. The residew rennith stepe up a long the hille, yn the toppe whereof is a fair paroche chirche.
> 　　　　　　　　　　　　　　　　　　(Leland)

The two parts are still recognizable amid the growth of the seaside resort of the 19th and 20th centuries: a typical hillside village clustering round its church, linked by roads not built for the motor car; and the harbour and its cottages some distance away. The port was Minehead's *raison d'être*. Leland remarked that the town on his visit in the 1540s was 'exceding ful of Irisch menne', and nowadays, in the summer, the natives are again outnumbered at least since Butlins opened their Holiday Camp in 1962.

The Irish connexion was the making of Minehead in the 15th century and later, for Ireland provided stock and wool for the West Somerset graziers and clothiers, and Minehead reaped the benefit. The church of St

May Day in Minehead: the hobby horse

Michael, standing nobly above the town on the slopes of North Hill, the Welsh *mynydd* or hill which gave the place its name, reflects the wealth of the town's merchants. It is a large and airy church with a tower to match having Dunster details. If there is early work in the walls, it has yet to be recognized, but the arcade is of the later 14th century and the nave not a great deal older. The chancel was rebuilt when the aisle was added, and later came the N vestry, formerly another chapel. Further additions were, in probable order, the tower, the screen with its delicate turret, and the porch – or at least its battlements, which before drastic restoration bore the Tudor Rose and the initials 'R.H.', probably for *Rex Henricus*, Henry (VIII) the King. Much more precise is the E window of the N chancel aisle, which bears the date 1529, the symbols of the Five Wounds of Christ, and, above, the inscription

> We prey to Jhu & M^c
> send owr neyburs safte.

A suitable prayer for a community of mariners.

Inside the church, now beautifully decorated and maintained, is a fine tomb on the N side of the sanctuary – a late-medieval Easter sepulchre to which an older figure of a priest has been added. The pulpit is of the early 17th century minus its tester, which an improving architect made into a table. But the greatest treasure of all is a medieval missal, beautiful enough on its own account, but of greater interest in that it belonged to Richard Fitzjames, a native of Bruton (q.v.), appointed by the canons of Bruton as vicar here beween 1485 and 1497, and Bishop of London from 1506 until his death in 1522.

Threatened with Spanish invasion in the 1580s, Minehead Quay was guarded by a battery of guns. At the turn of the century the port was still 'much frequented', and a new business had arrived: alabaster was quarried which 'for variety of mixtures and colours . . . passeth any . . . of this Kingdome if not others' for tombs and chimney pieces. By Defoe's time the production of serges for Ireland was 'indifferent', but there was still enough life in the town at election time until 1832, and at least some of her mariners had connexions with Virginia and the West Indies.

Minehead, like other Bristol Channel ports, began its history as a resort quite early. Bathing began in the late 18th century and a lodging house advertised leisure visits in 1800. But expansion was modest. The three points of settlement in the 15th century – the church, the quay, and a mill near the present town centre – only gradually began to grow together, and between 1801 and 1901 Minehead did little more than double its population. Here was a select resort for the Middle Class, offering races on the beach from 1865, but even as late as 1890 forbidding everyone over the age of 10 from bathing 'except from a bathing machine, tent, or other effective screen'. The railway came from Watchet in 1874, but the quiet, family holiday continued, comfortably centred from the First World War at establishments like the Strand Hotel, and entertained by such stars as Pavlova or Gladys Cooper playing at the Queen's Hall. The pace hardly quickened in the 1920s, though improvements to the sea front including the Blenheim Gardens (1925) extended Minehead's special, gentle charm. The family holiday resort has continued in a different way at Butlins.

The West Somerset Railway, closed in 1971, was reopened again in 1976, and under steam and diesel runs regular and special trips for the 14-mile journey to Bishops Lydeard (q.v.), making it the longest privately run railway in the country. Dunster, Washford (for Cleeve Abbey), Watchet, Williton, and Crowcombe (qq.v.) are along the route.

Montacute Som. 2 C3
Montacute has had at least three names: Logworesbeorh in the 7th century after one of the 12 monks at Glastonbury when St Patrick arrived; Bishopston (still a street name) after Tunbeorht, Abbot of Glastonbury and then Bishop of Winchester in the 9th century; and finally Montacute, after the castle built on the steep hill (*mons acutus*) overlooking the village (now covered in trees and called St Michael's Hill).

That castle, built by the Conqueror's half-brother the Count of Mortain, was a great insult to the native English, for it was the spot where the fragment of the Holy Cross had been found, the most precious relic that King Harold possessed, and the inspiration of his army at Hastings. And although the English failed to take it in 1068, the castle did not last long, for by *c.* 1102 the then Count of Mortain was forced to found a monastery and endow it with his own lands rather than face an open charge of treason. So, beneath the hill, beyond the present parish church, arose the Cluniac priory of St Peter and St Paul, endowed from the beginning with a castle, a borough, orchards and vineyards, a mill, and, by the late 12th century, a park. Subsequently the monks built a chapel and held fairs

Montacute

on the site of the castle, they extended the borough to include not only Middle Street but also the Borough and South Street, laid out around the monastic enclosure; and they developed the park on the s of the village whose bounds are still marked by a footpath through the woods (NT) and a road called Park Lane. The place became a little town, sending two men to Parliament in 1306, and in the 16th century a guildhall, shops, and shambles stood in its centre.

The monks took over the village church, but c. 1170–80 they built a new one; its chancel arch and some other fragments survive, though chancel, transepts, and N porch belong to the late 13th century, and the nave was at any rate remodelled in the later Middle Ages. The tower probably belongs to the early 16th century, sharing details with the Abbey gatehouse, built by Prior Thomas Chard (1514–32), and with the house in the borough whose gable end bears a carved panel with the fast-disappearing initials of Robert Shirborne, the last prior of Montacute (1532–9). The deliberately blank s face of the tower has more to do with the game of fives than with the fact that it faced the priory church.

In the N transept are monuments to the Phelips family beginning with the so-called tomb of David Phelips (d. 1484). Within little more than a century they became owners of much of the parish and builders of Montacute House (NT), the most spectacular Elizabethan house in the county – achieved through the machinations of Thomas Phelips (d. 1588) and the success in law and politics of his second son Sir Edward (d. 1614). The house, designed probably by William Arnold, has the dates 1598 and 1601 upon it.

Though clearly a Renaissance mansion it still bears many of the marks of a medieval building: the hall and screens passage are still there, and until the purchase of the 'Clifton Maybank' (Dorset) addition at the rear it was only one room deep. The pavilions at the corners of the formal garden in front of the house, linked by delicate balustrades crowned by obelisks, are not simply garden ornaments but the last vestiges of the outer walls and towers of the medieval castle plan. The misfortune of the family in the 19th century has left the house with little of the family furniture and pictures, but here is a house supremely to be enjoyed; the more so since the age of its creation is so fascinatingly illustrated in the superb collection of paintings from the National Portrait Gallery in the Long Gallery. There are to be found Tudor portraits of medieval kings, starkly formalized beside their own views of their magnificent selves; men and women from history who would have known the Phelipses even if they never came to Montacute.

The henpecked husband, condemned to 'ride the skimmington', seems curiously out of place facing a Renaissance stone screen in the hall; so, too, does Lord Curzon's bath, disguised in a cupboard in one of the bedrooms. His lordship rented the house for several years during the First World War, and is said to have awaited at Montacute his expected summons to the King in 1922 when the Conservatives won the General Election. His Majesty sent for Stanley Baldwin instead.

The house was bought from the Phelips family in 1931 by the Society for the Protection of Ancient Buildings, a body with Montacute connexions since its secretary, A. R. Powys, had spent part of his boyhood with his equally famous brothers Llewelyn, Theodore, Francis and John Cowper Powys in the village where their father was vicar.

Muchelney Som. 2 C2
The Benedictine Abbey of St Peter and St Paul, Muchelney (DoE), was founded probably by King Ine (d. 726); that was what the medieval monks used to claim with the aid of several forged charters, but archaeologists in the 1950s discovered a crypt under the choir which probably dated from the 8th century, thus showing that medieval forgers were not as bad as we sometimes think.

Muchelney means 'great island', and its site in the marshes was deliberately chosen to give the monks both security and solitude. The house had to be refounded by King Athelstan c. 950, and it lasted until 1538. Its estates, many of them between Muchelney and Ilminster in the often-flooded Isle Valley, were worth £447 at the Dissolution, shared between 11 monks, their servants, and farm hands – and there were plenty of those, including a gardener, a ploughman, shepherds, a laundress, a barber, a faggot maker, and 'le eggeman'.

Before the crash came there had been a lot of building. Although only the base of the church survives, it is clear that the earlier building had been encased in late-medieval stone panelling – exactly what happened to the Norman pillars in Sherborne Abbey nave. The 12th-century church at Muchelney had an apsidal E end with bubble chapels; and a similar chapel at the E of the s transept. A rectangular Lady Chapel was built c. 1360. The cloister lay to the s of the church, and beyond it the domestic buildings including the Abbot's Lodging. Part of the early-16th-century cloister, once used as a cider cellar, shows the high quality of the stonework. The Abbot's Lodging, comprising a kitchen, hall, and chambers above, has a fine parlour with elaborate fireplace and fitted oak linen-fold settle. Fragments of glass bear the initials of Abbot Thomas Broke (1505–22). The sites of the refectory, warming house, chapter house, and infirmary are known, and the reredorter still stands. Across the Drayton road, beyond the car park, is a 16th-century barn, and further E Almonry Farm, built in 1902 to replace the abbey almonry.

The village group is completed with church, cross, and priest's house. The church stands a few inches N of the Abbey church, and is all of the late Middle Ages, the ornate N and s chapels and the tower perhaps the latest additions. The tiles in the chancel were taken from the Abbey, and other earlier details, like carved fragments in cottages in the village, came from the same source.

Detail of the ceiling, Muchelney church

But the source of the remarkable painted nave roof is unknown – only that it seems to be of the early 17th century judging by what remains of the costume of the angels and cherubs in the firmament of sun, stars, and clouds. Much less attractive are the pulpit and lectern, made for the Lord Mayor's Chapel, Bristol, in 1830 and removed 60 years later. The barrel organ in the s gallery is still in working condition. Outside the E end of the church is a medieval tomb, also from the Abbey.

Across the road from the churchyard is the Priest's House (NT), almost exactly dated to 1308 when a vicar was first appointed. It then had a two-bay open hall, but alterations were made in the mid 14th century and *c.* 1475, and a floor was inserted over the hall *c.* 1550.

In the moors 2½ miles sw of Muchelney through Drayton, MIDELNEY MANOR stands on another 'island', an unspoilt Elizabethan house, or rather pair of houses, built to be shared by two Trevilian brothers. There is some 18th-century work inside, and behind a rare brick

mews; falconry was a popular sport in the valley of the River Isle.

Neroche Forest   Som. *see* **Broadway**

Nether Stowey   Som.   2 A1
Nether Stowey stands (now happily bypassed) on a main route beside the Quantocks; its name means 'stone way', clearly an important route even in Saxon times, when it linked the two extensive royal Saxon estates of Cannington and Williton. It is Nether to distinguish it from the village of Over Stowey, higher up the Quantock slopes. A 'poore village', Leland decided, when its former importance had evidently gone; and still a village, though grown in recent years, but retaining small shops and a general country air with the help of the stream and cobbles in Castle Street. It has remains of some magnificence, notably the motte-and-bailey castle at the top of the village, built probably by William Fitz-

Odo in the 11th century and held against King Stephen in 1138. Just below the castle mound is the site of a church. At the other end of the village, guarded by a gazebo and a high wall near the over-restored church, is Stowey Court, the 'goodly maner place of the Lorde Audeley's' which Leland saw next to its two deer parks. Audley's father had begun extensions which had progressed no further than foundations at the time of his execution in 1497 for leading an insurrection against Henry VII. The present house includes work of the late 16th and 18th centuries.

The Victorian clock-tower in the centre of the village, commemorating the Diamond Jubilee of 1897, replaced a rather ramshackle market cross, a reminder that in the 13th century the place had pretensions to status as a borough (at least by 1222), and from 1304 had a weekly market and an annual fair. It was never a large town, but it has associations with some remarkable people. Robert Parsons or Persons, born in the village, left it and his country to become a Jesuit priest in 1575. His return as a fugitive missionary to Elizabethan England for 'the preservation and augmentation of the faith of the Catholics in England' with the more saintly Edmund Campion is as thrilling a story of intrigue and escape as ever can be produced in the present century. Another remarkable cleric was Henry William Majendie, vicar of the parish 1790–3. Formerly tutor to Prince William, later William IV, and a canon of St George's Chapel, Windsor, he was considered an advanced and rash man for establishing a Sunday school in the parish. He later became successively Bishop of Chester (1800–9) and Bangor (1809–30).

Two houses in the village are famous not for themselves but for those who lived in them. In Castle Street is a substantial Georgian building called Poole House, the home of that cultured tanner Tom Poole, whose friendship was an anchor to the poet Coleridge. Poole in 1796 lent Coleridge a cottage at the end of his garden – in Lime Street (NT), and there for two years the Coleridges lived. 'This Lime-Tree Bower My Prison' refers to a day when he could not walk with Lamb and Wordsworth, both of whom, with Dorothy Wordsworth, Hazlitt, and publisher Cottle, met, walked or stayed with the Coleridges. The locals hardly appreciated these strange people in their midst, thinking them French spies. The Wordsworths stayed at the time at ALFOXTON PARK, now a hotel 2 miles W beyond HOLFORD (Dorothy Wordsworth called it Alfoxden), tramping the Quantocks, often at night, observing nature, and planning the *Lyrical Ballads*, including 'The Rime of the Ancient Mariner', the latter written in the cottage at Stowey, and taken over to the Wordsworths on 23 March 1798. Alfoxton Park, an early-18th-century house with a late-Georgian N side, was the home of the St Aubyn family. Holford church has a short tower with a saddleback roof, probably of the 13th century, but the rest was rebuilt in the mid 19th. In the churchyard lies Frederick Norton,

author of the popular musical *Chu-Chin Chow* first produced in 1916.

Nettlecombe   Som.   1 H2
Nestling in a little valley on the N edge of the Brendons just inside Exmoor National Park, the church and Court on the edge of a deer park stand almost the lone survivors of a medieval village. The property, owned from the mid 12th century by the Devon Raleghs (ancestors of Sir Walter), was inherited by the Cornish Trevelyans in the 15th through the marriage of John Trevelyan to a Ralegh great-niece in 1452. John was the 'Cornish Chough', the close royal favourite of Henry VI, whom Jack Cade and his followers claimed in 1450 had led the King astray. It seems likely that John built the earliest surviving part of the present house. In 1531 the house was let to John Sydenham on condition that he rebuilt the hall. Yet another John Trevelyan (d. 1623) built the present Great Hall, oriel, and porch (dated 1599) and probably other work, and his successors added a small dining room and chambers in 1641, parlour, drawing room, and dressing room in 1704, and the SW range in brick in contrast to the sandstone rubble and Ham stone dressings of the rest, in the mid and late 18th century.

The little red sandstone church nestling beside the Court has datable features of c. 1300 (the tomb recesses in the S (Ralegh) chapel), the 15th century (the tower), and 1522 (the N (Trevelyan) chapel), the latter, so Sir John Trevelyan requested in his will, to be dedicated to Our Lady and St George and 'in length of the said chaunsell and in bredethe of 11 or 12 foote'. The church has some remarkable treasures: the 15th-century font, with carvings representing the Seven Sacraments and Christ in Glory; original glass in the Trevelyan Chapel; and a chalice and paten, now in St Nicholas Church Museum, Bristol, the oldest piece of goldsmith's work in England whose date is known, for it carries the date letter B for 1479.

Nettlecombe Court, still owned by the descendants of the first John Trevelyan, has since 1967 been leased to the Field Studies Council as a Field Centre. It is named after Leonard Wills, a Birmingham manufacturer and naturalist.

North Cadbury   Som.   *see* **Cadbury**

Northover   Som.   *see* **Ilchester**

Norton Malreward   Avon *see* **Stanton Drew**

Norton St Philip   Som.   5 C5
Norton St Philip was one of the most important possessions of the Charterhouse at Hinton. It lay on the main road between Bath and Salisbury, and from 1255 a fair was held each year for three days around the patronal festival of St Philip and St James. The village proved an important collecting point for Mendip wool in the

The George Inn, Norton St Philip

Middle Ages, and still in Queen Elizabeth's reign linen and woollen cloth was being sold at the fair. And undoubtedly the focal point of the fair was the George Inn, 'an ancient and common inn called the George' as it was described in 1638. Many fanciful claims have been made for the building: oldest licensed premises; monastic guest house; built at the same time as the Charterhouse itself.

The oldest parts of the inn date from the late 14th century; so it will have witnessed the trouble in 1401 when the King's collector of wool-tax was set upon. 'No fewer than 100 mortal wounds' were inflicted on the unfortunate man, so it was reported, and hardly any of his men escaped alive. The building is one of the most famous in the county. It is of local brown stone with jettied timber-framed first and second floors in the front and a stone-slate roof. At the back is a polygonal stair turret, stone walls to full height, and cusped two-light windows.

Pepys and his household 'dined very well' at the George for 10 shillings in 1668, and the Duke of Monmouth made it his headquarters when he came in June 1685 after turning back from Bath. The legend that he was sniped at cannot be proved though there was certainly a skirmish here and one of Monmouth's Dorset men was seriously wounded by 'some heavy cutting instrument on his head at two places'. The doctor's bill for a very complicated operation was £5.

In Monmouth's time the inn had 35 beds to offer and stabling for 90 horses. The village still produced cloth known as 'Spanish medleys' in Defoe's time, but the loss of the main road later in the 18th century probably spelt the end of Norton's long tradition in cloth. The George, however, continues to offer hospitality as it has done for centuries.

The parish church, lower down this elegant and interesting village off the old main road, has in its s doorway traces of a 13th-century origin, and the nave was probably aisled in the 14th. Most of the rest is the expected Somerset Perpendicular; certainly expected in a clothing centre. But the tower is something of a puzzle, for it is said to be the gift (even the design) of Jeffrey Flower, a rich clothier, who died in 1644. Another indication of the longevity of medieval tradition.

Nunney Som. 5 C6
The focal point of the village is not the castle nor the church but the little market place beside the brook. A market was licensed by the Crown in 1260. Until the

Nunney Castle

18th century the village was an important clothing centre; Edward Flower, clothier (d. 1727), has left a memorial in the church and in fields towards the main road now covered by Local Authority housing. Three generations of evidently prosperous weavers have left their initials and dates on three adjoining houses in Horn Street, each a respectable example of the fashion of the day. Edge-tools took over from cloth in the 19th century.

But before all that the Delamares were lords here. Sir John in 1373 was licensed to crenellate his manor house, modelling it, so it has been said, on the Bastille; for he fought in France, whence came his wealth. But there are castles like this in the North of England. The result was hardly a military stronghold, for it stands beside a brook in the valley bottom.

The Castle (DoE) consisted of four drum towers forming a rectangular plan and providing accommodation of four floors. The Great Hall was on the second floor and a chapel at the top of the sw tower. The main roof was high pitched, and each tower had a conical top, the whole almost an English version of Ruritania. The Castle ceased to be a residence after damage during the Civil War; and William Whitchurch built himself the attractive Castle House, now Castle Farm, near by.

Between Castle and church the Nunney Brook runs past a spot which was used in cloth-making days as a 'pavement and place to wash wool'. The medieval market cross stands there now, rather incongruously, rescued from a worse fate as a garden monument in 1959.

The parish church, overlooking the Castle, suffered from restorers in the 19th century and death-watch beetle in the 1950s. There are remains of a 13th-century chancel, transepts of the mid-14th, and a nave which was aisled by *c.* 1300 but was rebuilt internally with new arcades at the time the Castle appeared. The wagon roof later to be virtually destroyed, probably dated, like the porch and tower, from the 16th century. But as usual, the Norman font is older than the rest, covered here with work of the 17th century; and older still are fragments of interlaced pattern from a Saxon cross.

On the wall above the nave arcade is a painting of St George with background motifs including the White Hart of Richard II. Three tombs, commemorating a 14th-century knight, a 15th-century knight and his lady, and an Elizabethan couple, have been identified, though without actual proof, as (respectively) a Delamare, Sir John Poulet (d. 1436), and Richard Prater, each in his turn lord of the manor Nunney Delamare.

Two miles SE over the ridgeway, TRUDOXHILL is noted for its early Congregational chapel, set beside the road at the bottom of the village, with an adjoining graveyard with yews which evokes well the spirit of early nonconformity. It is not quite as old as the datestone suggests, for it began life in 1699 as a home for Richard Newport and his wife, and was converted by them into a chapel in 1717. The interior has a tall pulpit, plain pews, and a small gallery.

One and a half miles E at MARSTON BIGOT is the former home of the Boyle family, Earls of Cork and Orrery. The mansion successfully disguises a 17th-century house which was extended in the early 18th century when formal gardens and cascades were created. Later in the century it was given a face-lift in the Palladian style, and more rooms were added in 1776 and the 19th century. Jeffrey Wyatville probably designed the loggia c. 1817. The house has recently been threatened with demolition, having been severely damaged during the war by army occupation, and then converted into flats.

The medieval church, at the end of the village street which disappeared when the park was created, probably in the 18th century, stood on the lawn in front of the house. It was removed during the improvements of 1787. The new church had a tower added in 1809 and the present chancel in 1845, when the whole building was 'Normanized'. So the most remarkable feature is the stained glass, from Flanders and the Rhineland, some of it dating back to 1500.

Oare Som. 6 D6
Almost within a stone's throw of the Devon border, in a remote and romantic setting in a valley, is a church which thousands visit not for its architectural merit, but for an event that never happened there! R. D. Blackmore's immortal story of the Ridds and the Doones in conflict on Exmoor, brought to such a climax at John Ridd's wedding to Lorna Doone in Oare church, is enough to make this place a focus of pilgrimage even if the Doones cannot actually be proved to have existed. Undoubtedly Blackmore knew Exmoor well, for his grandfather was rector of Oare from 1809 to 1842; there were real Ridds or Reds and Snowes; Yenworthy and

Parsonage farms are still standing, and Black Barrow Down, where John pursued Carver Doone, rises high above to the SE of Oare.

The local slatey sandstone is not the material for fine building and the plain church has nothing obviously earlier than the 15th century. It has a curious 'second' chancel, a smaller E extension to the original, and some late-18th- or early-19th-century fittings – box pews, pulpit, and reader's desk – which Blackmore must certainly have known (though the pulpit door would be hardly suitable for carrying Lorna back to Plover's Barrows (? Oareford Farm, 1½ miles SE).

The place was evidently romantic enough even before Blackmore wrote (1869); the Prince of Wales paid a visit in 1863, duly commemorated in a plaque in the church. Another plaque, on the county boundary beside Badgeworthy (*pron.* Badgery) Water, marks the centenary of *Lorna Doone*'s publication. The 'Doone Valley' lies beyond.

There are Ridds in another romantic churchyard at CULBONE 3 miles ENE of Oare, in a wooded valley just above the sea. Walk the 2 miles or so from Porlock Weir (q.v.) to the smallest complete parish church (so it is claimed) in England. The building is quite likely to be Saxon in origin: the tall nave is certainly high in proportion to its length and the N chancel window could also be pre-Norman. The 13th-century chancel arch is certainly an enlargement of an earlier one, and the porch was added to the late-12th-century nave at the same time. Once rendered and limewashed like most churches in the district, this is a little gem, made even more intriguing by the 19th-century spirelet. Inside, notice the late-14th-century screen, and the reredos and monument by C. F. A. Voysey an architect of national importance who worked for Lord and Lady Lovelace on several buildings on their estate.

There is a problem about the dedication of the church. Leland thought it might be to St Columbanus (see Cheddar); later writers have suggested St Coulban of Brittany, a hermit called Ceolburn, or even an otherwise unknown St Culbone. The old name of the place was Kitnor, which has been interpreted both as a hillslope frequented by kites and as 'Kil Benn', the church of St Benno, a 6th-century abbot from N Wales. James Hadley, of Withycombe near Dunster, left money in 1478 to places of pilgrimage including the chapel of St Culbone, so perhaps it may be the Breton saint after all whose chapel still remains an attraction today.

Odcombe Som. 2 C3
The church, with its high position, central tower, and circular churchyard has all the makings of an early Christian site, probably in succession to a pagan temple; but the restorers of 1874 took most of the clues, leaving only the square Norman font. Time also destroyed a famous pair of shoes which used to hang under the tower, the shoes of Thomas Coryate, the inveterate traveller

who was born in the rectory *c.* 1577. His *Crudities*, published in 1611, tell of his wanderings in Europe; he then went further afield, through the Middle East, and died in India in 1617.

One mile due E, but approached from the N, is BRYMPTON D'EVERCY, a group of house, gardens, church, and dower or chantry house of very great beauty and charm. The property was owned by the Sydenham family for nearly 300 years from 1434, but only slight traces of the first Sydenham house survive. The first obvious additions are *c.* 1520 and later in the 16th century, but the most striking part of the house is the S wing of the mid 17th century, like similar work at Hinton St George and Ashton Court (qq.v.) derived from copy-books of the period and not from Inigo Jones.

The Sydenhams sold Brympton in 1722; in 1731 it was bought by Francis Fane; his brother became Earl of Westmorland. The Fanes, and their descendants the Clive-Ponsonby-Fanes, have lived in the house, with some breaks, ever since. One feature of the house, which is open to the public, is a large modern 'bird's eye view' tapestry of the house and estate in the 18th century.

The church, close to the house, has a nave and S transept of *c.* 1300, a N transept of the later 14th century, followed by the chancel and then by the chancel chapel and the queer, top-heavy bellcot, the Sydenham contribution. The crowd of medieval monuments is presumably to departed D'Evercys. Above the 15th-century stone screen is a carved and painted beam, the remarkable survivor of a wooden loft which must have dominated such a small building. The screen itself has parallels not far away in Dorset at Thornford, Bradford Abbas, and Compton, evidence of the work of a local mason.

Brympton was always a small parish, but the village has long since disappeared. The Duke of Monmouth was fêted here by one of the successive Sir John Sydenhams (d. 1696) in 1680, the one usually called Sir John Posthumous not because he arrived after his father's death (as is usually claimed) though he was still very young when his father died, but because his grandmother's cousin also bore the name. Sir John's grandfather, also John (d. 1626), who lies in Brympton church, was evidently unusual: 'Report it, Sir' (so runs a line on his tomb), 'he died an honest man'.

Old Cleeve Som. *see* **Cleeve Abbey**

Old Sodbury Avon 5 C3
Soppa's fortified place, a Saxon settlement near an Iron Age hillfort, is the key to the place; the church on its knoll looks over its ancient parish, including the medieval 'new town' of Chipping Sodbury (q.v.), founded on its

Culbone church
Brympton House, Brympton D'Evercy

boundary. The church, close to farm and school above the village, is essentially a late-Norman building, though rather heavily restored. The chancel belongs to the 13th century and so, too, the transept arches, perhaps evidence of a central tower. The chancel was extended in the 19th century. In the N transept are two unidentifiable monuments: one is a late-14th-century wooden effigy of a knight, made at Bristol and now only one of five remaining; the other a mid-13th-century one, also a knight. A much later monument is to a remarkable man, David Hartley (d. 1813). Lord of the manor, Fellow of Merton College, Oxford, member of Parliament for Hull; but famous in a wider sense as 'Envoy Extraordinary and Plenipotentiary to the Court of Versailles for negotiating the peace with the United States of America in 1783'.

Down in the valley but still in the parish is the village of LITTLE SODBURY, notable not for its church of St Adeline (built 1859 to replace an earlier one) but for its manor house. The oldest parts, including open hall and porch, are of the late 15th century; a S wing with an oriel of the 16th, a 17th-century stair-well, and an 18th-century N range. It was the home of the Walsh family in the 16th century and for a short time, 1522–3, of William Tyndale, when he was tutor to the family. A less welcome visitation, so tradition says, was in the time of Maurice Walsh in 1556, when lightning passed through the house, killing one boy on the spot at dinner and six others and their father within two months, as a result of shock.

St Adeline, incidentally, seems somewhat obscure. She does not, under that spelling, occur in reference works on saints. Is she Adela, the early-8th-century nun who with her sister Irmina founded the Abbey of Trèves; is she Adelheid, the early-11th-century Abbess of Villich; or is she Adelhaid, wife successively of Lothair (d. 950) and of Otto of Saxony (d. 967)? The first seems the most likely.

Oldbury upon Severn Avon 5 B2
In the flat land beside the river, the towering modernity of the Severn Bridge or the sky-blue and grey mass of the nuclear power station (1966–7) are in striking contrast to a village whose name recalls what is thought to be an Iron Age (or is it Roman?) fort. Camp Road, one of the main streets, seems to coincide with the W part of the fortification, which covers approx. 10 acres. Another towering site was chosen for the parish church, a knoll which may possibly have been anciently fortified. A tradition attributed its remoteness to some supernatural power which destroyed what they had begun to build in the village, and only approved when they followed advice to yoke two heifers never milked, and to put their church wherever the animals stopped. That was not the end of disasters. The spire came down in the great storm of 1703; and much of the rest was destroyed by fire in 1897. What was left was heavily restored in 1899; the font, given by Edward Stafford

Howard, is an exact replica of the old Norman font; most other original details seem to be Perpendicular, though there are fragments of 18th-century work in the church-yard with the fine collection of 17th- and 18th-century table tombs. The view from the site is magnificent.

The church is dedicated to a local saint, Arild, a lady who, according to Leland, was martyred not far away at 'Kingston' (? Kington) near Thornbury by 'one Muncius a tiraunt, who cut off hir heade becawse she would not consent to lye with hym'. Her shrine was at the abbey in Gloucester (now the Cathedral), and her other church is at Oldbury on the Hill (Glos.).

Beyond Sheperdine, 3 miles N along the twisting lanes to the Severn bank, are the Windbound inn and Chapel House, formerly the chapel of St Mary on Severn, founded before 1350 when a chantry was established by Gilbert de Tyndene. Its priest is said to have also cared for a lighthouse. The chapel later became an alehouse and then a reading room for local watermen.

Samuel Rudder in the 18th century refers to local complaints that the large number of elm trees near the houses in the village made the air stagnant. The ravages of Dutch Elm disease might then have been welcomed.

Olveston   Avon   5   B3
Olveston was given to Bath Abbey by King Edwy by a charter of c. 955–9. The bounds of the estate referred to a landscape with thorn, oak, ash, and beech trees; an area of ancient settlement with a row of old stones and an old street, and a pit and a ridge named after the wolf. At the Dissolution of the Abbey the estate was sold to Sir Ralph Sadleir (1507–87), a diplomatist, one of Edward VI's Council, and later a commissioner to treat with the Scots concerning Mary Queen of Scots. The Dennis family, the local squires, lived at Olveston Court Farm, which is still a moated site with high wall, an early-Tudor gatehouse and other contemporary fragments. A brass to two members, wearing heraldic tabards, c. 1505 is on the E wall of the s transept in the parish church.

The present church began as a late-Norman building with a central tower between chancel and nave. Aisles and transepts were formed in the 14th century when the s porch was added. The spire and part of the tower fell in 1603, and the chancel was in consequence of the damage then rebuilt. The heavy pinnacles and parapet of the tower are dated 1606. Eighteenth-century monuments show how country families returned from Bristol to retire and die, including a builder and a celebrated surgeon. Three successive rectors, who held the living between them for a century, begin with Christopher Shute (d. 1767), who, rare for his time, 'constantly resided' for 24 years,

> charitably relieving the Distress'd, dispensing medicines, counsel, and comfort, to the Sick and Needy ...
> a man of Parts, a Genius Refin'd by a Knowledge of men and Books.

He was followed by John Camplin, STP (d. 1799), and then by Robert James Charleton, DD, who was vicar until 1844.

TOCKINGTON, ½ mile SE, is a secondary settlement around a large green, the focus of the market established in 1281. The manor house is of two principal phases in the 18th century, built for the Peach family, one of whom was Mayor of Bristol.

Orchardleigh   Som.   see **Beckington**

Othery   Som.   see **Weston Zoyland**

Otterhampton   Som.   see **Stogursey**

Penselwood   Som.   see **Wincanton**

Pensford   Avon   5   B5
Pensford is not an ancient parish, though it is still old by most reckoning. It was founded at a crossing of the River Chew, but on the borders of the two ancient parishes of Publow and Stanton Drew. The name Pensford may be old, but the place was usually known in the Middle Ages as St Thomas-at-Pensford, or simply as St Thomas, after the church in the village, dedicated to St Thomas Becket, and now no longer used for worship since a flood damaged it in 1968.

The river crossing is the key to the existence of Pensford, on a main route s of Bristol, and in sheep country. Leland called it 'a praty market townlet occupied with clothinge', and the Chew river even then drove a number of fulling mills. Spanish medleys were produced there at least until the beginning of the 18th century and the through traffic can be guessed when in the 1670s there were only 20 beds at its inns but stabling for 102 horses. In the 19th century it took on a different character, dominated by the 16 arches of the massive stone-and-brick railway viaduct built in 1873, and then influenced by three small coal mines, Rydons (in Stanton Drew) abandoned in the 1830s after only 20 years' work, Bromley (1893–1957), and Pensford Colliery (1909–1958). Bromley was the last pit in the Somerset coalfield to use horses to haul tubs underground. The 18th-century lock-up in the village is a fine building, at least from the outside.

PUBLOW, in its quiet valley beside the Chew, ½ mile NE, is a contrast to the almost industrial Pensford. Its fine tall tower is a gem in a beautiful setting, typical Somerset Perpendicular but with some original designs like the transom of lozenges. WOOLLARD, 1 mile E, has a medieval bridge spanning the Chew and an inn with some medieval details. COMPTON DANDO, the next village down the Chew (2 miles E of Woollard), has built into the NE buttress of the chancel a piece of Roman sculpture, evidently a figure of Jupiter, and now recognized as part of the great altar from the Temple in Bath (q.v.).

Pilton Som. 2 D1

Pilton is a scattered, higgledy-piggledy village in a valley on the edge of the Mendips, missed by the main Glastonbury–Shepton Mallet road, though the signs to Pilton Vineyard perhaps now encourage a stop. Pilton was Glastonbury land: its name, a Saxon boundary marker called *lang Pillis* in its daughter settlement of North Wootton (2 miles NW), and its neighbour Pylle (2 miles SE) all signify a pill or creek, now the low ground where the Whitelake river runs to join the Brue at Glastonbury. Here, one tradition says, St Joseph of Arimathea landed. Pilton lay on the edge of the Twelve Hides of Glastonbury, an area of peculiar jurisdiction, the actual boundary running through the parish church, in through the N door and out through the S. So during a formal perambulation monks, abbey officials, and tenants traipsed through church and churchyard before stopping for refreshment at the manor house below, once one of the many residences of the Abbots of Glastonbury.

The present house is a slightly curious Georgian affair, its pinnacles and castellated top odd companions for the central Venetian window. The turret on the S side and several small windows suggest a more ancient origin, and so, too, do the vaulted cellar, a dovecot, and what have been suggested as the remains of a cloister. The present grounds are planted with vines, the modern counterpart to the Abbey vineyards here in the 12th century, though now producing a Riesling of German origin. The Glastonbury link survives also across the valley in the gaunt ruins of a medieval barn; its gables are decorated with the symbols of the Evangelists as at the Abbey barn at Glastonbury, but its fine arch-braced roof disappeared in flames after a thunderstorm in 1963.

The church of St John stands on an awkward sloping site so that it has no S aisle. Its S door is fine Norman work, and the N aisle must have been added *c.* 1190. The tower was begun in the following century, though its top is Perpendicular, and so are the magnificent roofs of nave and aisles, with their fine angel busts. The 15th century glass in the chancel includes the figure of Thomas Overay, precentor of Wells 1472–93, who was by his office rector of Pilton, and responsible for the fabric of the chancel, and so probably the donor of the glass. He was a lawyer and a senior official in the diocese from 1467 until 1474, during the rule of the absentee Bishop Stillington. The screens probably include the work of Robert Carver who in 1498–9 was paid 3s. 6d. 'for makyng off the Trayle [the vine-leaf decoration] under the rodelofte' according to the accounts of the churchwardens. The same accounts refer to vestments given by the Abbot of Glastonbury and others, fragments of which survive. Other rare survivals are the musical instruments once used by the parish band before organs and robed choirs became the order of the day.

Pitminster Som. 2 A3

Nestling under the foothills of the Blackdowns 4 miles s of Taunton, it is a rather tortuous small village, in whose churchyard lie the ashes of A. W. Kinglake (1809–91), author of *Eothen*, a famous book of travel. Travel, too, affected the life of the Treat family, who left here in 1637 for the New World. Richard Treat, the father, had not always seen eye to eye with the authorities, like several of his kin, but beyond the Atlantic he became one of the patentees of Charles II's charter for Connecticut. His son Robert, baptised at Pitminster in 1624, was for 30 years governor of his father's colony. The Treat family put up a brass plate in 1902 to commemorate their connexion with the village.

The church itself, bearing many traces of a substantial building of the 13th century, is the last resting place of three members of the Colles family of Barton Grange, beginning with Humphrey (d. 1570), now consigned to the NW chapel under the tower. He was once in the chancel, which must have been uncomfortably cluttered with his son and grandson too. The font has been partly restored, but contains original carvings of St George and possibly St James.

The Colles' home, Barton Grange, was before the Dissolution an estate of Taunton Priory. One or two ancient trees in its park survive. It adjoined a larger park, POUNDISFORD, belonging to the Bishops of Winchester, lords of Taunton, who likewise had seen the possibilities of this rich stretch of level, wooded ground for the chase and kept here a herd of deer. In 1534 Poundisford came into the hands of two Taunton merchants, Roger and William Hill. The park was divided, and each built a house, Roger Poundisford Lodge, and William Poundisford Park. The latter, built soon after 1546, is an important architectural gem, belonging to a transitional period before the Elizabethan style was born. It is H-shaped, still with a small central hall, four-centred arched heads in the windows, and a detached kitchen (now the Wellhouse Restaurant). Inside is some fine plaster work, mostly of the later 16th century, but including a ceiling in the library of *c.* 1670. Poundisford Lodge, less well-known, is contemporary with the Park, and in similar style, though the richer Elizabethan ceilings are a little later, *c.* 1590.

A mile N of Poundisford Lodge is the village of TRULL, still not a Taunton suburb. Its church contains some magnificent rustic woodwork – pulpit of *c.* 1500 with undamaged carved figures, screens with original paint and the names of the donors, and splendid (if uncomfortable) benches of several different styles, the earliest dated 1510, the latest 1560 and signed by the craftsman. In between come the Instruments of the Passion, leaves, vases, and a splendid procession, not now in order, led by a crucifer, followed by the carriers of book, shrine, and taper, and finally the priest. In the chancel are two windows of 15th century glass.

Porlock Som. 4 E6

Porlock, thy verdant vale so fair to sight (Southey)

The pulpit, Trull church

'Enclosure by the harbour' is its Saxon name, and attacks from the sea by the Danes in 918 and then in 1052 by Harold, son of the outlawed Earl Godwin, suggest its importance, lying in a sheltered bay with North Hill on its E and Dunkery at its back. Thomas Gerard, in the 1630s, thought it was a bad harbour, but as an anchorage it figured on a map of Somerset's defences in the 1580s, sheltering small vessels behind a breakwater which gave its name to Porlock Weir (see below).

So its bay and not its harbour is the point to Porlock's origin; and it has resisted the tendency of other places to creep down to the beach. It still clusters round its ancient holy spot, the church of St Dubricius or Dyfrig, a 6th-century monk and bishop from the Herefordshire-Welsh borderland. His name here probably represents the work of one of his disciples rather than the saint himself, though Dyfrig was possibly Abbot of Caldey not far across the Channel. The church itself has traces of its ancient foundation in the fragments of Saxon cross-shaft in the w wall, but most of the building is essentially of the 13th century, with a late-14th-century s aisle and a N porch a century after that. The original E vestry is more common in the great Perpendicular churches of the 15th century (e.g. Langport and Crewkerne, qq.v.). Outside, its decapitated, shingled spire catches the eye, lost in a thunderstorm in the 17th century, not taken to Culbone (q.v.) by a giant. Inside there are late-medieval details to match the porch: the font, the Easter Sepulchre, and, most memorable of all, the Harington monument. Sir John Harington (d. 1418), knighted by Henry V during the Agincourt Campaign, lies beside the wife who outlived him for more than half a century. Since then, in increasingly defaced alabaster, they have for long gazed at a canopy in Dundry stone (see Introduction), not part of the original tomb, but what is left of a chantry Sir John had wished to found. Among Porlock's rectors were Adam Bellinden (1642–7), Bishop of

Porlock Bay from Porlock Hill

Aberdeen until ejected by the Presbyterian Scots in 1639, and Stephen Hales (1718–23), at the same time curate of Teddington (Middx.), scientist, inventor, and pioneer in the study of vegetable physiology.

Porlock's main street bears unmistakable marks of its popularity as a tourist centre, though its 15th-century manor house, called Doverhay (now an information centre), has a splendid traceried hall window.

Porlock Weir, 1½ miles w, is a delightful cluster of small hotels and cottages above a shingle bank and a disappearing harbour. Herrings were landed and cured here in the 17th century, and in the early 18th the Blathwayt family (of Dyrham q.v.) levied tolls on imports of salt, hide, limestone, and stockings and on exports of red haematite, herrings, oyster, and cloth. Porlock's yarn was sold in the Yarn Market at Dunster at the end of the century. The parish continues w into the wooded cliffs of the Lovelace estate, where the toll road winds its way towards Culbone and County Gate. The notorious Porlock hill, rising 1,350 ft in less than 3 miles, and in places with a gradient of 1 in 4, made Porlock for long 'the end of the world', where the inhabitants only travelled by foot or horseback or on a sort of 'sledge'. Such modes of transport were not too attractive to the poet Southey, though the beauty of the landscape enthralled him, and even a summer shower only served as catalyst for the poem 'To Porlock', composed at the Ship and printed by the *Morning Post* in 1799. At the Ship, too, he was introduced to laver, and ate it with relish ever after.

Portbury Avon *see* **Portishead**

Portishead Avon 5 A4
Portishead, and its neighbour Portbury (see below), take their names from the mouth of the Avon which served as harbour and anchorage long before the docks of the late 19th and 20th centuries transformed the coastline and river banks. Both settlements looked not to the sea but to the land, though Portishead Point was defended in the 16th century against Spanish invasion and garrisoned for the Crown in 1644. Invasion of another kind began in the 18th, when visitors coming by boat from Hotwells dined *al fresco* on the beach or in the woods. Battery Point was fortified again when Napoleon threatened, but from the 1820s villas began to appear on the cliffs overlooking the Bristol Channel, the Royal Hotel was opened in 1830, and a pier in 1849. By 1855 the local printed *Guide* described the baths as

> a singular contrivance by which the discoloured waters of the Channel [were] converted, by filtration, into a perfectly limpid element (without losing a grain of their saline impregnation).

The bath house survives (now The Saltings), and so do many villas such as Portishead House, formerly Eldon Villa, home of a Bristol wine merchant who financed the Emperor Napoleon III; and so does a fine terrace along the road to Battery Point, Classical changing to Jacobean.

Portishead was not to remain a select resort. Wharves for loading iron ore from Clapton (q.v.) for Wales preceded the commercial development which has almost swamped the country village and select resort. The railway came in 1864–7, the new pier in 1868–70, and the dock in 1879, all part of the greater complex of the Port of Bristol. The 20th century has added its own contribution to what is known as the Severnside Industrial Area. The Post Office receiving and transmission station is a vital link in the world's shipping network, and the two power stations (1929 and 1959) produce 396,000 kW by coal-fired boilers. The latest addition is the massive Royal Portbury Dock, E of the town, which has not yet achieved its potential.

Portishead church stands, by contrast, in a quiet tree-lined road, representing the earliest point of settlement. Its Norman font is the only reminder of its origin, for most of the church belongs to the mid 14th and 15th centuries and to a very successful extension eastward of 1878–9. Beside the church is the picturesque Court, a 16th-century house with a tall polygonal angle tower.

PORTBURY, 2 miles SE beside the Gordano motorway interchange, has a fine Norman church, now isolated from the village but evidently of importance as the centre of a hundred by the 11th century. Aisles were added c. 1300, and provided with stone seats all round the church. In the village is a medieval tower, now converted to form part of a dwelling. It is often called a priory, but was simply a manor house belonging to the Augustinian priory of Breamore (Hants).

Priddy Som. *see* **The Mendips**

Pucklechurch Avon 5 C4
Pucklechurch was an important place in Saxon times. Until 950 it was royal property, and at a residence here in 946 King Edmund, recognized from 944 as ruler of all England and overlord of the Scots, was killed when trying to prevent his steward from being murdered by Leofa, an outlaw. Edwy, Edmund's successor, gave the property to the monks of Glastonbury, where the murdered King was buried, to pray for his soul, and the charter recording his gift describes a large estate (including Wick and Abson, Westerleigh and Doynton) with place-names referring to caterpillars, wrens, oxen, beaver, waterhens, and geese. Perhaps more significant are a cinder ford, an old dairy farm, and an old dyke.

The place-name, Purcela's church, and the large estate suggest some ecclesiastical importance; and the church connexion was certainly important throughout the Middle Ages. It was owned by Glastonbury Abbey from 950 until King John's reign, and was then acquired by the Bishops of Bath and Wells. The bishops remained lords until 1548, when William Barlow was forced to give the estate to the Crown. Pucklechurch and Westerleigh were held for a time by Sir Nicholas Poyntz of Iron Acton (q.v.) and then by William Herbert, Earl of Pembroke.

Pucklechurch stands on a formerly important route from Bristol to Oxford and London. There was much coal-mining here in the early 18th century, the manufacture of felt hats, and quarries producing coarse black marble used for chimney-pieces and gravestones. It still successfully retains its village atmosphere despite considerable building and industrial expansion.

The church of St Thomas of Canterbury, with its fine tower, is a large 13th-century building with remarkably few additions, though it also includes a Norman door betraying its earlier origins. The N aisle was added in the 14th century, and the two medieval monuments – a lady and a civilian – belong to the same century. Equally anonymous was a deaf woman; commemorated by a 17th-century epitaph.

WESTERLEIGH 2½ miles N, has a 13th-century church largely rebuilt and extended in the 15th, when it was given a simple tower. The font is in the Norman style but is of the 17th century; the gallery, with some 17th-century panelling, was built in 1771. Dr Edward Fowler, Bishop of Gloucester 1691–1714, was born in the parish in 1632. As vicar of St Giles, Cripplegate, he was suspended for Whiggism in 1685, and influenced the clergy of London against reading James II's Declaration of Indulgence in 1687. His book *The Design of Christianity* resulted in a noted controversy with John Bunyan.

Putsham   Som. *see* **East Quantoxhead**

Puxton   Avon *see* **Banwell**

The Quantock Hills   Som.
The name of this range of hills comes from the Celtic word for circle or rim, and seen from across the Somerset Levels that is exactly what they are. They run from Quantoxhead (q.v.), almost on the Bristol Channel coast, nearly 13 miles SE to Thurloxton, rising to their highest points at Wills Neck (1,260 ft), Lydeard Hill, and at Cothelstone Hill. Along the top is the prehistoric ridgeway marked by beech avenues, Bronze Age barrows, cairns, and beacon mounds, a route followed by many later parish boundaries along lines that may well represent pre-Roman estate boundaries. Until the 18th century the rolling route was the main road between Taunton and the Channel coast, and carriages are known to have used it in the early 19th when the lower roads were impassable. The route is now for most of its length the exclusive preserve of the rider and the walker; and of the sheep, cattle, and horses which graze on the common lands of heath, bracken, and grass.

Archaeological finds on the hills date from the Middle Stone Age (c. 8,500–4,000/3,500 BC), but are principally of the Bronze Age. There are approx. 90 burial mounds, sometimes confused with simple piles of stones formed when land up here was being cleared for arable crops.

The barrows often form rough lines or clusters placed, it is thought, at the edge of a territory to guard it with the spirits of the dead. The Iron Age contributed Dowsborough hillfort overlooking Holford; inclosures for cattle like Trendle Ring above Bicknoller, Plainsfield above Cockercombe, Ruborough and Higher Castles in Broomfield; and linear ditches, of which the best known is Dead Woman's Ditch on Robin Upright's Hill. The tradition that the ditch was named after the wife of John Walford, murdered by her husband in 1789, will not do; the name appears before the deed was done, but Walford's Gibbet is almost certainly the site where the murderer met his end.

The Quantocks until the 13th century bore traces of a royal forest; they lay between the old Saxon royal estates of Cannington (q.v.) and Williton (q.v.), and their open country and native red deer made them obviously attractive to royal hunters. The deer and the attraction survive, and the meets of the Quantock Staghounds are popular local events both for hunters and for followers.

The northern half of the Quantock ridge, formed of the rather inhospitable purple-brown Hangman Grits, ends in a prominent headland above a narrow coastal strip. Its soils are not very fertile on the higher ground, and its heather and scrub oak long ago took over from medieval man's attempt to grow even the hardy rye. Sheep and cattle pasturage, turf-cutting, and timber have been its traditional use. The long, deep combes, so frequently incorporated in local names, have been planted with trees from the 18th century onwards. Further south the reddish soil over the Red Sandstone supports arable crops as well as high woodland, woodland which in this part of the Quantocks dates back to the late 7th century. The name Broomfield, one of the villages on the southern edge of the ridge, signifies open country characterized by its broom.

The hills are designated an area of Outstanding Natural Beauty and have been recognized as such at least since Coleridge and Wordsworth came to stay (see Nether Stowey and Introduction). Several pieces of land are owned by the NT (at Holford and Broomfield Hill). The Forestry Commission has created a Nature Trail (2½ miles long, near OVER STOWEY, complete with car parks) where the wide range of native and imported trees planted in the last 50 years may be studied. An Interpretation Centre has been established by the Somerset Trust for Nature Conservation at Fyne Court, BROOMFIELD, in what remains of the mansion where Andrew Crosse carried out his early experiments into electricity.

Radstock   Avon   5 C5
Radstock belongs to the industrial archaeologist and to the railway historian; its coal and railways have now both had their day, and will in time seem as remote as the Roman Fosse Way which runs near the town and gives the place its name – the settlement by the road.

The Quantocks

Roman industry was just up the hill towards Bath at Camerton; in modern times coal was found in the valley, and mining began on a large scale in 1763. For more than two centuries it dominated the scene, bringing wealth to the owners, local power to their agents, and employment to the hundreds who came from the land to live in the terraced houses which line the roads. The census population figures tell the story: 509 in 1801, 1,165 in 1831, 3,074 in 1881, 3,355 in 1901.

The coal, once hewn, had to be taken away; first by canal, from 1803 by tramway, and 50 years later by rail. The two railway companies forced their way into the narrow valley to compete with the Wellow Brook and eight roads. Two level crossings close together in the centre of the town did nothing for traffic flow, but at least the Somerset and Dorset railway, built in 1874, later offered more than branch services and coal trucks; for did not the great Pines Express from Liverpool and Manchester to Bournemouth run out of Green Park,

Bath, and down the valley to Radstock before breasting the 1 in 50 Mendip gradient for Shepton Mallet?

Pevsner found the town 'really desperately ugly' and regretted the lack of any building with dignity. The batches (spoil tips) were grassed and planted in pioneer fashion long before the last coal mine closed in 1973; but new buildings and industries have not been able to alter Radstock's mining character.

AMMERDOWN, 2 miles SE, the home of Lord Hylton, was designed by James Wyatt for Thomas Jolliffe in 1788 and extended in the 19th century. The house stands on the west of a ridge in gardens partly planned by Lutyens which merge into wooded parkland. A column $\frac{1}{2}$ mile SE is a memorial to the creator of the estate. The stables at the house have been converted for use as an Ecumenical Study Centre.

Redland Avon *see* **Westbury on Trym**

Rodden Som. *see* **Berkley**

Rudge Som. *see* **Beckington**

St Audries Som. *see* **East Quantoxhead**

Saltford Avon *see* **Keynsham**

Selworthy Som. 1 G1 (NT)
The ill-fated house at Holnicote, burnt three times since the end of the 18th century, was the second and often the favourite home of the Aclands of Killerton (Devon). Now a private Holiday Centre, it stands in the centre of an estate of 12,420 acres, most of which was given to the National Trust in 1944 by Sir Richard Dyke Acland. It stretches from the coast at Hurlstone Point to the heights of Dunkery Beacon (1,707 ft), and about half is still unenclosed hill and moor, and one-third of the rest is woodland. And not, by any means, uninteresting woodland; above Bossington there are evergreen oaks planted *c.* 1815 by Sir Thomas Dyke Acland (1787–1871); there are conifers at Luccombe from the 1920s, and Horner Woods have been declared an area of Special Scientific Interest with their 'high forest' and coppiced oak. Paths in Selworthy woods lead through oak, chestnut, scots pine, and silver fir, all planted by Sir Thomas, and on the moorland at Cloutsham is the beginning of a nature trail.

Within this area are the parishes of Selworthy, LUC-COMBE (late medieval additions to a 13th-century church in a picturesque, thatched-roof village) and STOKE PERO, so small and remote (and its church almost undatable) that with others it gave rise to the jingle

Oare, Culbone, and Stoke Pero
Parishes three no parson'll go.

But parsons *have* visited, and the church is still there. Selworthy parish covers a large part of the NT estate, and apart from the village, itself now not very large, are the hamlets of Allerford, Blackford, Bossington, Lynch, and Tivington. The first has a well-known packhorse bridge, clear enough reminder of the normal means of communication and trade here in the past. Lynch and Tivington both have medieval chapels, Blackford a medieval dovecot, and all with thatched and often whitewashed cottages.

Selworthy itself has three great attractions. The view from its churchyard across the valley to Dunkery is England at its best. Behind, on the steeply rising ground climbing eventually to Selworthy Beacon and the Iron Age Bury Castle (only reached from here by foot; by car only from Minehead) is Selworthy church, its s side a flamboyant work of 1538, made characteristic of w Somerset by its delicate transomed window patterns. The aisle roof is one of the finest Somerset timber roofs, its bosses decorated with the symbols of the Passion and other religious subjects. The rest of the church is of the 15th and early 16th century except for the plain 14th-century tower. The light and airy building, as deservedly popular as any in the county, has some nice 18th-century work including the w gallery and communion rails; and in the same delicate spirit the Aclands' pew converted from the chamber above the medieval porch.

Down below the church is a piece of picturesque paternalism; the thatched houses around the sloping green, cottage gardens, and leaded lights are another legacy of Sir Thomas Dyke Acland, who built this idyll for retired retainers in 1828 after the style of Blaise near Bristol (q.v.). Lady Acland's contribution was scarlet cloaks for the residents. One house is now the NT shop.

Sharpham Park Som. *see* **Street**

Shepton Beauchamp Som. *see* **Barrington**

Shepton Mallet Som. 5 B6
Shepton lies on the edge of the Mendips, and is one of several early Somerset 'sheep-farm' place names. Wool was thus the clue both to its foundation as a settlement and to its continuing prosperity. The Malet family, who also appear in the name, held Shepton of the Abbey of Glastonbury in 1166, but not long afterwards it passed through an heiress to other families and finally, in the 15th century, to the Duchy of Cornwall. The parish church is clear enough as a guide to Shepton's early significance, and by the 14th century it was a prosperous little town. A century later its clothiers were importing woad from Spain via Southampton for dyeing the cloth they made from wool bought from the Mendip farmers. By the early 17th century the local clothing families, the Barnards and the Strodes, were making fortunes from Spanish medleys, and 100 years later Defoe commented on the great prosperity of the area because of its knitted stockings and pure woollen cloth. The 17th-century terrace in Great Ostry and the individual houses of clothing masters in the lanes on the NE edge of the town remain a living, if now slightly crumbling, witness; for though silk manufacture replaced wool in the early 19th century, Shepton thereafter stagnated, saved from utter ruin, perhaps, by the railway (the great viaduct (*c.* 1855) used to thunder with the Pines Express), and the Anglo-Bavarian Brewery, and brought back to life in our century by the popularity of Showerings 'Babycham'.

The town was a good centre of communications, where the Fosse and other routes from Bristol to the south coast crossed an ancient Mendip ridgeway. The town's stabling for 108 horses in the 1680s indicates the volume of its traffic, still delightfully remembered in the Market Place in the sign declaring the mileage to London and other far away places where carriers might venture. The Market Place is another important thread in Shepton's history, with a market cross built in 1500 and endowed by Walter and Agnes Buklond. A contemporary inscription requests prayers for their souls, and a more modern one prohibits sales there except on market days, and then only the produce of farm, dairy, garden, and orchard. The square also contains the rather self-conscious remains of the town's medieval shambles or butchers' stalls. But all has a new face, the work of the Showering family. Derelict buildings between the High Street and the church have been replaced by shops, flats, and the Shepton Mallet Centre, offering facilities for cinema, theatre, banqueting, and other entertainment.

The church has become somewhat isolated behind the mass of this development, though its important early-Perpendicular tower suggests a building worth closer examination. Inside there is some fascinating archaeology, for is it not a late-Saxon or early-Norman church? The Transitional Norman arcades of *c.* 1190 obviously pierce earlier walls which, although thick, have Saxon long-and-short work high on the s side. The whole nave was raised gloriously in the 15th century to form a clerestory and then to support a new waggon roof, a magnificent specimen with 350 panels, even more bosses and rosettes and 36 angel supporters. That is where the eye turns first; and then to the early-13th-century chancel arch, the late-medieval stone pulpit, and the 18th-century organ case. Less pleasing are the aisles, widened out of proportion in the 19th.

The narrow streets of the town, especially NE of the church, reveal the splendour and the decline that was the Somerset clothing industry. There, too, is the prison, where Domesday Book and other treasures from the Public Record Office spent the Second World War in safety.

Two miles s of the town the Bath and West and Southern Counties Society established its permanent showground in 1965. The society, founded in 1777 to promote improvements in agriculture, arts, manufactures, and commerce, published a journal concentrating on agricultural advances between 1839 and 1940, and held annual shows first for its own members in Bath and from 1852 for the general public in various parts of southern England. The annual Mid-Somerset show is also held at Shepton, on a site at the sw edge of the town.

The Somerset Levels

At the heart of what is still the county of Somerset, between the Quantocks, the Mendips, and the coast, stretching inland w beyond Glastonbury and s to the edge of the Ham stone country, is an area of the greatest fascination. It is a landscape of willow trees but no hedges, of lush grass and summer milking units, of views appearing at a distance empty and barren, but bounded by low hills, punctuated by fascinating islands, and criss-crossed by waterways – drains, rhines (*pron.* reens) and ditches in descending order of size – which may at first frustrate the walker, but certainly more than satisfy the naturalist.

Commercial exploitation, archaeology, and natural science have between them been explaining the develop-

ment of the Levels. The original valley floor of 6000 BC some 90 ft and more below the present ground level, was in the next 2,000 years or so flooded by a rise in sea-level, due to the melting of polar ice. Blue-grey clay and silt was thus deposited, bringing the soil roughly up to its present level. The sea receded slightly, and, in the drying mud, reeds and sedge began to grow. The natural succession of water plants quite soon caused self-destruction, creating layers of decaying vegetation in a landscape of muddy pools and meandering rivers. In drier areas willow and alder began to spread, followed by ash, oak, and elm as their vegetation created firmer ground.

About 3000 BC an increase in rainfall reduced tree growth and produced the wet-loving cotton grass, heaths, and mosses; and the soil became acid, thus causing the bog by a complicated series of chemical changes, to grow, both upwards and outwards. Man was already here, and his sophisticated wooden roadways across the bog from islands and ridges of higher ground have been emerging through the work of archaeologists in advance of commercial peat cutting and drainage both N and S of the Poldens. The Sweet Track, the earliest trackway in Europe, and probably in the world, was built *c.* 4000 BC over the peat reed swamp, and probably linked Westhay with the Polden hills. Its materials – ash, hazel, holly, lime, elm, alder, willow, and oak – are in themselves a fine profile of the prehistoric landscape, and its technique and construction a triumph for prehistoric Somerset Man. Other trackways built in the following thousand years or so with different techniques, include the Walton Heath track, with hurdles of hazel and willow (2900 BC). Displays and restored sections are to be seen in the County Museum at Taunton (q.v.).

Trackways presuppose not only movement but settlement, and the so-called 'lake' villages of Meare and Glastonbury are the best-known, no longer thought to be exactly 'lake' villages, but lake-side settlements. And the lake that gave its name to Meare remained as a memory of the flooded Levels long after the settlements and trackways had disappeared. Roman occupation of at least parts of the area, and a thick brown clay deposit on some archaeological sites, suggest a succession of localized floods, but a general picture of marsh and wilderness, the 'fen fastnesses' where Alfred could retire to shelter from the Danes (see Athelney). Only the 'islands' afforded security, and are often found later with religious settlements. The possibility of a quay near Pilton and of boats at Glastonbury (qq.v.) is reality.

And then the erosion began. Inspired and encouraged by landlords, principally by the monks of Glastonbury and the canons of Wells, tenants built and maintained sea-walls, embanked rivers, and gradually worked from their island and marsh-side villages, draining and reinstating the land (see Weston Zoyland). None of this involved much co-ordination, and winter flooding as well as much litigation was the inevitable result. Between 1770 and 1833, however, co-ordinated efforts not only

A rhine on the Levels

attempted large-scale drainage, including the digging of the King's Sedgemoor Drain (1794), but also clay and silt was spread to alter the character of the soil. More difficult areas were and still are drained by pumping stations, the first in 1830. Greatest progress was made in the 1940s, first with the creation of the Huntspill Cut (assisted by the Golden Corner Pumping Station), as much to provide water for the Royal Ordnance Factory at Puriton as to improve drainage; and then the widening of the King's Sedgemoor Drain.

Flooding is not entirely ended; at least one farmer appreciates the annual deposit of silt and the wildfowl that come within his boundaries. Wild-fowling is now practised on a lesser scale than in the 18th century, when decoy pools were found all over the Levels. Plans for the use of peat-workings for recreation in the form of new lakes and nature reserves are the beginnings of a recognition that the Somerset Levels provide a unique landscape and are not the barren and misty acres that passers-by imagine.

Somerton Som. 2 C2

'Ancient Capital of Wessex' proclaim the road signs at this grey stone town on the edge of a ridge overlooking the level grounds of Sedgemoor. The ridge was part of the estates of the Saxon royal house, though the centre of Saxon rule was wherever the king happened to be. The real claims to capital status are the place-name and the fact that from 1278 until 1371 the town was the site of the county gaol and the meeting-place of the circuit and shire courts. Did these come from Ilchester (q.v.) because of a more ancient tradition, for certainly the county name is interpreted as the people of Somerset (the *Sumorsaete*) who looked to Somerton as their centre of influence.

Somerton's street pattern was once cruciform, meeting at a cross-roads NW of the church, but a speculative development of the late 13th century created the present delightful market-place with its 17th-century 'town hall' and market cross. In the 18th century Somerton's Spring Fair for fat cattle attracted buyers from London, and in

Market-place, Somerton

the event of invasion by Napoleon in Devon the moors below the town were to be the concentration point for cattle from the South West. The town was bypassed by the early railways in the county, and is missed by the main roads. It almost fossilized during the 19th, but thus was preserved its now jealously-guarded centre, including the tree-lined Broad Street (formerly Pig Street) and Cow Square, with its elegant town houses. Old Hall perhaps represents the medieval court house. Several of the town's old inns survive around the market-place, the White Hart certainly of medieval origin with traces of a galleried courtyard.

St Michael's church, on the N side of the market-place, dates from the early 13th century. The nave was rebuilt with aisles in the mid 14th and the fine timber roof is *c.* 1510. The church belonged to Muchelney Abbey (q.v.) in the Middle Ages; the abbey tithe barn, much rebuilt, is used by an international antiques business.

Harbin Arnold (d. 1782) left a rent-charge of eight guineas to provide bread on Sunday afternoons for four of the oldest and poorest families in the parish, but his munificence only lasted for 40 years. A more permanent

memorial are two of the three brass chandeliers in the nave, dedicated

> To God's Glory and the Honor of the Church of
> England.

Sir John Betjeman claimed that these words inspired him when he was writing *English Parish Churches.*

Alabaster was quarried on the slopes of the ridge which runs N from Somerton towards Street (q.v.) from Roman times (a villa was found at Littleton during the 19th century), and there were 'plasterparys' quarries (gypsum) there in the 14th. Great Breach Wood is a Nature Reserve. The parish of COMPTON DUNDON, 4 miles N of Somerton, is really two villages, Compton on the E and Dundon on the W, the latter named after the prominent hill topped with an Iron Age fort with remarkably-preserved ramparts. The church at Dundon has a curious pulpit of 1638, approached through the thickness of the wall where the medieval rood-loft stair once emerged. On the ridge above Compton stands a monument, topped by a naval crown, to the memory of Vice-Admiral Sir Samuel Hood, Baronet, of nearby Butleigh Wootton who died at Madras in 1814. He was a member of a remarkable family which produced in the previous generation two other naval leaders, Samuel, Lord Hood (d. 1816), who fought with Rodney in the West Indies, and his brother Alexander, Lord Bridport (d. 1814), who took a leading part in the battle off Ushant in 1794 known as the 'Glorious First of June'.

South Cadbury Som. *see* **Cadbury**

South Petherton Som. 2 C3

'The *tun* by the Parrett' was an important place in Saxon times: the site of a royal 'palace' (perhaps in the valley s of the church), and a mission centre, still reflected in the large church prominently set above the village. But somehow, even with these advantages, it never became a town despite its market and midsummer fair, for it is bypassed by the main trade routes. For that reason it has retained considerable charm, and its bustle shows how small shops and personal service still have genuine appeal.

The carving of *Sagittarius* and the lion (cf. Stoke sub Hamdon) in the s porch and some walling at the w end of the chancel are the oldest fragments in the church, which underwent major rebuilding in the late 13th and early 14th centuries. The s transept and nave were rebuilt again in the 15th when the N porch and the top stage of the octagonal central tower were built. The church was heavily restored in the 19th century, partly by Blomfield and Sedding, leaving the nave with a dull Victorian look, though later work on the s transept has revealed its medieval magnificence, a proper setting for one of Somerset's best brasses, on the tomb of Sir Giles Daubeney (d. 1446) and his first wife. There is a separate brass to his second wife (d. 1442). The cross-legged knight, found in a local quarry, is probably Sir Philip Daubeney (d. 1294). Henry Compton (d. 1603) kneels uncomfortably facing his wife on the E wall of the transept. Compton inherited part of the manor of Wigborough, in the s of the parish; his daughter Alice married a man rejoicing in the name of Emorb Johnson, so named to distinguish him from his father, whose name was Brome! In the N transept (the vestry) is a monument to William Sandys (d. 1679), a local squire who lived at 'King Ina's Palace' (see below) and who, so his inscription declares, was a faithful Anglican who hated extremism and enthusiasm of all kinds, and especially that which he found in the civil and religious troubles of his own lifetime.

Another dislike of enthusiasm was shown by the vicar who dismissed his curate, Thomas Coke, for making the services of the church too popular. Coke met John Wesley at Kingston St Mary and with Lady Huntingdon's preachers Coke brought life to South Petherton's religious practices. He was removed in 1777 but bought a new house in the village in 1778. He was later to be the first Secretary of the Methodist Conference and first Superintendent and Bishop of the American Methodist Church.

The Daubeneys, owners of the main manor from c. 1225, built a house in the valley NE of the village centre in the 14th century. The E end was rebuilt in the early 16th century, probably by Giles, Lord Daubeney, KG (d. 1508), the work including a beautiful two-storeyed bay window. The whole was restored in the 19th century when the name 'King Ina's Palace' came into use.

The rich agricultural land in the parish gave no incentive for enclosure, and traces of the open fields may still be seen w of the village. Only in the 19th century was there any appreciable growth in industries other than farming, mostly connected with the locally-grown flax, and with a small amount of gloving. The open stalls in the market-place ceased to be used by 1870, and the arcades of the market hall were filled in. But substantial houses in South Street and Palmer Street show how prosperous the parish was in the 17th and 18th centuries.

Stanton Drew Avon 5 B5

The stone circles beside the river Chew form a prehistoric site of the greatest importance. There are three circles with associated avenues, a probable chamber tomb known as the Cove, a single stone called Hauteville's Quoit, two other stones called Middle Ham, the whole forming a complex over half a mile across, dating from the Beaker Period of the Bronze Age (2000–1600 BC).

It used to be thought that the 'Drew' part of the village name had some connexion with druids, on the probably correct assumption that the stones had some religious significance. While the interpretation of the place-name is not tenable, it is a fact that the Drew or Drogo family also held at least two manors in Devon that have megalithic remains.

The stones are of three kinds: dolomitic conglomerate, and limestone quarried in the immediate region, and sandstone of uncertain origin. The largest circle is approx. 350 ft in diameter, and 27 of the original 30 stones survive. A site like this has encouraged many traditions. John Aubrey visited his grandmother at Stanton in 1664 and heard the local tale that the stones were a petrified wedding. People pointed out to him the bride, the parson, and the cook; later visitors were shown the fiddler and dancers. There were other traditions that the stones could not be counted nor drawn, and any who tried would be immediately struck down or come to a sudden end as a result of their boldness. Hauteville's Quoit, across the river in Norton Malreward, was, people said, either rolled down Maes Knoll or otherwise hurled to its place by an enraged Sir John Hauteville, frustrated by getting such a poor reward as Norton from Edward I. Only the existence of Sir John has any historical reality (see Chew Magna).

Stavordale Som. *see* **Wincanton**

Steart   Som. *see* **Stogursey**

Steep Holm   Avon *see* **Weston-super-Mare**

Stockland Bristol   Som. *see* **Stogursey**

Stocklinch   Som. *see* **Barrington**

Stogursey   Som.   2 A1

Stogursey, or Stoke Courcy, from the family of de Curci who owned it in the 12th century, is a village which used to be a town. Between 1100 and 1107 William de Falaise and his wife Geva gave the church of St Andrew to the Abbey of Lonlay in their native Normandy, and monks were sent over from the mother house to administer the property and form a small religious community. The priory suffered, like most 'alien' houses, during the wars with France, and was small throughout its life, probably only a prior and two or three monks. An inventory of the conventual buildings in 1324 described only a hall, the prior's chamber, his store-room, kitchen, brewery,

bakery, and barn. Among the furniture were six trestles in the hall, but only one bed in the whole establishment. After years under Crown control, the property was handed over to the newly-founded Eton College c. 1440. The College still owns land in the parish and appoints clergy to the living. All that is certainly left of the priory buildings is a circular dovecot.

The former priory church, at the end of the village, is undoubtedly the most impressive Norman building in the county, and its architectural development reflects very accurately the fortunes of the priory. It was begun on an ambitious scale, presumably by William de Falaise, c. 1070, and the massive crossing and tower stands witness to Norman prosperity and ambition. The completed church then consisted of nave, transepts with E apses, and a short apsidal chancel; a form common enough in Normandy. Late in the next century, c. 1180, following the successful establishment and possible expansion of the religious community, the chancel was lengthened and given aisles. The late-Norman zig-zag work is well in evidence in the choir arcades, made all

Stone circle, Stanton Drew

the more impressive because of the higher level of the E end.

After all this magnificence, the typical Somerset rebuilding of the later Middle Ages was confined to the nave – the work of the parish, not of the dead or dying priory. And even here the work was confined, as far as survival goes, to new windows, a rood-screen and benches, the last made, it seems, between 1524 and 1528. Several of them have clear Renaissance elements, and one has what looks remarkably like a spoonbill. And there are, in the s chapel, which became the chapel of the Vernay family of FAIRFIELD (1 mile W), and later of their descendants the Palmers, the tombs of William de Vernay (d. 1333) and John de Vernay (d. 1447/8). The former was actually buried in Hillfarrance and only his heart lies here – hence the effigy holds that vital organ; the latter had to appear before the Archbishop of Canterbury for shouting at the vicar in English during a service, though he apparently ended his days as a lodger in the Priory. Another William de Vernay is said to have been licensed to build a wall with seven round towers to defend his mansion at Fairfield. The present house, not normally open to the public, was begun by Thomas Palmer (d. 1583) and was completed by his grandson, also Thomas (d. 1605). It certainly incorporates late-medieval features and was remodelled in the 18th century.

Stogursey also boasts a castle, still with substantial remains, though at present hardly appreciated. It has a circular tower, a gatehouse and a curtain wall, built in the 12th century and rebuilt in the 13th and 14th. The first castle here, *c.*1100, was probably occupied by William de Falaise; by 1166 it was the home of the de Curcis. A new tower was built in the 1490s but by 1538 the whole building was in decay. An ingenious use of a stream still provides water for the moat and once went on to drive the manor mill. The de Curcis also probably developed the village in the early 13th century into a borough with urban characteristics (Stogursey actually sent representatives to one of Edward III's Parliaments). The house plots in the centre of the village still bear traces of their urban nature, and the frontage lines indicate a large open market square between the remains of the market cross and Church Street.

Between Stogursey, the Parrett, and the coast is a for-gotten corner of Somerset; flat marshlands to add to the rich variety of the county. COMBWICH (*pron.* Cummidge) lies 4 miles E, a little port on the Parrett, with a 19th-century look and somehow a little foreign, belonging to the E coast. It was an outport of Bridgwater in medieval times, and boasted a church in the 14th century, not to be confused with the present Victorian–Decorated pile. Almost certainly the place has an ancient origin, for here the Parrett could be forded until a century or so ago. In the 19th century the local bricks and tiles were the main product, for local buildings including a fives wall,

Combwich

and for export. After a decline a new wharf was built in 1958 to take heavy machinery for the Hinkley Point nuclear power station, whose two reactors (2 miles NW) dominate the coast for miles (hence also the surprisingly well-maintained road). Narrow, open roads lead through the marshes, once dotted with windmills, to OTTERHAMPTON and STOCKLAND BRISTOL, to STEART and STOLFORD, to a coastline that is peculiar to the Channel, where mudflats at low tide are still crossed by Stolford fishermen with sledges as they go out to their distant nets. It is a coastline which, because of marked changes in tide levels, was in 7000 B.C. 3 miles nearer Wales; a coast which at Stolford was covered in forest in 2500 B.C., and which now at Steart Island forms a National Nature Reserve for Whitefronted geese, a wide variety of duck, and an important source of Spartina grass to consolidate the sea defences not only of Somerset but of other exposed coastlines throughout the world.

Stoke Bishop   Avon *see* **Westbury on Trym**

Stoke Gifford   Avon   5 B3
Sandwiched a little uncomfortably between the modern phenomena of motorway and railway, Stoke's added name recalls its Domesday owner, Osbern Giffard, though from Edward III's early years it was held by the ubiquitous Berkeleys, one of whom, Sir Richard, built a mansion here at the end of Elizabeth I's reign. It is said to have been damaged during the Civil War, and was restored if not substantially rebuilt by Norborne Berkeley *c.* 1760. Berkeley, MP for Gloucestershire, was appointed Groom of the Bedchamber on George III's accession in 1760, became Lord Lieutenant of Gloucestershire in 1762, and in 1764 was created Lord Botetourt. He was appointed to the unenviable post of Governor of Virginia in 1768, evidently in an attempt to restore his financial strength, but died two years later.

> A very courtier, [wrote Horace Walpole] who was ruined in his fortune, was sent governor to Virginia, where resided some of the ablest of the American patriots, yet in the two years that he lived to govern them his soothing flattering manners had so wrought in the province, that his death was bewailed with the most general and affectionate concern.

A magnificent statue voted by the Virginia Assembly was erected over his grave in William and Mary College, Williamsburg, USA.

Botetourt's house, later used as a hospital, is in the Classical style, contrasting with its early-19th-century Gothick porch and parapet. Its site, on an artificial terrace still flanked by the balustrades of Sir Richard Berkeley's house, gave it fine views over its parkland and lake. The hospital chapel was formerly an orangery of *c.* 1700 and thus also belonged to the older house. In the grounds are the remains of an obelisk, and a sarcophagus commemorating the winner of the St. Leger.

The parish church is also of the Classical spirit, though it is essentially of the 14th century, with a solid Norman font and 15th-century windows. The N aisle and chapel were added in the 18th century, necessitating a new chancel arch; the N chapel, now occupied by the organ, was built (complete with fireplace for essential comfort) as the private chapel for the Duchess of Beaufort, Lord Botetourt's sister and heir.

Stoke Pero   Som. *see* **Selworthy**

Stoke sub Hamdon   Som.   2 C3
In the shadow of the steep slopes of Ham Hill, the village of Stoke is really two villages, and has been since the time of Domesday and before. East Stoke has the church, a rare example of high-class Norman work for Somerset, with fine chancel arch decorated with billet, zig-zag, and lozenge ornament, original corbel table at the chancel eaves and, most notable of all, the figure over the N door. There the tympanum has a relief of a tree of life carrying three birds, flanked by two animals and an archer. About 1200 the tower base was added as a N transept with a good example of Transitional vaulting. The upper part of the tower was added in the 13th century and the parapet in the 15th. The S transept and the porch were built probably at the end of the 13th century, but thereafter the alterations have been only in detail, notably the W window of the late 14th century with reticulated tracery.

A tomb in the S transept is thought to contain the remains of Reginald de Monkton (d. 1307) first provost of Stoke College. This was founded as part of the manorhouse complex in West Stoke, the main village. There, under the present Castle Farm, are the remains of a house which John Beauchamp was licensed to crenellate in 1333. But the last male Beauchamp died in 1361, and after the death of Sir Matthew Gournay, husband of the Beauchamp widow, in 1406 the property was no longer lived in. It passed to the Duchy of Cornwall in 1443. Leland saw 'very notable ruins of a great manor place or castle' and the chapel of St Nicholas, in his time full of Beauchamp tombs, and with Gournay's brass in front of the choir screen. Already in 1540 there were signs of decay, but still masses were said there three times a week by the provost of a college who had a 'large house' in the village.

This large house is Stoke Priory (NT) in North Street, originally the home of a community of priests who from their foundation in 1304 were charged to say five daily masses for the Beauchamps in the manorial chapel of St Nicholas. The College was dissolved in 1548 and the chapel has disappeared as well as the manor house, gatehouse, and other associated buildings leaving only the line of the outer wall. The 'large house' has become a farm complex and includes a hall, domestic quarters, barns, and a dovecot. Most of the buildings are of the 15th century or later.

Stoke was one of the last villages to abandon its openfield agriculture, perhaps in part because gloving had made the village prosperous. Gloves also divided the village between church and chapel: the ostentation of the chapel in North Street is no accident.

Three miles NE is TINTINHULL, now a spreading, almost suburban village, at its centre a triangular green with important houses at its edge. St Margaret's church, almost hidden behind Tintinhull Court, is a Somerset rarity, an early-13th-century rectangular one-cell church with chancel arch inserted in the 14th century and a N tower whose top stage was added in 1516–17. The porch was built in 1441–2, the benches made in 1511–12 (note the extra seats at their ends).

Tintinhull Court, next door, was the medieval rectory and includes at its front a small projecting room of *c.* 1500, though most of the building is of the 17th and 18th centuries. The Dower House, facing up the green, was called 'new' in 1687 and was built by the dominant family, the Nappers. Along Farm Street is Tintinhull

Tintinhull House

House (NT), a Napper conversion of the early 18th century, which is now set in gardens established early in the 20th century worth travelling miles to see.

Stolford Som. *see* **Stogursey**

Stratton-on-the-Fosse Som. 5 B6
A Mendip village which seems at first sight to live up to its name – a settlement on the street; the main road follows the course of the Roman Fosse Way. The old village centre around the church is easily missed, partly because of the dominance of Downside on the other side of the road.

Like several Mendip churches this one has good 18th-century features: the chancel (1765), the Knatchbull chapel (*c.* 1780), and the nave ceiling; perhaps evidence of the prosperity brought by coal, mined here by the Duchy of Cornwall in the 15th century and exploited until 1968. The church is dedicated to St Vigor, the family name of the Norman tenants of the Domesday lord, the Bishop of Coutances. St Vigor was a 6th-century Bishop of Bayeux, known for his attacks on idolatry, who gave his name to St Vigeur-le-Grand, near Bayeaux, where he founded a monastery. His appearance here is a direct link with the church's founder, perhaps the Domesday lord, the Bishop of Coutances, or some Norman tenant who came from the Bayeux region.

On the w side of the Fosse stand the impressive buildings of Downside, a Benedictine Abbey and a Public School. The community traces its origin to 1607 at Douai. It came to this country in 1795 when the French Revolution was making life uncomfortable on the continent, and settled first at Acton Burnell (Salop). Downside House (*c.* 1700) and estate were brought in 1814, and buildings have been added regularly ever since as both school and community grew. The school has remained and expanded in impressive wings and quads near the original house, while the monastery has moved to higher ground to the N and now clusters round the abbey church.

In many ways the church is a mirror of the medieval cathedral, for it is not in a single style nor by any means by a single hand, thanks in part to the changing opinions of the community. It began with the N transept by Dunn and Hansom (1872) and continued with the crossing and S transept, the ambulatory and the radiating chapels. Thomas Garner designed the chancel (1901–5), but the dominant hand is that of Sir Giles Gilbert Scott, who built the nave (1923–5) and the upper part of the tower (1938), a magnificent landmark for miles around. Pevsner remarks on the 'almost Spanish effusiveness' which 'on the grandest French cathedral precedent' combines styles ranging from the Early English of the N transept to the Perpendicular of the chancel. The interior is noticeably void of monuments, but includes the tomb of Cardinal Gasquet (d. 1929), a great medieval historian. The church remains unfinished, lacking two and a half bays, but plans are in hand for completion.

Street Som. 2 C1

At first sight Street is a town with little to offer the visitor, the view from the bypass of large car parks in front of factory buildings suggesting a modern foundation. And so, in many ways, Street is: a 19th-century industrial town, but based on an industry that has left relatively fews scars. It is the home of Clarks, whose shoes are now made in many parts of the world. The firm was established in 1825 when Cyrus Clark, fell-monger and wool-stapler, started in business on his own. His brother James joined him in 1828 in making sheepskin rugs, and in his spare time made the famous sheepskin slippers, the 'Brown Petersburgs' or 'Brown Peters', from skins too small for rugs. Within 20 years slippers and shoes had outstripped rugs. And Street grew as the business grew, its buildings in a uniform grey lias which at first seems to lack character. But they have a unity and, near the factory, an almost garden-city atmosphere, which is worth further examination.

The Clarks are a Quaker family, and factory and Friends' Meeting House (1850) stand close together. The factory incorporates the first building of 1829 and a clock-tower of 1897. The building contains a fascinating and well-displayed museum illustrating both the development of the shoe from Roman times and the history of the firm. Quaker views on temperance and social justice are reflected in the establishment of a workers' club and library by 1885, a temperance hotel (the Bear Inn) in 1894, and the Institute (Crispin Hall) in 1894–5. Further down the street the former Board School (now a furniture shop) was built from the profits made on army clothing in the Crimean War by a firm that was forced to accept the contracts on humanitarian grounds, but which could not benefit itself from the profits of war of which they disapproved.

But if Street owes its existence as a busy town and shopping centre to Clarks, under whom it expanded from just under 1,000 inhabitants when the firm began to nearly 4,000 by the end of the century, it has a well-hidden history going back to the Dark Ages. A Roman road running to the E of the town gave the place its name, and settlement began near it, in the area where the parish church now stands. That church, now dedicated to the Holy Trinity, is a 13th-century building which in the Middle Ages was known as the chapel of St Gildas. Gildas (c. 500–c. 570) was a great figure in the Celtic Church and especially in Welsh monastic life; c. 540 he wrote the *De excidio Britanniae*, an attack on British leaders of church and state at their failure against Saxon advance. For a time he lived on Flat Holm in the Bristol Channel, but died at his monastery in Britanny, the abbey of St Gildas-de-Rhuys. Relics were brought from there to Glastonbury, perhaps in the 11th century, and Street's chapel, one of the Abbey's possessions, may have been dedicated in Gildas's honour at the time.

Street, or rather Leigh (1 mile S), also claims a connexion with St Kea, for its name as far back as 725 was Lantokai, meaning 'the church of St Kea'. He probably came from Glastonbury, and is said to have acquired a bell from 'a skilful bell-founder named Gildas'. Is that his near neighbour, the Saint? Most of St Kea's missionary work was done in Devon and Cornwall, but like Gildas he probably went to Brittany and died there. He was apparently efficacious for toothache and children's diseases, and is associated in his Legend with a stag. That Legend also tells how Kea came back from Brittany to try and restore peace between Arthur and Mordred, but coming too late, all he could do was to persuade Guinevere to become a nun.

But Street is a modern place; near the church is Strode College incorporating a theatre, and 1 mile SE is the centre of Millfield, a school of international repute.

Two miles W is WALTON, a long village with farm-houses still recognizable in the main street, typical of a village whose lands were mostly in the marshlands. The 'Old Parsonage' next to the church is an attractive late-medieval building with transomed and traceried windows and a most complicated plan.

SHARPHAM PARK, 1 mile NW, like Walton part of the Glastonbury estates, was created by the 14th century and probably by 1260. A house, which has been much altered since, was there in the time of Abbot Nicholas Frome (1420–55) but this 'poore lodge', as Leland called it, was turned into a 'maner place' by Abbot Richard Bere (1493–1524). There in September 1539 Henry VIII's Visitors examined Abbot Richard Whiting, and then sent him 'a very weak man and sickly' to the Tower of London, before his trial at Wells and execution on Glastonbury Tor.

Edward Dyer (d. 1607), poet and friend of Sir Philip Sydney, was born at Sharpham Park, the son of Thomas Dyer the Crown tenant. Henry Fielding the novelist was born there in 1707 when his mother was visiting her family home.

Sutton Bingham Som. *see* **East Coker**

Tarr Steps Som. *see* **Exmoor**

Taunton Som. 2 A2

Taunton is the county town of Somerset. This is not, as in most counties, an historic position, for Somerset's administration has only been totally concentrated here since 1936, though assizes were held in the town from medieval times, and visits of the judges created, as in other assize towns, a 'season' when the spectacle of felons by day was expunged by theatres and balls by night. And beside all this, the town has for even longer had an administrative function as a Saxon borough and as the centre of the vast estates of the medieval Bishops of Winchester.

Yet Taunton began as a military outpost built by King Ine before 722, and it seems likely that a missionary centre was soon established. This minster, which with its surrounding estates was bought from the Crown by Bishop Denewulf of Winchester in 904, may have stood (according to latest theories) within the outer precincts of the later castle and just outside what came to be the medieval borough. In *c.* 1120 this minster, with daughter chapels in the surrounding countryside (e.g. Bishop's Hull, Trull (qq.v)) became a house of Augustinian canons, and in 1158 it was given a new site, outside the town's E defences. Part of its huge graveyard was recently uncovered and one side of the precinct gateway, for long known as Priory Barn, still stands by the County Cricket Ground.

The removal of the old minster was achieved to extend the castle. Its site on low ground beside the Tone emphasizes its non-military function, though the great square keep (now the Castle Hotel garden), added by the Prince-Bishop Henry of Blois to the works of Bishop William Giffard (1107–29) and some unknown predecessors, is still imposing. The first great hall and chamber were replaced *c.* 1245–9 by new buildings under Bishop William Ralegh, providing a new hall, private chambers, and chapel joined to each other round an inner bailey by circular angle towers. Further work was done late in the Middle Ages: the apparently 17th-century Castle House is a 15th-century timber building, and the Ham stone gatehouse was erected by Bishop Walter Langton in 1495. Beyond the gate over the inner moat is an outer bailey, its limits marked by the 13th-century Castle Bow, the Municipal Buildings (the E end built at the edge of the moat as a grammar school by Bishop Richard Fox in 1522) and by some early brickwork forming the inside of the front hall of the Castle Hotel.

The subsequent history of the castle includes minor repairs, alterations, damage and neglect by successive Bishops of Winchester and their officers, the siege of the

The font, St James's, Taunton

town when Robert Blake held out for Parliament in 1644–5, and the use of the great hall to hold the assizes (most notably by Chief Justice George Jeffreys in his Bloody Assize after Monmouth's Rebellion in 1685). In 1873 the castle was saved by the Somerset Archaeological Society and has been their home ever since. Their fine collections, improved and extended since 1958 under the care of the Somerset County Council, instructively illustrate many aspects of the prehistory and history of the ancient county of Somerset.

Taunton was an early clothing centre with fulling mills established early in the 13th century. The grandeur of its two churches – St Mary's a little self-conscious since the vista of Hammett Street was opened in 1788 – is a sure reflection of the town's prosperity. Both towers, a splendid sight especially from the train, have been rebuilt, St James's a little less accurately than the other. St James's seems more modest now, but one wide bay in its otherwise rather long arcade suggests a former crossing tower. The church's unquestioned magnificence is in its font, a little crude but as ornate as anything in the county. St Mary's is more flamboyant, and the eye is forced immediately up the slender piers to the angels and the painted roof. This was the townsmen's church; between 1488 and 1514 they left money for the tower,

St Mary's, Taunton

and the porch has the date 1508. Inside, the nave has double aisles, the second arcade on the N being the earliest recognizable part, dating from the 13th century. At the end of Henry VIII's reign the altars standing in the side chapels and before several pillars must have made the church something little less than a cathedral in colour and magnificence.

Taunton's clothiers turned to Nonconformity in the 17th century and the town was known for its prosperity and its independence, though where politics and religion drew the town towards Robert Blake and Parliament in the Civil War, innate caution made the leading citizens hesitate when Monmouth was proclaimed King here in 1685. The same innate caution or less overwhelming commercial pressure than elsewhere has fortunately preserved a sprinkling of medieval buildings even in the centre of the town, notably the timber-framed and gabled houses in Fore Street; and others lie behind more modern façades. Elsewhere, the wide streets, often with refreshing glimpses of the Blackdowns or the Quantocks, have still enough mellow brick (see especially the Crescent 1807) to recall an earlier age. Thomas Gerard in the early 17th century commended the 'faire and pleasant towne' for its

> largenes ... the bewtie of the streetes and markett place ... the sweet situation ... [and] a rich soyle.

The traveller, finding the town with a main railway station and a motorway, would commend also its good communications, which have made Taunton something of a regional centre for a wide range of commercial administration and distribution, and still the market centre of a rich agricultural region as it was 1,000 years ago.

Temple Combe Som. *see* **Milborne Port**

Thornbury Avon 5 B3

'Idelnes muche reynithe there', wrote Leland in the 1540s, for disaster had struck the once-thriving clothing town. The 'poore tenaunts' of various properties around the town had in their time 'not without many curses' suffered all the disadvantages of an improving landlord, taking their rich corn and grass land to expand his parks, but the fall of the Staffords of Thornbury castle contributed greatly to economic decline. Thornbury also owed its rise to the owners of the castle. There was a market here at Domesday, and for centuries the town was the centre of a feudal honor, the Honor of Gloucester, a trace of which still survives in High Street, in the Classical form of the Old Register Office. The Earls of Gloucester had a 'castle' here, referred to in the early 14th century, which passed to the Stafford family. This house, or part of it, was pulled down by Edward Stafford, Duke of Buckingham, who began, what still remains, a magnificent building which is part palace and part castle. The castle is not open to the public, but enough can be glimpsed through the windows in the N wall of the

churchyard to reveal late medieval architecture at its best.

What survives is in fact unfinished, for the Duke of Buckingham was executed in 1521 (see Hinton Charterhouse). By that time he had partially completed three sides of a courtyard, the fourth comprising the hall of the earlier house. The side facing the church is the most famous, recognized and copied in its details after Pugin's study of it in the 1830s. This is the palace, with echoes of Henry VII's chapel at Westminster and new work at Windsor, overlooking a privy garden with – at least in Leland's time – a wooden gallery, and hence the curious windows towards the church. One chimney on this range, facing into the courtyard, is a splendid conceit of moulded brick, with badges of the Staffords – the knot – and the date 1514.

The W side of the courtyard is pure castle: a grand gatehouse begun in 1511, and a polygonal tower with machicolated parapet. It faces an outer court now appearing ruinous, which was never finished: 'certeyne gates, and towres in it castelle lyke' were built, but only rising four or five yards even in the 1540s, 'and so remaynithe a token of a noble peace of worke purposid'.

Leland speaks of a temporary roof over the buildings after Buckingham's sudden demise, and Henry VIII and Anne Boleyn are said to have stayed there in 1539, but its history thereafter is not clear until work in the 19th century, largely by Salvin in 1854, brought much of the castle into use as a dwelling. A survey made in James I's reign refers not only to state rooms but to domestic quarters not now recognizable and probably now demolished, including wet and dry larders, privy bakehouse, boiling house, great kitchen, privy kitchen with lodgings for the cooks, cellars, buttery, and sculleries. The present fame of Thornbury Castle is as a restaurant of national repute since 1966. The diner approaches the great gatehouse in Buckingham's unfinished outer court through a vineyard planted in 1972; not, perhaps, what the Duke of Buckingham had planned.

Thornbury church, close beside the castle, is of a size and grandeur to be expected of a town with such a history. The tower, with its superb pierced and turreted crown, dominates. 'A fayre pece of worke', remarked Leland, who added that 'the hole savinge the chauncell' was built within living memory. This presents a difficulty. The chancel is certainly of the 14th century, though apparently later than the consecration of the high altar in 1309 unless it is advanced work, possible since the builders were the monks of Tewkesbury as rectors of Thornbury. The late Norman N and s doorways in the nave and the font are perhaps too late to support a tradition of rebuilding by Robert FitzHamon, and more likely to be the work of Robert, Earl of Gloucester (d. 1147), FitzHamon's son-in-law, and illegitimate son of Henry I.

The rest of the nave clearly belongs to the late Middle

Ages, and although precise ascription is not possible the clues are plentiful enough: carvings on hood moulds, windows, and pinnacles around the exterior show Stafford Knots in plenty, a rose, a sunburst and what is usually called a peascod but is in fact broom. The Staffords had royal, Plantagenet blood (hence the broom); and the rose and the sun in splendour are, if nothing else, characteristic of a period of political unrest where to be exclusively for York or Lancaster was dangerous if not fatal. Humphrey Stafford, 1st Duke of Buckingham, died at Northampton in 1460 fighting for Lancaster against York; Henry, the 2nd Duke (d. 1483) supported Richard, Duke of Gloucester, and then rebelled against him after he became King; Edward, the 3rd Duke (d. 1521), aspired (so Wolsey claimed) to the throne on his own account.

Later members of the family were necessarily more circumspect, Sir John (d. 1624) managing (so his modest memorial in the chancel declares) to follow the 'frail and slippery course of a soldier and courtier' for 47 years under Queen Elizabeth and James I, and was for much of that time constable of Bristol castle. The last Stafford occupant of Thornbury castle, and lord of the manor in remarkable succession, turned to a profession that epito-

mized the traditions of his ancestors: Sir Algar Howard (1880–1970) was Garter King of Arms from 1944 until 1950.

The church is curiously bereft of pre-Reformation detail inside to match its external magnificence. Plans by the 3rd Duke to found a college for a dean, sub-dean, 8 priests, 4 clerks, and 8 choristers seem to have come to naught, but there were four chantries here in the 1540s.

The town of Thornbury lies some distance to the s of church and castle, though modern residential development is joining them together. The alignment of the streets reveals the history of the town, a new creation by Robert de Clare, Earl of Gloucester, between 1243 and 1262: three streets converging on a large market place, perhaps the whole area bounded by High, Silver, and St Mary Streets. The splendidly irregular street frontages throughout the town comprise a fine collection of buildings dating from the early 15th century, happily preserved, as in so many places, through hard times. By the late 18th century the clothing industry was 'entirely lost' though women and children did some spinning. The reason for this was that the turnpike road left Thornbury isolated. Its market and three fairs, its booth hall, corn-

Thornbury Castle

market house and shambles gradually became redundant. The splendid white lion over the hotel of that name now presides, however, over considerable bustle. Thornbury in the 1970s has become a desirable residential place away from Bristol, almost trebling in size within a decade, and thus creating the pressure for development which has in the past been the death of country towns. ALVESTON, 1 mile s, is a characteristically scattered settlement, stretching a mile between Alveston Down and the old parish church. Modern houses have filled and more than filled the gaps between cottages and farmhouses of the 18th and 19th centuries on the w of the A38, leaving untouched on the other side the hamlet called the Street, with a 17th-century farmhouse, a late-Georgian house called the Grove, and their associated cottages and buildings. Isolated too, more than a mile s of the village (if it is that), is the former parish church of St Helen. Only its Perpendicular tower and a fragment of the N nave wall are standing, but a doorway in the wall is clearly of Norman work, and the roughly circular churchyard, now bounded in part by Old Church Farmhouse (16th-century and later), suggests an early religious site. So, too, does the dedication, to St Helen, mother of the Emperor Constantine, and found more commonly in the North of England. The church was abandoned in 1885 for one on the main road at Rudgeway. The Norman font came from the old church. At the time, presumably, it was thought that the new church would form the centre of the village, but is itself now nearly as isolated from the heart of Alveston as its predecessor.

Tintinhull   Som. *see* **StokesubHamdon**

Tockington   Avon *see* **Olveston**

Trudoxhill   Som. *see* **Nunney**

Trull   Som. *see* **Pitminster**

Ubley   Avon *see* **Chew Magna**

Uphill   Avon *see* **Weston-super-Mare**

Walton   Som. *see* **Street**

Watchet   Som. 1 H1
Watchet is a busy little working port where Midlands-produced tractors are exported to Portugal; the home of paper manufacturers since the 17th century, who make the little Washford river an unusual colour and temperature; and the product of a great deal of fascinating history. Its name means 'under wood' and is Celtic; and the high ground behind the town was, so the field-names declare, once heavily wooded. The Celtic influence, too, is clear; there were trading links with Wales from the Middle Ages, and from the 13th century

onwards many inhabitants had Welsh names; and best of all is the name of the parish, not Watchet but St Decuman's.

St Decuman was probably a 6th-century Welsh monk from Pembrokeshire who met an unprovoked and untimely death by decapitation while at prayer. A religious centre was established here, and within its parish several hamlets grew up including Watchet which, by Alfred's time, was defended against possible enemy attack. Twice the little town was ravaged by the Danes in the 10th century, but it survived and its mint suggests thriving business. But worse than enemy attack was the relentless damage of the sea. The Saxon defences seem to have gone, and St Decuman's church too, it seems, had to be moved to its safer but lonely position over the hill, where only the top of its tall tower can be seen from the town. The present church certainly dates only from the 13th century.

The church is isolated from the town, but near the old rectory farm, held by successive rich prebendaries of the cathedral at Wells. The prosperity of the parish in the later Middle Ages is clear from the church building: it is large for the district, and its enriched N arcade has piers with niches, some still occupied and more than a trifle crude. Its medieval rood screen and roofs are of good quality; and the pulpit and communion rails are Jacobean.

The tombs in the Wyndham chapel begin with John (d. 1572) and his wife Florence (d. 1596). She had two funerals, having been declared dead soon after her marriage. Her inadvertent saviour was the local sexton, whose crude attempts to remove a ring from her finger in the vault the night after the first funeral roused Florence and more than terrified the thief. Much more impressive, but now denuded of its canopy, is the tomb of John's father, Sir John (d. 1574), a curiously archaic structure without Renaissance detail, though the brass figures are firmly Elizabethan. At the w end of the chapel is the family pew, decorated with luscious foliage and dated 1688.

Wedmore   Som. 4 H6
The origin of the place-name has caused even the experts some difficulty: 'moor for hunting', says one; 'moor liable to flood', says another. And early popular etymology changed the meaning yet again to 'moor of the agreement, pledge or reconciliation', for people well remembered that here in 878, at a solemn religious ceremony, the newly baptised Danish king, Guthrum, underwent the solemn chrisom-loosing which thereafter marked him as no longer a threatening, pagan invader, but a Christian leader of a settled people. The 'Peace of Wedmore' marked the acceptance of the fact that eastern England was now the Danelaw. But why Wedmore?

It was royal property, and not far from Aller (q.v.), the place where Guthrum was baptised; and not far, too, from Alfred's island refuge of Athelney (q.v.). Wedmore was another such 'island', and a retreat like the others both strategic and spiritual. Wedmore 'island' is in the Axe valley beneath the Mendip scarp, and within easy reach of the royal palace at Cheddar (q.v.). There is a tradition of a Saxon palace here, too; what is perhaps more likely is a religious settlement, for where else but at a religious site should the great chrisom ceremony take place? There was certainly a church at Wedmore by 1075, and its several chapels – Mark, Biddisham, Allerton, and Mudgeley – strongly suggest an early Saxon minster. So, too, does the present church fabric, much of which dates in essence to c. 1200.

The most magnificent feature of the church is undoubtedly the s doorway, and the similarity with Wells (q.v.) is obvious. But then Wedmore had been given to Bishop Giso as long ago as 1062, and the Deans of Wells had held a manor here since 1136. So the same designers and craftsmen were almost certainly employed. And to them are owed not only the doorway but also the crossing and probably the chancel, once evidently lit each side by a row of lancets. The Perpendicular work which at first seems to dominate is more restrained, and perhaps earlier here than usual: the upper stages of the tower and porch, parapets and large windows in nave, aisles, and transepts, leaving the w end almost more in glass than in stone. Inside there are few traces of similar magnificence: two murals of St Christopher, one painted over the other, and some flamboyant ironwork on the door, repaired, but surely not first made, in 1677.

The village itself lies low between two parts of the 'island', and Pilcorn Street there may indicate an ancient quay. If the hoard of 10th- and 11th-century coins found in the churchyard is not clear evidence of local commerce, the weekly market and annual fair granted in 1255 suggest as much. There is evidence of local enterprise in other ways. Captain Thomas Hodges, commemorated in the church, was killed at the siege of Antwerp in 1583, and had his heart sent home to Wedmore. A descendant, George, followed his military example, but managed to die in his own bed in 1630. Enterprise and experiment later in the century was shown by John Westover, a local surgeon but with far more than a local reputation, whose successful treatment of mental patients in quarters adjoining his own house (Porch House) he recorded in his journal between 1685 and 1700, not only detailing their behaviour but also his charges for their board and lodging.

Hannah More established a Sunday school in Wedmore in 1799, and in face of opposition from vicar and gentry it survived, though the parish remained, according to Martha More, 'depraved and shocking as ever', despite their efforts. A more enlightened vicar, S. H. A. Hervey (1876–98), excavated a building at Mudgeley too early and too unscientifically to prove that it was Alfred's palace, published the *Wedmore Chronicle*, a more valuable contribution to the history of his parish, founded the local Musical Society, played cricket for the

village, walked miles in the countryside, and enjoyed tennis. He lived to be almost a hundred.

Wellington   Som.   2 A2
The town that gave title to one of our greatest soldiers has had a much less distinguished history, though the place-name, which seems to mean the *tun* of the temple clearing, suggests an ancient religious spot, perhaps sited on the highest point in the flat valley where the parish church now stands. It was still only an agricultural settlement at Domesday, but by then it was one of the estates of the Bishop of Wells, having been given to Sherborne by King Edward the Elder in 904 and transferred when the see of Wells was founded in 909.

By 1279 a borough had been established, though as a money-raising venture it was hardly a success, worth to the bishop in the 1360s only just over £4 a year in rent and £3 in court fines. In 1548 Bishop Barlow was obliged to give up possession of the town and manor to Protector Somerset as part of the spoliation of the see, but Somerset's fall brought it to the Crown, where it remained until sold to Sir John Popham (d. 1607), whose own estimation of himself is no doubt reflected in the flamboyance of his monument in the parish church. He was, it is true, a dominating figure: successively Solicitor- and Attorney-General, and from 1592 Chief Justice of the Queen's Bench; Speaker of the House of Commons in 1581 confident enough to say, when Queen Elizabeth asked him what had passed in the Lower House: 'If it please your Majesty, seven weeks.' Frequently accused of brutality as a judge he was involved in the main State Trials of his time, including those of Mary, Queen of Scots, of Sir Walter Ralegh, and of the Gunpowder Plotters.

Thomas Gerard, writing in 1633, referred to his 'wholesome severity towards wandering roagues', one reason why Popham was interested in a colony in North America, where disbanded soldiers, beggars, and highwaymen could be sent. The 'goodly house' he built was in 1633 'still the greatest ornament' of the town, but it was levelled by the Royalists under Sir Richard Grenville in 1645, for Sir Francis Popham and Wellington with him were Parliamentarians in sympathy.

A good market town in Gerard's time; the centre of a prosperous area of serge production when Celia Fiennes came in the 1690s. But something soon went wrong, and a quarter of a century later Defoe called it a 'low, dirty place', full of the beggars that Popham would have abhorred. Cloth-making continued, and by the end of the 18th century had revived again, led by the Fox family, not only prosperous manufacturers but also bankers, who continue in business at Tonedale, N of the town, where Thomas and Elizabeth Were had fulling mills in 1754. Bricks and tiles were made E of the town from 1842, and the 19th century also saw brave attempts at reviving Wellington's agricultural importance, notably in the establishment of a market and the erection of the market house in 1832–3. Today the wide main street, curiously interrupted by the market house, still has both the breadth and the air of a market town, and much of its charm lies in the brick Georgian and early Victorian frontages and the small, personal shops.

The church, almost isolated at the E end of the town, is more impressive from the outside than within: tall, red sandstone tower, clerestory and embattled aisles and chapels, all Perpendicular, and much renewed. Only the early-14th-century effigy of a priest in the chancel is definitely earlier; and perhaps the best part of the church is no longer there, but in the County Museum at Taunton. This is the late-14th-century painted stone reredos, with tiers of figures below a Crucifixion, discovered forming part of the flooring during restoration.

On a spur of the Blackdown hills 3 miles s stands the WELLINGTON MONUMENT (NT), not quite what Thomas Lee the younger of Barnstaple and the committee of local gentry envisaged in 1815 when they opened a subscription fund to 'perpetuate the memory of Wellington' on the estate bought for him by a grateful nation in 1813. The monument, topped by a massive statue in cast iron, was to have at its base a series of circular steps, brass cannon from Waterloo, and three cottages, each to house a wartime veteran. And each year on 18 June, the anniversary, a revel called 'The Wake of Waterloo' was to be held near by. But the money did not exactly flow, despite the reported 10,000 present at the foundation-stone laying by Lord Somerville in 1817, and Wellington's only visit in 1819. For some years it remained in an unfinished state, and the present triangular column (built that way at half the cost of a square one according to the first architect), was completed in its modified form by C. E. Giles in 1854. After recent repairs its 235 narrow stairs will well reward the climber; even at its base the views over the Brendons and Exmoor are magnificent.

The country around Wellington includes several houses, of which the best-known is COTHAY, beside the young River Tone, a mile w of Thorne St Margaret, 'one of the most perfect smaller English manor houses of the late C15' (Pevsner), behind an embattled gatehouse. It includes some rare wall paintings with both religious and secular subjects, and some early-17th-century additions. Slightly earlier is GREENHAM BARTON, 1 mile s of Cothay, built by the same family, the Bluets, and still preserving a two-storeyed porch of c. 1400 and an open hall with inserted windows of the early 16th century. WELLISFORD MANOR, ½ mile N of Thorne St Margaret, is a brick house of c. 1700, not a usual material at that time in Somerset, but possibly showing Devon influence, for this is very near the border, and in the valley that is still the main route to the South-West.

Wells Som. 5 B6

The clear natural springs of water bubbling now in the bottom of a pool in the bishop's garden where the cathedral is so beautifully reflected, gave Wells both its ori-

gin, perhaps in prehistoric times, and its name. 'The minster by the great spring' mentioned in 766 and by tradition founded by King Ine (d. 726) became the seat of Athelm, the first bishop of the Somerset people, when the huge see of Sherborne was divided in 909, and for a century and a half it so remained until Bishop John de Villula (1088–1122) removed his seat to Bath. The old minster continued, but the regular religious life around cloister and refectory, established on the continental pattern by Bishop Giso (1061–88), probably came to an end.

Robert of Lewes, Bishop of Bath 1136–66, set Wells on its feet again by re-establishing a permanent and independent group of clergy under a dean, and 24 estates or 'prebends' were set aside as income for them. The medieval and later buildings around the cathedral which formed the Liberty – a city within a city – housed the successors of Robert's clergy; not only the dean but precentor, chancellor, treasurer, and other prebendaries, whose duty it was, in person or by deputy, to maintain the regular worship of God, the purpose of the life of a cathedral.

But Bishop Robert did more than this. He was responsible for building a new cathedral (for so it was again, with a bishop's seat or *cathedra* here as well as at Bath, though he was still simply 'Bishop of Bath'), which was consecrated in 1148. A hundred days remission were offered on that day to all who should keep the anniversary by a visit to Wells. And before 1160 he issued a charter which marks the beginning of independence for the town and another stage in its physical development. Henceforth the three fairs were no longer to be held in the cathedral and its porch, but in 'broad places' elsewhere; and the townsmen were to be quit of toll there. It is not quite clear just what all this implies, but excavation on the s side of the cathedral is suggesting that the Saxo-Norman minster-cathedral may have been on a slightly different alignment from the present one, pointing rather sw down to face the market place. Was Bishop Robert trying to move the market-place from the front of his new (or newly furbished) cathedral?

Bishop Reginald (1174–91) was more radical, for c. 1180 he began the present cathedral on a different alignment, uncluttered by established parts of the town, and in a style that is the earliest form of English Gothic. Reginald and his successor Jocelin of Wells (1206–42, and the first Bishop of Bath and Wells) built at the same time as Glastonbury was rising from its ashes. Its Lady Chapel was consecrated in 1191, though that was clearly old-fashioned in style and Wells distinctly revolutionary. The new work had perhaps reached the transepts from the E very quickly, judging from the introduction of a different stone; and there was another break just w of the N porch, which probably marks the period (1209–13) when Bishop Jocelin was driven out of England by the Interdict, and Dean Alexander, the other moving spirit, died. Jocelin consecrated the building in 1239,

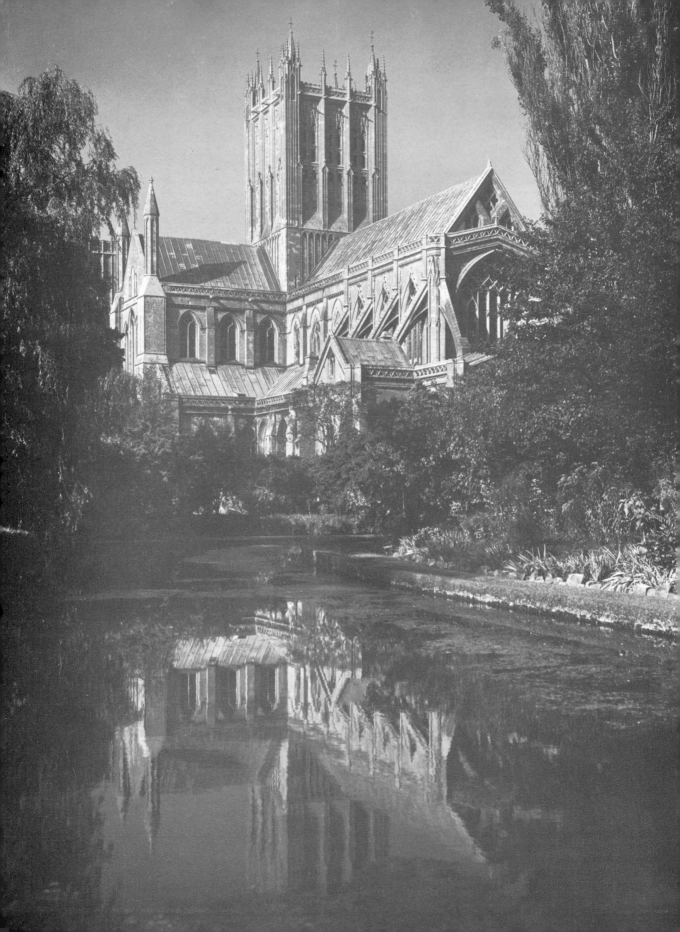

OPPOSITE: *Wells Cathedral*
ABOVE: *The Crossing, Wells Cathedral*

and finally abandoned the old cathedral, but it was still not finished: the chapter house undercroft and stairs came soon after *c.* 1250, the chapter house itself by 1307, the Lady Chapel *c.* 1319. Other important alterations within suggest continuous work until the 1340s in a style which, with work at St Augustine's, Bristol (now the Cathedral), 'represents the most original treatment of space in architecture of which any country at that time was capable' (Pevsner). These new developments involved raising the central tower *c.* 1315–*c.* 1322, originally with a high steeple, and soon to prove so heavy that the foundations gave way, to be saved eventually (*c.* 1340–50) by the graceful and ingenious scissor-arches which are so much a feature of the interior. Meanwhile the choir and E end, including the retrochoir, the Lady Chapel, and the haunting chapter house were built, finished perhaps in the late 1330s. The cathedral as it is now was almost complete except for the w front.

For some the w front is near perfection, for others a

failure; for very many it is seen as a single concept, whereas in truth a century and a half separates the front from the sw or Harewell tower, and another 50 years lies between Harewell and the NW or Bubwith tower. The great screen with its Purbeck shafts and its now sadly defaced figures (in process of restoration) is in spite of his general doubts, according to Pevsner 'the richest receptacle of C13 sculpture in England'. In its complete state it had 176 life-size statues, 49 biblical scenes, 30 angel busts, a frieze of the Resurrection in 85 panels and, in the centre, the Virgin and Child, the Coronation of the Virgin, and Christ in Judgement, flanked by archangels and apostles.

Bishop Nicholas Bubwith (1408–24) left money not only for the NW tower but had also financed the E cloister and library, on the foundations of Bishop Jocelin's work. East of this cloister lies the key to the earlier cathedral. Between *c.* 1478 and *c.* 1487 a Lady Chapel was built here by Bishop Robert Stillington, though the first time

BELOW: *Capital in the south transept, Wells Cathedral*   OPPOSITE: *Chapter House steps, Wells Cathedral*

West Front, Wells Cathedral

he entered was his last, at his funeral in 1491. Underneath still lies an earlier Lady Chapel, but on a curious alignment. This seems to be proof enough that an even earlier building of considerable importance had dictated this curiosity, and archaeological evidence, still incomplete, seems to suggest the site of the Saxo-Norman cathedral of Giso, and the minster which Athelm raised to cathedral status.

Monuments inside the cathedral (and many removed to the cloisters in a 19th-century restoration) tell not only the history of the building but that of the diocese at large. Jocelin brought the remains of his Saxon predecessors from the old cathedral presumably in the 1220s (and allowed them to be jumbled in the process), and placed them in the choir aisles. There, too, are Bishops William of Bitton I (d. 1264) and II (d. 1274), natives of Bitton (q.v.), and illustrative of how a single family could corner church patronage without the least suspicion of scandal and indeed with an odour of sanctity. In the NE transept lies Dean Godelee, under whom so much of the second and distinctive work at the eastern end of the cathedral was done. In the N chancel aisle is Bishop

Ralph of Shrewsbury (d. 1363), occupier of the see during the disturbing times of the 1340s and credited with turning the Bishop's Palace into a castle during a quarrel with the townsmen. Another legacy of Bishop Ralph is the College of Vicars Choral (1348), whose Close of houses, chapel, and hall on the N side of the cathedral, altered in the 15th century and recently restored, is a fine and rare piece of street planning. On the S side of the presbytery is Bishop Thomas Bekynton (d. 1465), commemorated by a tomb with cadaver below and himself in mass vestments above, planned in the greatest detail by the bishop himself and consecrated in 1452, 13 years before his death (*see* Beckington). His monument is outside as well as in:

He has indeed, at his own proper pains and charges, conferred such a splendour on this city, as well as by strongly fortifying the church with gates and towers and walls, as by constructing on the grandest scale the palace in which he resides and the other surrounding buildings, that he deserves to be called not the founder merely, but rather the splendour and ornament of the church.   (*William Worcestre's Itinaries*)

So a contemporary eulogist; and certainly Bishop Thomas built the three gateways into the cathedral green, including the Chain Gate to allow the Vicars Choral to arrive in choir in the dry, the 'Bishop's Eye' leading to the Palace Green, a substantial part of the Palace itself, the properties on the N side of the Market Place ('New Works'), and an improved water supply from a well-head in the Palace gardens. His executors added fireplaces and chimneys to the houses in Vicars' Close and a library over the chapel.

There is a nice contrast, reflecting well the different architectural styles, between the simple 12th-century nave and aisles, almost entirely without later ornament or furnishing, and the more ornate E end, with its fine contemporary (though jumbled) glass, tombs, chapels, and sculpture. The delicate chantries of Bishop Bubwith and Dr Hugh Sugar are thus the more effective, the latter now the entrance to a striking and monumental pulpit given by Bishop Knight. Its Renaissance forms are no surprise to those who have visited his house at Horton (q.v.).

Wells, it has been suggested, is visited more for its 14th-century clock than for its cathedral, and the crowds watching the jerky procession and Jack Blandifer the striker perhaps bear out the accusation. The swans on the moat surrounding the Bishop's Palace are equally famous and not much less mechanical in their behaviour. Beyond the gatehouse is a range of buildings which almost match the cathedral in age – a central block of undercroft and presence chamber built by Bishop Jocelin soon after returning to his native city from Bath, in the years after creating a park in meadows beyond St Andrew's stream in 1207. Bishop Robert Burnell (1275–92) built the great hall, and replaced Jocelin's chapel with the present one, fitted curiously between the two blocks. Bishop Bekynton built the N range, where the present Bishop lives, together with a tall gatehouse and cloister now swept away. The romantic impression of the site owes more than a little to artifice. The hall lost its roof in the 16th century, but some of its walls lasted until the 19th, when a bishop pulled them down to make the whole more picturesque.

The cluster of medieval buildings around the cathedral are not all that Wells has to offer. Shop-fronts in its main streets almost without exception hide high-quality medieval houses behind them, for Wells was an important place, if not entirely in its own right. The Bishop was a political as well as a spiritual figure; diocesan and chapter together were owners of vast estates and valuable jurisdictions. Visitors to the precinct and the Palace brought business to the town. From the 14th century, if not earlier, Wells was the largest urban centre in Somerset, and even at the end of the 17th century its inns provided far more beds and stabling for far more horses than its nearest rival, Bath. Still in the 18th century its cloth market attracted clothiers from W Somerset. Its attractions (and the consequences in traffic prob-

lems and alternative solutions) are still obvious, notably the streams of water flowing in the streets, its many local businesses, its noble parish church, and its genuine individuality.

St Cuthbert's gaunt tower, though unfortunately seen by many behind a red-brick terrace, is ample evidence of the prosperity of medieval Wells. But it is not, as it seems, a church of the 15th century, for inside there are taller piers with 13th-century capitals than ever seen before – or rather what has happened is that the late-medieval masons raised the nave simply by raising the 13th-century piers and reusing the original capitals. But this is not the earliest work on the site, though only a broken Norman pillar piscina can be seen. More relevant to origins is the dedication to King Alfred's patron saint, Cuthbert. Were there two Saxon churches in such close proximity, and if so what does that suggest? A substantial settlement independent of the minster-cathedral; perhaps even a royal residence?

Certainly the 13th-century church was substantial and cruciform, for the central tower collapsed in 1561 (the wardens earlier said they could not dismantle the rood-screen lest such a thing should happen). The Perpendicular work thus included the new W tower with its splendid tower arch, the flamboyant nave roof, and the eastern chapels, and the tragically defaced transept reredoses.

There is still more in Wells to be seen and discovered. Just behind St Cuthbert's are the so-called Bubwith Almshouses, with chapel, almshouse, and guildhall founded in 1436. St Thomas's Chapel (before 1191), St John's Priory (c. 1210), and Mountery College (c. 1400) have disappeared until they can be recovered by archaeology. But it is not only medieval Wells that has been overtaken. At the height of railway enthusiasm Bishop Lord Arthur Hervey could travel throughout the county with ease from any one of the three termini which served the city before 1876. Development in the last 30 years has almost doubled the size of the town and engulfed the railways as well as the surrounding countryside. Only the cathedral and Palace still (for the moment) look over fields as they have ever done.

West Cranmore Som. *see* **Doulting**

Westbury on Trym Avon 5 B4
There is still a noticeable 'village' atmosphere about Westbury: older houses, irregular roads, the parish church, and, down beside the little River Trym, what remains of Westbury College (NT). Expanding Bristol has encircled the place, and its ancient parish, once stretching from Avonmouth almost into the heart of the city, has been dismembered. But that great parish is certainly a clue to the origin of a place that was of considerable significance before Bristol emerged to greatness.

It has been claimed that Westbury was founded c. 716 as a mission centre. It was certainly in existence in 824 when it was given to Worcester cathedral priory in settlement of a dispute with the church of Berkeley witnessed at Westbury by a huge crowd of 210 priests. The church seems to have been destroyed by the Danes raiding up the Channel and the Avon at the end of Edgar's reign, but St Oswald, Bishop of Worcester, refounded it as a Benedictine monastery *c.* 693–4, probably the first Reformed monastic settlement in the country. Disaster struck again when 12 monks left in 972 to start a new house at Ramsey (Cambs.). There were new beginnings *c.* 1093, but this project had lapsed by 1112, leaving the church for a time solely parochial.

By the time of Bishop Walter de Cantilupe (1237–66), however, Westbury had been refounded as a secular college of a dean and several prebendaries, and the early-13th-century arcades, chancel arch, and s aisle of the church suggest a date early in Cantilupe's time or even earlier for its establishment. In 1286 Bishop Godfrey Giffard increased its membership and value in an abortive attempt to make Westbury a joint cathedral with Worcester, to create the kind of balance which had been working for years in Bath and Wells, and as a practical administrative solution in a large diocese with a growing city at its southern edge.

Two centuries later another Bishop of Worcester and a native of Westbury, John Carpenter (1444–76), for a time styled himself 'Bishop of Worcester and Westbury'. He rebuilt the college which, as Camden later wrote, looked 'more like a Castle than a College, with a faire gate and divers towers and with a strong wall embattled'. What remains after Prince Rupert burnt it in 1643, lest it should be defended by the Parliamentarians, is the huge, four-storeyed gatehouse, a piece of the wall, and a circular angle tower. It was given to the NT in 1907. Carpenter's college, rededicated to the Holy Trinity, included a dean and five prebendaries, priests, almsmen, choristers, and later a schoolmaster; and by the time the college was dissolved in 1544 there were 39 people living and working in the community.

The parish church reflects the new lease of life in the late 15th century. The tower belongs to the period, and includes a figure of the bishop above the w window; so, too, do the details of the nave – windows, clerestory, battlements, porch, and rood-loft turrets. But the chancel and its flanking chapels were entirely rebuilt, probably when Henry Sampson was Dean between 1458 and 1469, and the work apparently included a painted stone-and-alabaster reredos. Bishop Carpenter was himself buried in the crypt below the chancel, in a chapel originally decorated with frescoes apparently representing his funeral procession from Worcester. Only the cadaver from his tomb, on the s side of the sanctuary, survived destruction in the 17th century. The present tomb was built by Carpenter's own college, Oriel at Oxford, in 1853.

Among the holders of Westbury prebends in the 14th century were William Melton (Chancellor of England,

Archbishop of York 1317–40), John de Stratford (Chancellor, Archbishop of Canterbury 1333–48) and William of Edington (Bishop of Winchester 1346–66). John Wyclif (see Aust) held a prebend 1362–84, and another member of the college was the pugnacious Cornishman John Trevisa, translator of Latin prose into English and, as vicar of Berkeley before he came to Westbury, a thorn in the flesh of the then Dean. In the 15th century the most famous Dean was the former Bristol merchant prince William Canynge, who retired from commerce and was head of the college 1469–74. His 'clerical' effigy now in St Mary Redcliffe, Bristol, may perhaps have come from the se or Canynges Chapel in Westbury church, consecrated by Bishop Alcock when both Canynges and Carpenter were dead.

Westbury and its neighbours Stoke Bishop, Kingsweston, Redland, and Cotham, only began to lose their identity to the expanding Bristol in the 19th century, although scattered gentlemen's residences appeared from the 17th century after the break-up of the ecclesiastical estates. STOKE BISHOP, given by Ealdorman Aethelred of Mercia to the monastery of Berkeley and later transferred to the Bishops of Worcester, was first defined by a charter claimed to date from 883, and its bounds included lead diggings on the edge of Clifton Down. The bishops' house was followed (1669), by that of Sir Robert Cann (now a theological college). Adjoining was Sneyd park, another episcopal estate, which later passed to Sir Ralph Sadleir and then also to the Canns. All that remains to recall the mansion is the Observatory on the Downs, built as a belvedere. The bishops' park and Stoke itself were developed with substantial houses for prosperous Bristolians in the 1870s and 1880s. SEA MILLS, on the N bank of the Avon at the edge of the old park, was the Roman port of *Abona*, and its commercial possibilities were revived for a time in the early 18th century, only to be 'utterly abandoned' by the 1770s.

A mile w of Westbury Sir Edward Southwell commissioned Vanbrugh to build KINGSWESTON HOUSE *c.* 1710. A magnificent, rather monumental pile, it is topped with a fantastic arrangement of chimneys on arches, giving the effect of some sort of castellation. The gardens include a banqueting house for outside parties, and elegant lodges, the whole standing on a prominent site which once gave a splendid view NW to the sea, a view hardly enhanced by industrial Avonmouth. The house has a staircase without visible means of support, but most interior details are of the later 18th century and after.

REDLAND was also in the ancient parish of Westbury. It was developed in an elegant way in the 18th century beginning with Redland Court (1735) and Redland Chapel (1741–3). The chapel, which contains busts of John Cossins (a retired London grocer) and his wife by Rysbrack, is a fine, unspoilt example of a proprietary chapel of considerable elegance. It has some very good

Kingsweston House

woodcarving by Thomas Paty, and is unencumbered with later Anglican additions. The whole building, standing on its pretty green, is an oasis in the midst of streets of large houses of the 1860s. Neighbouring COTHAM also had its 18th-century beginnings, notably in the shape of a house built on Durdham Down as a summer residence for a Bristol worthy. Its expansion came in the 1870s with small-scale villas, in the planned Alexandra Park, with streets named to honour Sir Walter Scott.

Westbury sub Mendip   Som. *see* **The Mendips**

Westerleigh   Avon *see* **Pucklechurch**

Weston-super-Mare   Avon   4 H5
The growth of Weston-super-Mare has been nothing short of phenomenal. From a fishing village squeezed between undrained moor and the sea, with a population of 163 in 1811, it was, 100 years later, the largest town in Somerset after Bath. By 1971 it topped the 50,000 mark. The foundation of the resort is difficult to explain, for the regular and almost complete disappearance of the sea beyond acres of mud is not an obvious attraction. Indeed, the village of Uphill (see below) had more attractions for Hannah More when she wanted to convalesce in 1773, and in 1797 apartments were offered with the added possibility of pleasure boats and passage vessels to Flat Holm, Steep Holm, and the Welsh coast. About 1791 the Revd William Leeves, vicar of Wrington and a friend of Miss More, built a summer cottage at Weston (now part of the thatched Cottage Restaurant). He won more popular fame for his air to the ballad *Auld Robin Gray*.

Weston was owned by the Pigott family, and their agent, Richard Parsley, was the real founder of the

Weston-super-Mare

town's (and his own) fortune. He financed the building of the first hotel (The Royal) in 1810, though it closed a year later (when its contents included 31 beds, 23 mattresses, a 'four motion beer machine', and a bathing machine, the second on the Severn estuary). The hotel opened again in 1814 when a coach service from Bristol began. The town then began to expand after the surrounding land was inclosed in 1815. Hot-and-cold baths were established at Knightstone in 1822. The railway arrived early in 1841, and the population doubled to over 4,000 in the next decade. In the 1850s and 1860s terraces and crescents spread from Knightstone to Italianate and Tudor villa properties at Montpelier and the Boulevard (how significant the names), some enhanced by their sites in the grounds of the former magnificent Villa Rosa.

The churches, as Pevsner says, are curiously much less interesting than the houses. The old parish church, St John's, has a Norman font but was rebuilt in 1824 and enlarged later. In the mid 19th century it was a stronghold of Low Church tradition, its chancel, observed a critic, leaving no room for the most 'ingenious processionist' to place furniture or acolytes. Much more acceptable to him was Tractarian Uphill, where 'soft hats, straight collars, long coats, and short sermons' proclaimed a different style of churchmanship.

Medical opinion recommended Weston 'for delicate children, especially from India, the anaemic and scrofulous; for convalescents and cases of neurasthenia, nervous breakdown, chronic albuminaria and chronic bronchitis', and claimed to have the lowest death-rate of any British resort. Weston's ozone and iodine have continued their efficacious work and the resort is still a haven for thousands each year.

The town has found other activities besides entertaining holidaymakers. The Royal Potteries, founded in 1847, received an 'honourable mention' at the 1851 Exhibition, and became 'Royal' for the flower pots, urns, tiles, and terracotta figures supplied to the Royal Parks. Much of Somerset County Council's administration was centred at Weston until 1935. From 1885 the English end of the transatlantic telegraph cable was in the town, and some of Marconi's early radio messages were sent and received from Brean Down in 1896–7.

Worlebury Camp, on the headland N of the town, is a 10-acre Iron-Age fortress, with hut circles and pits which contained a mass of human skeletons, evidently the victims of a massacre. WOODSPRING (more correctly WORSPRING) PRIORY, 4 miles N, beyond Kewstoke, was a small house of Augustinian canons founded here in the 1220s in honour of the Holy Trinity, the Virgin, and St Thomas of Canterbury by William de Courtenay, a grandson of one of St Thomas's murderers, Reginald FitzUrse. Unusually, the monastic church with its tower survive, together with a barn and the outline of the cloister. It is owned by the Landmark Trust, and open to the public.

STEEP HOLM, 6 miles W in the Channel, was the site of a small priory in the 13th century, and in the 19th boasted an inn whose keeper kept a bear and who paid scant regard to the excise. An artillery battery was established in 1867. Since 1929 the island has been a nature reserve now owned by the Kenneth Allsop Memorial Trust. The protected wildlife includes a rare Mediterranean peony, *Paeonia Mascula*.

If ever a place-name was misleading it is UPHILL, 1 mile S of Weston: for the 'hill' means not a hill but a pill or creek. It is likely to have been a port in Roman times; troops were assembled here for the campaign against Owen Glendower in Wales in the early 15th century; and when invasion was threatened in the 16th the creek was defended by guns in a round tower.

The old church above the creek, its nave now open to the sky, is a Norman building, though the tower was probably rebuilt in the 15th or 16th century, when the rood-screen, stair, pulpit, and S window were inserted. A new church was built in the village in 1844 though Old St Nicholas has not been abandoned. It contains the font from the old church: an elaborate 13th-century stem of leaves and crockets and an octagonal bowl perhaps recut two centuries later.

Weston Zoyland   Som.   2 B1

The 'zoy' element in this name, also found in MIDDLE-ZOY and CHEDZOY (where it is pronounced 'zey'), refers to a stream name now gone, such as 'Sow' or 'Sowe', and the Saxon word 'eg' for island (as in eyot in the Thames). The same island element occurs in OTHERY, the 'other island'. All these villages stood in the Somerset Levels surrounded, if not by permanent water, at least by marshland crossed at best by causeways. The whole area belonged to the monks of Glastonbury, who in the century before 1240 encouraged their tenants to undertake large-scale reclamation. Nearly 1,000 acres of rich grazing and corn land were added to the 'islands' by

their efforts, benefiting both landlord and tenant. By the early 14th century, in fact, Middlezoy, Othery, and Weston had more people liable to tax than towns like Crewkerne and Yeovil. This prosperity is clearly indicated in their parish churches, with their evidence of the Glastonbury connexion: the initials of Abbot Richard Bere (1493–1524) appear on the porch at Chedzoy, benches at Othery, and the S transept at Weston Zoyland. The churches illustrate the history of the area well: the 13th-century expansion after land reclamation can be seen in the nave arcade at Chedzoy with its circular piers and simple capitals and the slightly later chancels at Chedzoy and Middlezoy. Othery is essentially of the 14th century, but the 15th was here, as elsewhere in the county, the greatest age of building: new windows everywhere, to give maximum light; the clerestory at Chedzoy, most of Middlezoy and Weston; and the towers of all four, making their bold declarations to the wide skies. The medieval furnishings, too, have a unity – work largely of the later Middle Ages, though a bench end at Chedzoy was made during the Catholic Renaissance under Queen Mary (1553–8). And it is not accidental that Othery and Chedzoy still possess fragments of medieval embroidery. The monks at Glastonbury did not imagine, even at the last, that the Dissolution was upon them. Their people could hardly have thought otherwise, and the remote Somerset Levels of the 16th century were no place for innovations. Yet each church has striking individual characteristics: Middlezoy, its position on the high point of its 'island', the village clustering tightly round its churchyard; Weston Zoyland, the finest of all the group, with its magnificent medieval roof and its screen, complete with loft and rood – a splendid and surprising product of the 1930s.

Weston Zoyland has a place in national history, for the level ground to the NW of the village is the site of the battle of Sedgemoor, the final and decisive action in the ill-fated rebellion of James, Duke of Monmouth, against James II in 1685. In the parish register is an account of the battle on 6 July:

> The jniadgement began between one and two of the clock in the morning. It contineued near one hour and halfe. Their was kild upon the spott of the king's souldiers sixtenn, five of them buried in the church, the rest in church yeard ... theire was kild of the rebils upon the spott about 300; hanged with us 22 ... About 500 prisoners brought into our church, of which there was 79 wounded and 5 of them died of thire wounds in our church.

After the prisoners left, two men were paid a large sum to clean up, the building was fumigated (with frankincense, saltpetre, and resin), and windows and seats needed minor repairs. A week after the battle Weston people were complaining that the great common grave for the rebels was not properly covered, though they had been forced not only to dig it in the first place, but also to provide gallows, gibbets, and chains for sum-

mary treatment for rebels not fortunate enough to be killed in battle. The butchery continued in a more legal fashion at Taunton (q.v.).

Whitelackington Som. *see* **Ilminster**

Wickwar Avon 5 C3

Wickwar began life as a farmstead (wick) which after the Conquest belonged to the Warre family. The village, clustered around the church, was developed in the late 13th century with the addition of what came to be the main street, the present High Street. A market was established in 1285, and Wickwar became a borough, with its own government. It was always one of the smallest towns in Gloucestershire, too near the larger market towns of Wotton-under-Edge and Chipping Sodbury to prosper. Leland called it 'a pretty clothing townlet' in the 1540s, and cloth-making continued into the 18th century. Women and children were fully employed spinning for factories in Stroud, and others were involved in the town's brewing industry.

The old Tudor manor house near the church, known as Pool House, was pulled down in the 19th century, and all that remains is its terraced site and a sculpture of St John the Baptist, dated 1496, in the church. The 'town' has a nice collection of stuccoed and rendered houses which give Wickwar a kind of urban flavour – including the Town Hall of *c.* 1795 with its arched openings and bellcote, and several 17th- and 18th-century buildings.

The old grammar school (1684) was founded by Alexander Hosea, a native of the town who, like Dick Whittington, ran away to London and made his fortune. He left two houses in Holborn and £600 to the corporation for a school for children of poor parents, though on no account should the parson be the schoolmaster. The school did not live up to expectation; Latin was rarely, if ever, taught, though from 1835 there was to be a master for 40 boys and a mistress for 30 girls.

Only in 1841 did the population top the 1,000 mark, and then only because of the workers digging the railway tunnel under the 'village' end. The round tower near the church is its ventilating shaft.

Williton Som. 1 H1

This busy place on the holiday route to West Somerset owes its urban 'feel' to the 19th century, when it became the centre of a Poor Law union and hence of local government. The dignified old workhouse survives as a hospital. Williton's earlier claim to fame as the home of Sir Reginald FitzUrse, one of Becket's murderers, has never been forgotten, and one result was that half the manor was given or sold by FitzUrse to the Order of Knights Templar, possibly to raise money to pay for a

penitential journey to Rome and to the Holy Land. The property passed subsequently to the Knights Hospitaller, and was still called the manor of Williton Hospital in the 17th century.

The church of St Peter stands in a village setting to the w of the town, at the end of a triangular green and by a farmyard, well away from the shops. It has no churchyard, for it was a Chapel of the church of St Decuman, though it had its own priest from the late 12th century. Relations between the two were sometimes strained, and in the early 15th century the people of Williton had to promise to visit St Decuman's church four times a year, including the feat of the Saint and the feast of his Translation (probably from the old church to the new). Later in the century they were ordered not to play 'tenez' against the chapel walls, and in the later 1630s to cease playing fives there.

The church itself is small, though it was extended and over-restored in 1838. It possesses, however, an unusual alabaster font made in Watchet in 1666 for £3 5s., presumably replacing an older one 'cast down' by Nicholas Lukis, a troublesome parishioner, in 1657.

Orchard Wyndham, the home of the Wyndhams since the early 16th century, lies 1 mile sw of the town in extensive grounds (not open to the public). It is of complicated plan, but probably dates from the 14th century when it was the home of the Orchard family. John Wyndham acquired the house when he married the heiress Elizabeth Sydenham in 1528, and Wyndhams have lived there ever since, as squires, Baronets, or Earls of Egremont. Here, for instance, lived Sir William Wyndham (1688–1740), a High Tory who was Chancellor of the Exchequer under Queen Anne in 1713 at the age of 24. On the accession of George I he found himself in the Tower for his Jacobite sympathies, and never again held political office, although he always held the respect even of his political opponents. Swift made him a member of the Lilliputian Senate under the guise of Gumdahm. In his time the gardens of Orchard Wyndham were looked after by a local man who contracted to maintain the walks and 'vistos', tend the vines and espaliers, plant peas and french beans in the kitchen garden, and pick all the walnuts in the park, leaving only enough for the family.

Charles Wyndham his son (1710–63) inherited the earldom of Egremont and estates in six counties. He served for a while as Secretary of State under Lord Bute and spent most of his time at Petworth (Sussex). George, Earl of Egremont, his son (1751–1837), a supporter of the Turf and of Fine Arts, is said to have given £1,200,000 to charity in the last six years of his life. After the death of the 4th Earl in 1845 the title lapsed, but Wyndhams still live in the house.

Weston Zoyland church

Wimbleball Reservoir Som. *see* **Dulverton**

Wincanton Som. 3 E2

Wincanton, the settlement on the Cale (whose tributary in the 10th century was the Wincawel) is on an uncomfortable hillside site above the river crossing. This site was the key to its existence and to its life: in 1686 it could offer beds for 50 guests and stabling for 254 horses, for it was on the main London–Exeter coach road. Heavier 20th-century traffic has brought a complicated traffic system and finally a bypass.

It was called a borough in the early 14th century, perhaps because of the new High Street development added to the village around the church; and in the 16th century it had a weekly market. It depended greatly on cloth-making, and Defoe notes its fine Spanish medleys and the coarser dowlas and ticking. The elegant 18th-century houses and inns in the main streets are a result of this prosperity as well as the consequence of a disastrous fire in 1747. Some 200 looms were still working at the end of the century, and in 1811 nearly two-thirds of the population were clothworkers. But the challenge from the North of England could not be faced and the trade collapsed, though there was compensation, for the town became the head of a Poor Law union in 1836 and from 1855 felt the benefits of the railway. The parish church reflects in its outer s aisle (1735) Wincanton's 18th-century prosperity, but in its Victorian rebuilding (which destroyed Nathaniel Ireson's chancel and clerestory) something of its decline. The town is now a busy shopping centre for the scattered villages of SE Somerset, and achieves national importance during the National Hunt race-meetings at the course on the hill.

Wincanton achieved some wider fame when Nathaniel Ireson (d. 1769), a master builder from Warwickshire, settled here *c.* 1726. He built several houses in the town and others in the county including Crowcombe Court (*c.* 1734), Ven House near Milborne Port (*c.* 1725), Mells Park (1725), and Berkley House (1730–2) (qq.v.), besides additions to churches at Bruton (q.v.) and Redlynch. He opened a quarry, and having found large quantities of clay, also made bricks and became a potter.

Between 1804 and 1812 the town was host to over 300 French prisoners of war, mostly officers on parole. They amused themselves with operatic and theatrical entertainments; one or two married local girls, some fathered children, others died and were buried in the churchyard. They left as suddenly as they came, to march to Kelso to be exchanged for British prisoners in French hands.

STAVORDALE PRIORY, 3 miles NE, stands in a remote wooded landscape, the church of a house of Augustinian canons founded by 1243 and rebuilt by John Stourton, who left money in his will for the church and cloister to be glazed. The rebuilding was completed by 1443 but the house, never rich, was finally taken over by Taunton Priory in 1533. The Zouch family were living there by

1548. It is not open to the public.

PENSELWOOD, 1 mile further E, next to the Dorset and Wiltshire borders, is the normally accepted site for the battle of Peonnan which opened the West County in 658 to the Saxon invader. Kenwalch's Castle, a fortification in Castle Wood N of the village, is named after Cenwealh, the Saxon victor. The church of St Michael has a Norman s doorway and a Norman font.

Winterbourne Avon 5 B3

The old village, named after the stream which only became a river in the winter, moved up to the Bristol road at least by the late 14th century, for a market was granted there in 1393. The oldest surviving house there seems to be Winterbourne House (now part of a school), which may be 16th-century. There are several others of the 17th century, including Hicks Farm (1650). Rudder in the late 18th century described the roadside settlement as 'like a market town'; the market had thus by his time ceased at least in a formal sense.

So what is left of the old village is down Church Lane (turning opposite Riding High School): the church, traces of the manor house complex, Court Farm, and some cottages. The manor complex includes a circular dovecot, the earthworks of a garden, and some fishponds. The church dates from the 12th century; the chancel was built then and the nave and s tower not much later, though new windows were inserted everywhere in the 14th century, probably when the N chancel chapel was built to house the chantry founded in 1351 by Thomas, Lord Bradeston. Perhaps at the same time the tower was formed into a second chapel and decorated with roses and the figure of a knight. The Bradeston chapel contains the tombs of several members of the Bradeston family, and a notable brass, probably to Agnes, Lady Bradeston (d. 1369). It was the oldest brass in the former county of Gloucester.

Among the monumental inscriptions is one to Thomas Mountjoy, a local surgeon, who died in 1797 at the age of 64.

> He was noted through England, Ireland and Wales for his knowledge and success in cureing the diseases of Weakly and Ricketty children and Ruptures which he practised successfully for forty years by an Original Receipt which had been in the family for near two hundred years.

His secret was presumably passed on, since his daughter married a surgeon from Rotherham. Another former Winterbourne inhabitant, Amy (d. 1662), wife of Thomas Symes, was declared to be an 'honor to her family', through her 'exemplary life and manners'—during which in 20 years she produced for her husband 12 sons and 6 daughters.

Not far away, a member of the same family came to the district 'to seek a repose'. John Symes (d. 1661) is recorded on a brass in the church at FRAMPTON COTTERELL, 2 miles NE, where he had come into 'long and horrible exile' from his home at Poundisford (q.v.), near Taunton, 'in the late unhappy times of rebellion'. MP for Somerset in 1624, Sheriff, Deputy Lieutenant, Justice of the Peace, his talents were, so his memorial says, 'not hid in a napkin'. He died at the age of 88 years, 7 months, and 17 days, leaving over 100 living descendants.

Frampton might appear, save for its church (the tower is Perpendicular, the rest rebuilt in 1858), to be almost a new town, for like Winterbourne it is a Bristol outer-suburb. The 'farm on the river Frome', distinguished from many other Framptons by the name of its 13th-century owners, the Cotels, has, in fact, a long industrial history. By the mid 17th century it was the principal centre of felt hat manufacture in the Bristol region, later so prominent that the famous London hatters, Christy's, had a factory here between 1818 and 1864. In the 19th century, too, haematite was mined here in quantity, 68,000 tons being extracted between 1862 and 1874.

Witham Friary Som. 2 E1 (*pron.* Wit-ham)
Even now a little remote, Witham in Selwood Forest was chosen in 1178–9 as the site of the first Carthusian monastery in England, founded by Henry II in part expiation for the murder of Archbishop Thomas à Becket. The first monks came from the s of France, and found both the place and people hostile, but the third prior, Hugh of Avalon (d. 1200), was made of the stuff of saints, and the foundation prospered even after he became Bishop of Lincoln in 1186.

In Hugh's time at Witham the cloister and its surrounding buildings were at least begun in stone, but the *conversi*, the lay brethren, still lived in wooden huts. This was the way with the contemplative Carthusians: simple cells grouped around a great cloister, with a relatively small and simple church; and a community some distance away where the lay brethren who worked the fields might live together. And Witham Friary, the village, is the 'frèrery', the lay settlement, clustering still round its little church with three bays of simple rib-vaulting of *c.* 1200 with an E apse, the whole restored and extended in 1876. South of the church is one further Carthusian relic: the rectangular dovecot, converted into a parish room.

The cloister lies ½ mile E near Witham Hall Farm. The railway now divides the turf-covered site of the church and cloister from the monastic fishponds, a sad end for a house that none could fault at the Dissolution in 1539. If in its later years it did not live up to the standard set by St Hugh, yet it attracted a learned man like Master John Blakman, a Cambridge don, and biographer of Henry VI, who told the story of how the innocent king was embarrassed by the nude bathing at Bath.

Wiveliscombe Som. 1 H2
There is a feeling that you have come to the end of the world when you come to Wiveliscombe, not because it

is backward, but simply that it lies at the end of what looks like an impasse, for it nestles in the green folds of the Brendons, its skyline marked by the red sandstone of its church tower and the red brick of its impressive but now empty brewery. The area was not too remote for the Romans, who built a fort at Nunnington Park, and a hoard of 3rd- and 4th-century coins found there indicates how long they stayed. The place was also an early church centre, and the Bishops of Bath and Wells were lords of the manor here at least from 1042 until the early 19th century. The remains of their manor house, sometimes referred to rather grandly as a palace, are incorporated in cottages SE of the church and include a 14th-century archway leading to ground called Palace Green, where a century or so ago still stood some other buildings including a barn. It was Bishop Ralph of Shrewsbury's favourite residence in the 14th century, and one of his successors, William Knight (see Horton), presumably in remembrance of days enjoyed there, left money to be given to the poor there 'at the oversight of the curate and two honest men of the parish'. His coat of arms, carved in wood, hangs in the church. Some fragments of the manor house, including a crowned Tudor rose, are now incorporated in the buildings NW of the church.

The church itself is unusual. The medieval building was by 1827 unsafe, a huge crack running up one side of the tower. All that now remains of it are perhaps two windows at the E end of the crypt, for it was entirely demolished and replaced by the present building in a vaguely Perpendicular style but with the porportions of a galleried preaching house of the 18th century. It is an early work of Richard Carver, then of Bridgwater and later of Taunton, and it is still a remarkably untouched example of early Gothick, even to the delightful but uncomfortable pews. There are, of course, traces of earlier things – the bowl of a Norman font, the sounding-board of a Jacobean pulpit, the tomb of Humphrey and Margery Wyndham (d. 1622 and 1620 respectively), she 71, he 84 whose epitaph includes the couplet

Here lies a paire, whome for their equall loves
Let after ages terme the Turtle Doves;

and a record of the building and plan of the seating of a gallery in 1705, with the names of the singers of 'tenor and treble' on one side and 'bassus and treble' on the other.

Wiveliscombe church played a notable rôle during the Second World War as the refuge for a large collection of ecclesiastical and other treasures: glass, plate, records, books, furniture, and pictures from churches and other buildings all over England were stored in the crypt. Here, in a scheme organized by the Central Council for the Care of Churches, were housed, for instance, the 15th-century E window of St Peter Mancroft, Norwich; the records from the Guildhall, London; the 8th-century St Chad's Gospel from Lichfield; the entire library of the French Protestant church in London; maritime relics from Portsmouth Cathedral; treasures from London synagogues; and furniture and glass from several City churches which would otherwise have been destroyed.

In the 18th century the town was an important centre of cloth-making, producing blanketings, shrouds, baize, and especially penistones, a type of cloth stretched beyond its limit which in rain would shrink rapidly. Such cloth was popular with West Indian slave-owners, the suits they provided soon becoming as good as straight jackets after a tropical downpour. In the 19th century the place was famous for Hancock's beer and as Kilvert says in his *Diary* as the home of the 'celebrated piano-maker' Mr Collard. Taunton Vale Industries now produce a wide range of decorative kitchen and dining-room giftware for a world-wide market.

Woodspring Avon *see* **Weston-super-Mare**

Wookey Hole Som. 5 A6
Wookey Hole, where the River Axe emerges from its underground lair in the Mendip Hills, has been a tourist attraction at least since the 15th century. William Worcestre, servant of Sir John Fastolf and antiquarian, described

> a certain narrow entry where to begin with is the image of a man called the Porter. One must ask leave from the Porter to enter the hall of Wookey, and the people carry with them ... sheaves of reed sedge to light the hall. It is as big as Westminster Hall and stalactites hang from the vault which is wondrously arched over with stone.... the passage through which one enters the hall is about half a furlong in length ... between the passage and the hall is a broad lake crossed by 500 stone steps ... and if a man goes off the steps he falls into the water...

He went on to mention the 'kitchen', the 'Parlour', and an office called an 'oast'; and in it 'the figure of a woman clothed and spinning with ... a distaff held beneath her girdle'. This figure later generations have known as 'Witch of Wookey', whose activities as maimer of cattle, torturer of the old, and destroyer of the young has not lessened her attraction.

Thanks to the work of H. E. Balch and later cave explorers, as many as 25 chambers have been discovered deep under Mendip, though only a few are accessible to visitors. Their archaeology tells the story of their regular use by men from *c.* 250 B.C. to *c.* 400 A.D.: pottery, weaving equipment, coins, part of a horse's bridle, and evidence of the use of coal and of storage of grain show how the caves were home to generations; but evidence of human sacrifice suggests not only an origin for the Witch Legend but also points to the abrupt end of the Great Cave as a dwelling in the 4th century.

But even all this evidence is small compared to the bones found in an adjoining rock shelter, called Hyena Den; bones of animals dating back to the Palaeolithic age, perhaps to 50000 B.C. – bones of lion, mammoth, bear,

woolly rhinoceros, wild horse, deer, fox, and hare, nearly all chewed by hyenas who occasionally had to share their home with Palaeolithic men, who left behind them some flint tools and broken marrow bones.

The industrial buildings at Wookey Hole may be something of a surprise; and their contents even more so. At least since the early 17th century the emergent Axe has been harnessed to make paper, and the present buildings were put up by the Hodgkinson family from the mid 19th century. High-quality hand-made paper was made here until 1972, and the whole property was sold in 1973 to Madame Tussaud's. Since that time there have been notable changes: part of the mill houses Lady Bangor's famous collection of fairground objects, themselves made between 1870 and 1939, including organs, gallopers from roundabouts, cars from scenic railways, and many other pieces of a now almost vanished culture, resplendent in the colours and detail that could hardly be studied when the fairground was at work at night, and often at high speed.

Another part of the mill has become the working store-room and studio for Madame Tussaud's exhibition. Heads, bodies, and limbs of those whose fame has faded, and costumes and crowns, ready to take their place again in Baker Street, are there arranged neatly on shelves, together with the plaster negative moulds of those of current fame.

Paper is again made on the premises by hand, bringing industry back to this remarkable site which offers such a range of the evidence of man's activity in so small a compass. The rejected heads on the shelves of Madame Tussaud's storerooms are often quoted as evidence of the fickleness of fame; the flint tools in the Hyena Den are at least a comfort to ordinary mortals.

Woollard Avon *see* **Pensford**

Wrington Avon 5 A5
There is an urban air about the village which suggests some past prosperity; and the parish church and wide streets are more precise evidence. From Saxon times until 1539 Wrington was a valuable part of Glastonbury Abbey's vast estate, and the abbot's sheep grazed on the high ground in large numbers. A fair was founded in 1332 which lasted until the beginning of the 18th century. The end of the Abbey's rule brought Wrington into a different orbit, for it was sold in 1546 to Sir Henry Capel, an Essex man. His descendants were ardent royalists, but managed to appoint one of the country's leading Presbyterians, Samuel Crooke, to the rectory in 1602. Perhaps in those early days Dr Crooke was not so bold in his opinions; and on his death in 1649 the Capels themselves were in no position to remedy the matter: Sir Arthur Capel, 1st Lord Capel, lost his head only a few weeks after his King, and Crooke was replaced by another Presbyterian, Dr Francis Roberts. He, perhaps with Capel help, made his peace at the Restoration,

Wookey Hole

1961 the population was 3,898; in 1971 10,176.

But the church represents an ancient and important foundation. It was a minster or mission station in the 9th century and later, like similar centres, was absorbed by the cathedral priory at Worcester. Evidence of this antiquity is sparse, but a Norman window in the s transept and clear indications of a central tower of the 13th century or earlier point in the same direction. Eastward expansion also in the 13th century is suggested by the chancel arcades. The 15th century put in new windows, some glass still remaining, a rood-loft, the wall painting of St Christopher and a water-mill, and the font. Traditional furnishings have been abandoned in favour of a central altar totally surrounded by moveable seats.

Lead ore, calamine, and coal were mined in the parish in the 18th century, but agriculture (mostly dairying and grazing) could not be improved by inclosure largely because of the poor coal carriers, who would have been put out of business by the disappearance of waste land.

Yate Court Farm stands on the site of a house Ralph de Willington was licensed to fortify in 1293-4. It was garrisoned by Parliament during the Civil War in 1644, burnt, and not rebuilt. Thomas Neal, born in the parish *c.* 1519, was a noted Greek and Hebrew scholar and theologian at Oxford, where from 1559 for 10 years he was Queen's Professor of Hebrew. His Catholic views were recalled in his epitaph at Cassington (Oxfordshire); he was perhaps the ultimate authority for the Catholic story of Archbishop Parker's consecration in the Nag's Head.

Yatton   Avon   5   A5
Yatton has one of those rare churches (in Somerset like Croscombe, Pilton, and Tintinhull (qq.v.)), where the survival of early churchwardens' accounts allows precise dating of parts of the church, as well as giving fascinating details of furnishings and of the means by which the money for the work was raised. Much of Yatton parish lies on the marshlands of the Yeo, and the wardens in 1528 paid for repairs to a sluice at Wemberham, and later for the regular scouring of the river. During the wave of extreme Protestantism under Edward VI, even the great silver processional cross, bought in 1499 for £18, was sold, 'and the money bestowyd upon the makyng of a sirten skusse (sluice) agenste the rage of the salte water'. The discovery of a Roman villa and boathouse by the Yeo at Wemberham (2 miles sw) indicates an established use of the Yeo and some of the marshlands at an early date.

Yatton was originally a large parish, one manor there belonging to the Bishops of Wells in the 11th century and another forming a prebend of the cathedral in *c.* 1135. Cleeve and Claverham were both part of the medieval parish, and contributed to church funds through their own officials, known as lightmen. And these contributions were incredibly generous, considering there were few families like the Newtons of Court de Wyck (a medieval house burnt down in the early 19th

served the next Arthur Capel, Earl of Essex, in Ireland, and died at peace with all men in 1675. Two other figures of national importance have Wrington links. The philosopher, John Locke, was born in 1632 in a house near the church; and Hannah More (d. 1833), pioneer of education among the Mendip country children, lived at Cowslip Green and later at Barley Wood, both in the large parish.

The church is more impressive and welcoming outside than in. Its unity of design gives the appearance of a single build, but careful examination reveals a building of several generations. The chancel is of *c.* 1300, and the tower preceded the clerestory in the late Middle Ages. Internal alterations continued until the Reformation, for a new chapel in front of the screen was dedicated to St Erasmus as late as 1545. The tower so impressed Sir Charles Barry that he used its proportions in his Victoria Tower at the Palace of Westminster. He also designed the reredos.

Yate   Avon   5   C3
Yate, the gateway to the royal forest of Kingswood, occurs as early as 779, and yet it is a new town, founded only in 1966. Acres of rather desolate – some say unplanned – housing spread from a large shopping centre SE of the church, a building that stands on the edge of the new development, near the only bit of the old village that survives. Recent growth has been phenomenal: in

century), and most parishioners were yeomen and labourers.

The church they so much loved was clearly cruciform in Norman times, but its central tower and certainly the s transept were rebuilt in the late 13th century; probably, too, the N transept, though the tomb recesses there are of the early 14th century. There was a great rebuilding in the early 15th century when the chancel, nave, clerestory, and aisles were renewed, the mouldings at the crossing altered to suit current fashion, and the w front created, the whole in the fine, grey Dundry stone which shows its perfection in the magnificent s porch, with Somerset blind panelling seen at its best. The tower was raised and the spire built in 1456, perhaps when the nave had been finished, though the spire showed signs of weakness in the 1580s, and was left as a safe if inelegant stump in 1595.

Yatton Church

Beyond the N transept is a chapel which houses the fine tombs of Sir Richard Newton (d. 1448), a judge of the Common Pleas under Henry VI, his son Sir John Newton (d. 1488), and their wives. This 'newe chapell of Saint John the Evangelist within the churche' as it was described in 1499, is all that obviously remains of the late-medieval magnificence of Yatton: the chapels of SS. James, Katherine, Thomas, George, Nicholas, and Christopher have gone; so has the rood-screen and loft, made in the 1450s, carved, painted, gilded, and decorated with over 80 images. Of the rich and costly vestments all that survives is a 15th-century velvet dalmatic, saved by conversion to a pall. The new organ of 1528 was at least replaced 300 years later by one of some distinction, in origin an instrument built by the Jordans for Bath Abbey and bought from the Bishop's Palace at Wells in 1842. With it came the two carved figures now at the w end of the church.

Adjoining the N side of the church a 'chapter house' and offices have been built to give more room for a growing community, for Yatton's population has nearly doubled in the last decade. The new buildings serve very much as once did a group of cottages on the N edge of the churchyard, almshouse from 1621, but before then the medieval church house (see Crowcombe) the social centre of the parish, where church ales were held to raise funds for building and maintenance. South-east of the church is the 15th-century prebendal house or old rectory, with a fine N front, another reminder of the richness of the agricultural land of the Somerset marshes.

Yeovil Som. 2 D3
'I cannot commend the towne for the beauty of it, yet of late some have begun to new build': so Thomas Gerard, writing in the 1630s. Leland had called it 'meately welle buildyd', and thought it stood 'pleasauntly' on its 'rokky hille'. Gerard's comment would suit the 20th century; for since the last war, and notably in the last 10 years, the needs of traffic have been made paramount. A medieval half-timbered inn, the George, was demolished to widen Middle Street – and then the street was pedestrianized; and Handford Manor, the best representative of Yeovil Georgian, has a doubtful future.

What survives is the parish church of St John ('faire and lyghtesom' said Leland), begun by Robert Sambourne, rector 1362–82, and still under construction at his death. The designer was probably William Wynford, master mason at Wells. Only the small crypt under the chancel may be a little earlier. Gerard commended it as a 'large and curious structure ... nothing but faire windows and pillars' – the genius of Wynford. Before the Reformation there were five chantries inside the church and one outside, and a staff including singing boys and lay clerks. All that remains of this magnificence is the rare brass lectern of *c.* 1450, given it seems by Brother Martin Forester part of whose effigy is engraved on it. The lectern is said to be one of five desk lecterns of the period and the only one in a parish church.

The market in the 17th century was noted for its cheese, regularly taken to adjoining counties, and for its hemp and linen thread. The town houses still glimpsed above shop fronts show prosperity in the 18th and 19th centuries based on silk, gloving, and the market. During the 19th century its population rose from 2,774 to 11,704 and more than doubled in the next 70 years thanks to the introduction of engineering by the Petter factory, followed by the present manufacture of helicopters by Westlands. Yeovil still retains an important cattle mar-

ket drawing business from a wide hinterland which reaches well into Dorset.

One and a half miles s is BARWICK (*pron.* Barrick), where the park around Barwick House is dotted with early-19th-century follies including a spire over a Gothic *umbrello*, known as Jack the Treacle-Eater. The church, which looks over the village to the late-17th-century Barwick Farm, has a Norman font and a 17th-century transeptal tower. Of particular interest are the datable aisle (*c.* 1489) and the stalls and pews, all *c.* 1530 and including spirited scenes of hunting and shooting.

Yeovilton   Som. *see* **Ilchester**

St John's, Yeovil

Further Reading

General
Aston, M. and Leech, R. H. *Historic Towns in Somerset* (1977)
Bettey, J. H. *Rural Life in Wessex, 1500–1900* (1977)
Bromwich, D. and Dunning, R. W. *Victorian and Edwardian Somerset from Old Photographs* (1977)
Connor, A. B. *Monumental Brasses in Somerset* (1970)
Dunning, R. W. *A History of Somerset* (1978)
Ekwall, E. *The Oxford Dictionary of English Place-Names* (4th edn. 1970)
Farr, G. *Somerset Harbours* (1954)
Leech, R. H. *Small Medieval Towns in Avon* (1975)
MacInnes, C. M. and Whittard, W. F. (eds.) *Bristol and its Adjoining Counties* (repr. 1973)
Moore, J. S. (ed.) *Avon Local History Handbook* (1979)
Pevsner, N. B. L. *The Buildings of England: Somerset* (2 vols. 1958)
Rudder, S. *A New History of Gloucestershire* (1779, repr. 1977)
Smith, A. H. *Place-Names of Gloucestershire* (4 vols. 1964–5)
Smith, B. S. and Ralph, E. *A History of Bristol and Gloucestershire* (1972)
Verey, D. C. W. *The Buildings of England: Gloucestershire* (2 vols. 1970)
Victoria History of Gloucestershire (5 vols. 1907–76, in progress)
Victoria History of Somerset (4 vols. 1906–78, in progress)
Walker, F. *The Bristol Region* (1972)
Wickham, A. K. *Churches of Somerset* (new edn. 1965)
Woodforde, C. *Stained Glass in Somerset, 1250–1830* (repr. 1970)

Landscape
Atthill, R. *Old Mendip* (1971)
Atthill, R. (ed.) *Mendip: a New Study* (1976)
Billingsley, J. *General View of the Agriculture of Somerset* (1797)
Burton, S. H. *Exmoor* (3rd edn. 1978)
Coysh, A. W., Mason, E. J., and Waite, V. *The Mendips* (4th edn. 1977)
Darby, H. C. and Finn, R. W. *The Domesday Geography of South-West England* (1967)
Finberg, H. P. R. *The Gloucestershire Landscape* (1975)
Hawkins, D. *Avalon and Sedgemoor* (1973)
Lawrence, B. *Quantock Country* (1952)
MacDermot, E. T. (ed. Sellick, R. J.) *A History of the Forest of Exmoor* (1973)
Orwin, C. S. and Sellick, R. J. *The Reclamation of Exmoor Forest* (2nd edn. 1970)
Peel, J. H. B. *Portrait of Exmoor* (1970)
Storer, B. *Sedgemoor, its History and Natural History* (1972)
Waite, V. *Portrait of the Quantocks* (2nd edn. 1969)
Williams, M. *The Draining of the Somerset Levels* (1970)

Archaeology, history, and folklore
Alcock, L. *'By South Cadbury is that Camelot...'* (1972)
Ashe, G. *Camelot and the Vision of Albion* (1971)

FURTHER READING

Barnes, T. G. *Somerset, 1625–40* (1961)

Buchanan, A. and Cossons, N. *Industrial Archaeology of the Bristol Region* (1969)

Day, J. *Bristol Brass: the History of the Industry* (1973)

Dobson, D. P. *Somerset* (The County Archaeologies) (1931)

Down, C. G. and Warrington, A. J. *The History of the Somerset Coalfield* (n.d.)

Dunning, R. W. (ed.) *Christianity in Somerset* (1976)

Finberg, H. P. R. (ed.) *Gloucestershire Studies* (1951)

Gough, J. W. *The Mines of Mendip* (2nd edn. 1967)

Grinsell, L. V. *The Archaeology of Exmoor* (1970)

Hembry, P. M. *The Bishops of Bath and Wells, 1540–1640* (1967)

Little, B. *The Monmouth Episode* (1956)

McGrath, P. and Cannon, J. (eds.) *Essays in Bristol and Gloucestershire History* (1976)

Palmer, K. *Oral Folk Tales of Wessex* (1973)

Palmer, K. *The Folklore of Somerset* (1976)

Pearce, S. M. *The Kingdom of Dumnonia* (1978)

Porter, H. M. *The Celtic Church in Somerset* (1971)

Tongue, R. L. (ed. Briggs, K. M.) *Somerset Folklore* (1965)

Treharne, R. F. *The Glastonbury Legends* (new edn. 1975)

Trench, C. Chenevix *The Western Rising* (1969)

Underdown, D. *Somerset in the Civil War and the Interregnum* (1973)

Wroughton, J. *The Civil War in Bath and North Somerset* (1973)

Travellers and diarists

Bates, E. H. (ed.) *Gerard's Survey of Somerset 1633* (Somerset Record Society xv, 1900, repr. 1973)

Defoe, D. (ed. Cole, G. D. H.) *A Tour through the whole Island of Great Britain* (1927)

Fiennes, C. (ed. Morris, C.) *The Journeys of Celia Fiennes* (1949)

Kilvert, F. (ed. Plomer, W.) *Kilvert's Diary* (3 vols. illus. 1977)

Lawrence, B. *Coleridge and Wordsworth in Somerset* (1970)

Leland, J. (ed. Smith, L. T.) *Itineraries* (5 vols. repr. 1964)

Skinner, J. (eds. Coombs, H. and P.) *Journal of a Somerset Rector* (1971)

Woodforde, J. (ed. Beresford, J.) *The Diary of a Country Parson* (5 vols. repr. 1968)

Worcestre, W. (ed. Harvey, J. H.) *Itineraries* (1969)

Bath and Bristol

Carus-Wilson, E. M. *Medieval Merchant Venturers* (1954)

Crick, C. *Victorian Buildings in Bristol* (1975)

Cunliffe, B. *Roman Bath Discovered* (1971)

Gadd, D. *Georgian Summer* (1971)

Gomme, A. H., Jenner, M., and Little, B. *Bristol: An Architectural History* (1979)

Haddon, J. *Bath* (1973)

Ison, W. *The Georgian Buildings of Bath* (repr. 1969)

Little, B. *The City and County of Bristol* (1954)

McGrath, P. *The Merchant Venturers of Bristol* (1975)

Robertson, C. *Bath: An Architectural Guide* (1975)

Photograph Credits

Index

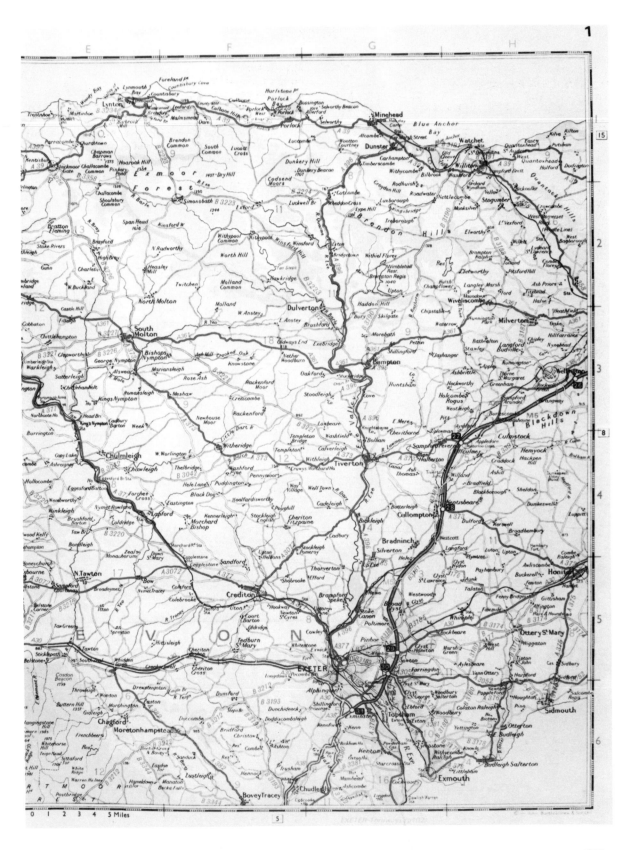

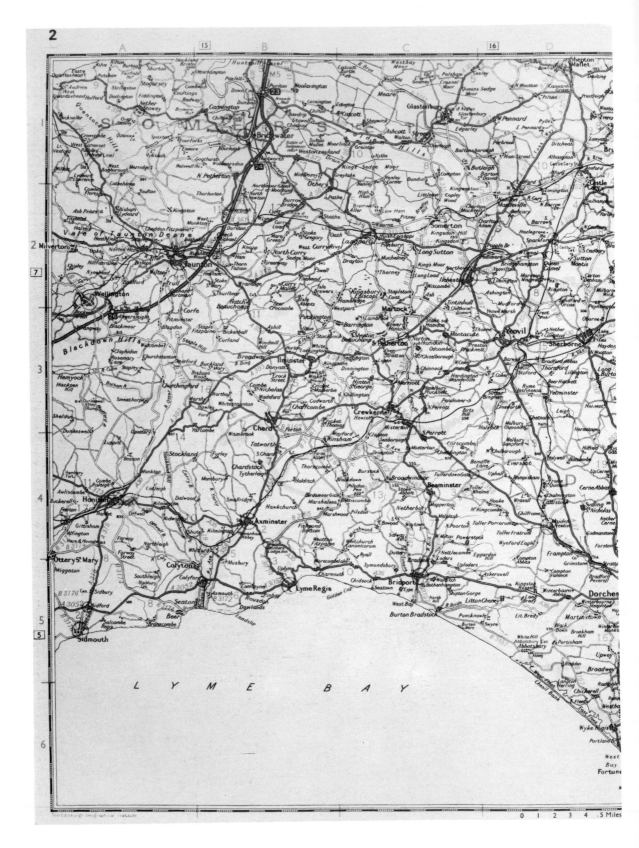

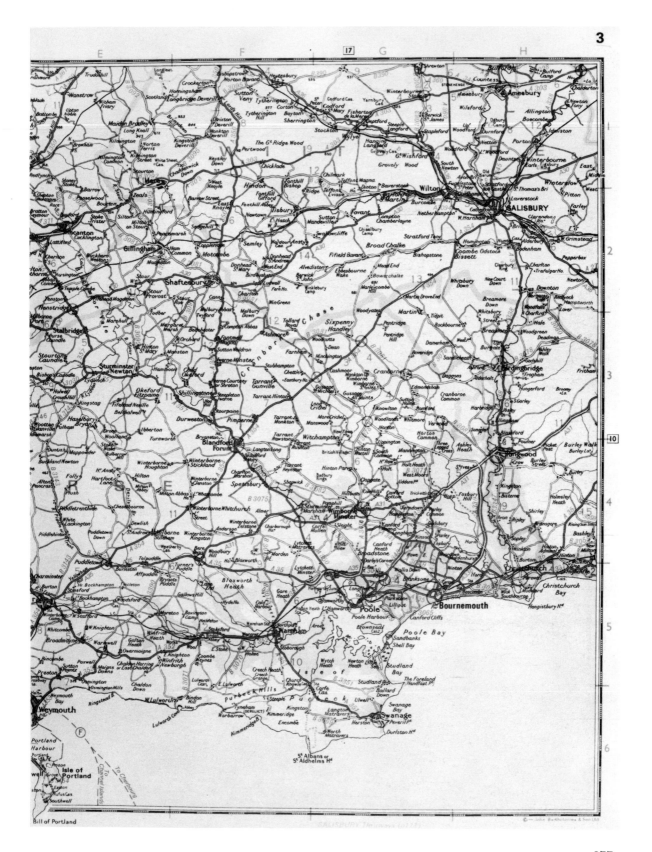

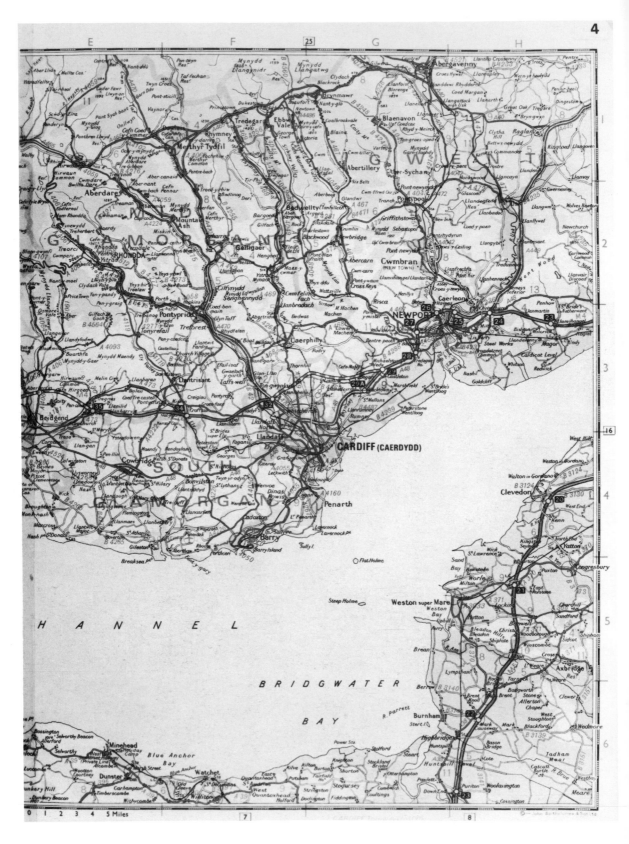

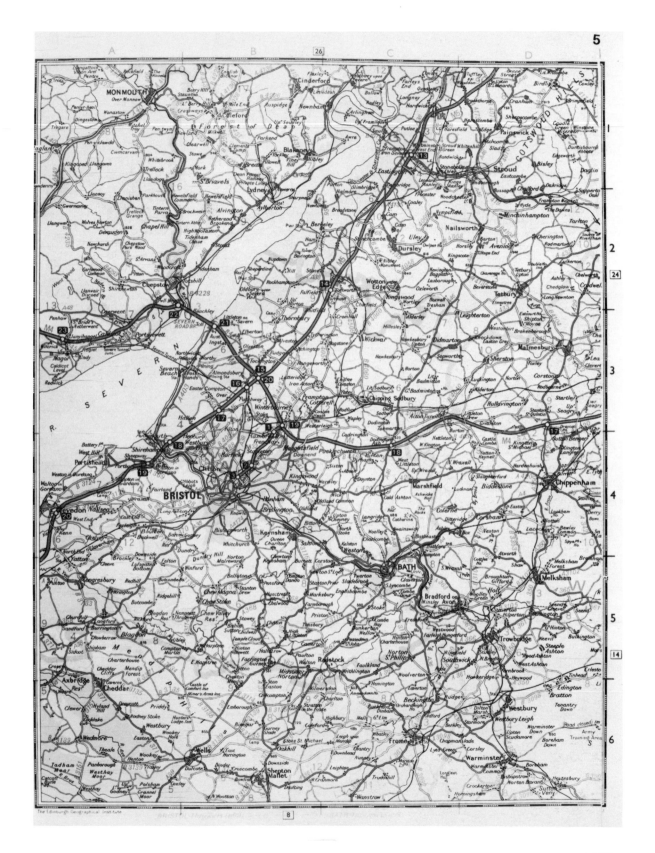

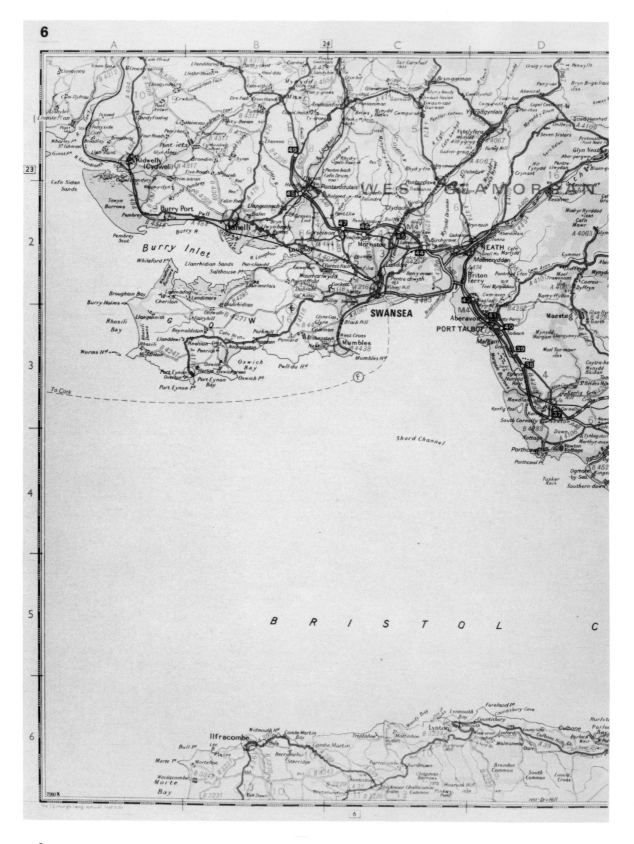